VISIT US AT

w w w . s y n g r e s s . c o m   WITHDRAWN

Syngress is committed to publishing high-quality books for IT Professionals and delivering those books in media and formats that fit the demands of our customers. We are also committed to extending the utility of the book you purchase via additional materials available from our Web site.

SOLUTIONS WEB SITE

To register your book, visit www.syngress.com/solutions. Once registered, you can access our solutions@syngress.com Web pages. There you may find an assortment of value-added features such as free e-booklets related to the topic of this book, URLs of related Web sites, FAQs from the book, corrections, and any updates from the author(s).

ULTIMATE CDs

Our Ultimate CD product line offers our readers budget-conscious compilations of some of our best-selling backlist titles in Adobe PDF form. These CDs are the perfect way to extend your reference library on key topics pertaining to your area of expertise, including Cisco Engineering, Microsoft Windows System Administration, CyberCrime Investigation, Open Source Security, and Firewall Configuration, to name a few.

DOWNLOADABLE E-BOOKS

For readers who can't wait for hard copy, we offer most of our titles in downloadable Adobe PDF form. These e-books are often available weeks before hard copies, and are priced affordably.

SYNGRESS OUTLET

Our outlet store at syngress.com features overstocked, out-of-print, or slightly hurt books at significant savings.

SITE LICENSING

Syngress has a well-established program for site licensing our e-books onto servers in corporations, educational institutions, and large organizations. Contact us at sales@syngress.com for more information.

CUSTOM PUBLISHING

Many organizations welcome the ability to combine parts of multiple Syngress books, as well as their own content, into a single volume for their own internal use. Contact us at sales@syngress.com for more information.

SYNGRESS®

Essential Computer Security

EVERYONE'S GUIDE TO E-MAIL, INTERNET, AND WIRELESS SECURITY

Tony Bradley CISSP-ISSAP, About.com's Guide
for Internet/Network Security

Harlan Carvey Technical Editor

MVP
Microsoft
Most Valuable
Professional

KEY	SERIAL NUMBER
001	HJIRTCV764
002	PO9873D5FG
003	829KM8NJH2
004	FGT53MMN92
005	CVPLQ6WQ23
006	VBP965T5T5
007	HJJJ863WD3E
008	2987GVTWMK
009	629MP5SDJT
010	IMWQ295T6T

PUBLISHED BY
Syngress Publishing, Inc.
800 Hingham Street
Rockland, MA 02370

Essential Computer Security: Everyone's Guide to Email, Internet, and Wireless Security

Printed in Canada.
1 2 3 4 5 6 7 8 9 0
ISBN: 1-59749-114-4

Publisher: Andrew Williams
Acquisitions Editor: Gary Byrne
Technical Editor: Harlan Carvey
Cover Designer: Michael Kavish

Page Layout and Art: Patricia Lupien
Copy Editors: Michelle Melani, Mike McGee
Indexer: Richard Carlson

Distributed by O'Reilly Media, Inc. in the United States and Canada.
For information on rights, translations, and bulk sales, contact Matt Pedersen, Director of Sales and Rights, at Syngress Publishing; email matt@syngress.com or fax to 781-681-3585.

Acknowledgments

Syngress would like to acknowledge the following people for their kindness and support in making this book possible.

Syngress books are now distributed in the United States and Canada by O'Reilly Media, Inc. The enthusiasm and work ethic at O'Reilly are incredible, and we would like to thank everyone there for their time and efforts to bring Syngress books to market: Tim O'Reilly, Laura Baldwin, Mark Brokering, Mike Leonard, Donna Selenko, Bonnie Sheehan, Cindy Davis, Grant Kikkert, Opol Matsutaro, Steve Hazelwood, Mark Wilson, Rick Brown, Tim Hinton, Kyle Hart, Sara Winge, Peter Pardo, Leslie Crandell, Regina Aggio Wilkinson, Pascal Honscher, Preston Paull, Susan Thompson, Bruce Stewart, Laura Schmier, Sue Willing, Mark Jacobsen, Betsy Waliszewski, Kathryn Barrett, John Chodacki, Rob Bullington, Kerry Beck, Karen Montgomery, and Patrick Dirden.

The incredibly hardworking team at Elsevier Science, including Jonathan Bunkell, Ian Seager, Duncan Enright, David Burton, Rosanna Ramacciotti, Robert Fairbrother, Miguel Sanchez, Klaus Beran, Emma Wyatt, Krista Leppiko, Marcel Koppes, Judy Chappell, Radek Janousek, Rosie Moss, David Lockley, Nicola Haden, Bill Kennedy, Martina Morris, Kai Wuerfl-Davidek, Christiane Leipersberger, Yvonne Grueneklee, Nadia Balavoine, and Chris Reinders for making certain that our vision remains worldwide in scope.

David Buckland, Marie Chieng, Lucy Chong, Leslie Lim, Audrey Gan, Pang Ai Hua, Joseph Chan, June Lim, and Siti Zuraidah Ahmad of Pansing Distributors for the enthusiasm with which they receive our books.

David Scott, Tricia Wilden, Marilla Burgess, Annette Scott, Andrew Swaffer, Stephen O'Donoghue, Bec Lowe, Mark Langley, and Anyo Geddes of Woodslane for distributing our books throughout Australia, New Zealand, Papua New Guinea, Fiji, Tonga, Solomon Islands, and the Cook Islands.

Dedication

I want to thank my kids for giving me the motivation to create this book. Jordan, Dalton, Paige, Teegan, Ethan, and Noah are all wonderful, fabulous kids—each in his or her own way—and I am lucky to be their Dad. I also want to welcome Addison, the newest addition to the Bradley family.

I can't say enough to thank my wife. It may be sappy for a dedication in a technical book, but Nicki is my Sunshine. She is more giving, loving, thoughtful, and devoted than anyone else I have ever known. She brings joy to my world and inspires me to be better than I am. I can only hope that I give her even a fraction of what she gives me.

> "Far away there in the Sunshine are my highest aspirations. I may not reach them, but I can look up and see their beauty, believe in them, and try to follow where they lead."
>
> —Louisa May Alcott

Author Acknowledgments

I need to express my deepest appreciation to Syngress Publishing for helping me get this book published. This project began a couple years ago and got side-lined. Syngress believed in the purpose of the book and worked with me to make it happen.

I want to extend my personal thanks to Gary Byrne, Amy Pedersen, and Andrew Williams. Each of them has worked as hard as I have—maybe harder—to make sure this book got to you. It isn't easy keeping me on schedule, but they were relentless…in a good way.

I also want to thank Harlan Carvey for providing his technical expertise as the technical editor for the book, and Paul Summit and Larry Chaffin for their zero-hour contributions to help us make our deadlines.

Lead Author

Tony Bradley (CISSP-ISSAP) is the Guide for the Internet/Network Security site on About.com, a part of The New York Times Company. He has written for a variety of other Web sites and publications, including *PC World*, SearchSecurity.com, WindowsNetworking.com, *Smart Computing* magazine, and *Information Security* magazine. Currently a security architect and consultant for a Fortune 100 company, Tony has driven security policies and technologies for antivirus and incident response for Fortune 500 companies, and he has been network administrator and technical support for smaller companies.

Tony is a CISSP (Certified Information Systems Security Professional) and ISSAP (Information Systems Security Architecture Professional). He is Microsoft Certified as an MCSE (Microsoft Certified Systems Engineer) and MCSA (Microsoft Certified Systems Administrator) in Windows 2000 and an MCP (Microsoft Certified Professional) in Windows NT. Tony is recognized by Microsoft as an MVP (Most Valuable Professional) in Windows security.

On his About.com site, Tony has on average over 600,000 page views per month and 25,000 subscribers to his weekly newsletter. He created a 10-part Computer Security 101 Class that has had thousands of participants since its creation and continues to gain popularity through word of mouth. Aside from his Web site and magazine contributions, Tony is also coauthor of *Hacker's Challenge 3* (ISBN: 0072263040) and a contributing author to *Winternals: Defragmentation, Recovery, and Administration Field Guide* (ISBN: 1597490792) and *Combating Spyware in the Enterprise* (ISBN: 1597490644).

Contributing Authors

Larry Chaffin is the CEO/Chairman of Pluto Networks, a world-wide network consulting company specializing in VoIP, WLAN, and Security. He is an accomplished author. He was a coauthor on *Managing Cisco Secure Networks* (ISBN: 1931836566) and contributed to *Skype Me* (ISBN: 1597490326), *Practical VoIP Security* (ISBN: 1597490601), and *Configuring Check Point NGX VPN-1/Firewall-1* (ISBN: 1597490318). He also wrote *Building a VoIP Network with Nortel's MS5100* (ISBN: 1597490784) and coauthored/ghostwrote 11 other technology books for VoIP, WLAN, security, and optical technologies. Larry has more than 29 vendor certifications from companies such as Avaya, Cisco, HP, IBM, isc2, Juniper, Microsoft, Nortel, PMI, and VMware. Larry has been a principal architect in 22 countries for many Fortune 100 companies designing VoIP, security, WLAN, and optical networks; he is viewed by his peers as one of the most well-respected experts in the field of VoIP and security in the world. Larry has spent countless hours teaching and conducting seminars/workshops around the world in the field of Voice/VoIP, security, and wireless networks. Larry is currently working on a follow-up to *Building a VoIP Network with Nortel's Multimedia Communication Server 5100* as well as new books on Cisco VoIP networks, practical VoIP case studies, and wasted taxpayer money in a state-run network.

Larry cowrote Chapter 5.

Jennifer Davis is a senior system administrator with Decru, a Network Appliance company. Decru develops storage security solutions that help system administrators protect data. Jennifer specializes in scripting, systems automation, integration and troubleshooting, and security administration.

Jennifer is a member of USENIX, SAGE, LoPSA, and BayLISA. She is based in Silicon Valley, California.

Jennifer wrote Appendix B.

Paul Summitt (MCSE, CCNA, MCP+I, MCP) holds a master's degree in mass communication. Paul has served as a network, an Exchange, and a database administrator, as well as a Web and application developer. Paul has written on virtual reality and Web development and has served as technical editor for several books on Microsoft technologies. Paul lives in Columbia, MO, with his life and writing partner, Mary.

Paul cowrote Chapter 7.

Technical Editor

Harlan Carvey (CISSP) is a computer forensics engineer with ISS/IBM. He is based out of the Northern Virginia area and provides emergency response services to ISS clients. His background includes vulnerability assessments and penetration testing, as well as incident response and computer forensics for clients in the federal government and commercial sectors. Harlan also has a great deal of experience developing and conducting hands-on functional incident response training for commercial and government clients.

Harlan holds a BSEE degree from the Virginia Military Institute and an MSEE degree from the Naval Postgraduate School. Harlan has presented at Usenix, BlackHat, DefCon, and HTCIA conferences. In addition, he is a prolific writer, and his articles have been published in journals and on Web sites. He is the author of *Windows Forensics and Incident Recovery*.

Contents

Foreword xix

Intro xxi

Part I: Bare Essentials 1

Chapter 1 Basic Windows Security 3
   Introduction 4
   Why Do You Need to Be Secure? 4
   Why Are You at Risk? 5
      Malware 5
      Weak Passwords 6
      Physical Security 6
      Network "Neighbors" 6
      Logging In 7
      User Accounts 7
         Limiting the Number of Accounts 9
         Disabling the Guest Account 11
         Renaming the Administrator Account 12
         Creating a Dummy Administrator Account 13
      Security Groups 13
      Windows XP Home Account Types 15
      FAT32 versus NTFS 16
      File and Folder Security 16
         Keeping It Simple .17
         Sharing and Security 18
      Windows Services 21
      Hidden File Extensions .24
      Screen Saver 25
   Summary 28
   Additional Resources 28

Chapter 2 Passwords 29

Introduction 30
Password Power 30
    The Keys to Your Data 32
    Selecting Strong Passwords 33
Password Cracking .35
Storing Your Passwords 36
One Super-Powerful Password 37
Summary 39
Additional Resources 39

Chapter 3 Viruses, Worms, and Other Malware 41

Introduction 42
Malware Terms 42
The History of Malware 43
    Protect Yourself with Antivirus Software 44
    Keep Your Antivirus Software Updated 47
    How Not to Get Infected 49
    Do You Think You're Infected? 49
Summary 52
Additional Resources 52

Chapter 4 Patching 53

Introduction 54
Patch Terminology .54
Why Should I Patch? 55
How Do I Know What to Patch? 56
    Patching Precautions 60
Summary 64
Additional Resources 64

Part II: More Essential Security 65

Chapter 5 Perimeter Security. 67

Introduction 68
From Moats and Bridges to Firewalls and Filters 68
Firewalls 69
    Network Traffic Flow 70
        Routers and Ports 71

Packet Routing and Filtering 72
Stateful Inspection 73
Application Gateways and Application Proxy Firewalls . .74
Personal and Cable/DSL Router Firewalls 74
Intrusion Detection and Prevention 80
Summary 84
Additional Resources 84

Chapter 6 E-mail Safety. 85
Introduction 86
The Evolution of E-mail 86
E-mail Security Concerns 86
Opening Attachments 87
Web-Based versus POP3 E-mail 91
Spoofed Addresses 92
Spam 93
Hoaxes and Phishing 97
Summary 102
Additional Resources 102

Chapter 7 Web Surfing Privacy and Safety 103
Introduction 104
The Revolutionary World Wide Web 104
Web Security Concerns 106
Cookies 106
Privacy and Anonymous Surfing 109
Getting in the Zone 112
Shopping Safely: SSL and Certificates 116
Financial Transactions 117
Content Filtering and Childproofing 119
Summary 121
Additional Resources 121

Chapter 8 Wireless Network Security 123
Introduction 124
The Basics of Wireless Networks 124
802.11b 126
802.11a 127
802.11g 127

Next-Generation Protocols 127
Basic Wireless Network Security Measures 128
Secure Your Home Wireless Network 128
Change the SSID 129
Configure Your Home Wireless Network 130
Restrict Access to Your Home Wireless Network . . .130
Use Encryption in Your Home Wireless Network . .131
Review Your Logs 132
Use Public Wireless Networks Safely 133
Install Up-to-Date Antivirus Software 133
Install a Personal Firewall 133
Additional Hotspot Security Measures 134
Verify Your Hotspot Connection 134
Watch Your Back 135
Use Encryption and Password Protection 135
Don't Linger 136
Use a VPN 136
Use Web-Based E-mail .136
Summary 137
Additional Resources 137

Chapter 9 Spyware and Adware 139
Introduction 140
What Is Adware? 140
What Is Spyware? 144
Getting Rid of Spyware 145
Summary 150
Additional Resources 150

Part III: Testing and Maintenance 151

Chapter 10 Keeping Things Secure 153
Introduction 154
General PC Maintenance 154
Disk Cleanup 155
Erase the PageFile 157
Disk Defragmenter 158
Scheduled Tasks 159
Patches and Updates 161
Windows XP Security Center 162

Summary 164
Additional Resources 164

Chapter 11 When Disaster Strikes 165

Introduction 166
Check the Event Logs 166
Enable Security Auditing 167
Review Your Firewall Logs 170
Scan Your Computer 171
Restore Your System 173
Start from Scratch 174
Restore Your Data 175
Call In the Pros .175
Summary 176
Additional Resources 177

Chapter 12 Microsoft Alternatives: Inside the Linux Desktop 179

Introduction 180
Common Desktop Environments 180
    Gnome 181
    KDE 183
    Common Features 184
    Install Both, Make One the Default 185
    Alternative Window Managers 185
The X Window System and Window Managers 185
    X Window Servers versus Window Managers 186
    Window Managers as
    Alternative Desktop Environments 188
E-mail and Personal Information Management Clients 190
    Evolution 190
        Evolution, Microsoft
        Exchange, Novell GroupWise, and OpenExchange . .192
    KDE Suite/KMail 192
        Kontact 192
    Aethera 193
    Mozilla Mail/Thunderbird 194
        Thunderbird .195

Sylpheed 195
Essential Information 196
E-mail and PIM Software .196
Migrating Mail 197
   Migrating from Outlook or Outlook Express 197
   Importing Outlook Mail into Mozilla 198
   LibPST 199
   Importing Outlook Mail into Evolution 199
   Document Standards .201
   The Hard Way 201
Web Browsers 202
Mozilla 202
   Mozilla and Microsoft CHAP 203
Firefox 203
Galeon 204
Konqueror 205
Opera 205
Migrating Bookmarks 206
Browser Plug-Ins 206
   Macromedia Flash and Shockwave/Director 206
   RealPlayer 207
   Adobe Acrobat Reader 208
Office Application Suites 209
OpenOffice.org 209
   Limitations: Macros and PDF Files 212
   Future Plans 213
StarOffice 213
KOffice 213
Hancom Office 214
Running Windows Applications on Linux 214
Compatibility Layer Software 215
   Wine 216
   Code Weavers' CrossOver Office 216
Summary 218
Additional Resources 218

Part IV: Security Resources **219**

Appendix A Essential Network Communications **221**
Introduction 222
Computer Protocols 222
Communication Ports 223
TCP and UDP Protocols .223
Understanding IP Addresses and DNS 224
Managing IP Addresses 226
Firewalls 227

Appendix B Case Study: SOHO
(Five Computers, Printer, Servers, etc.) **229**
Introduction 230
    Using netstat to Determine Open Ports on a System . .230
    Determining More Information with lsof 235
    Using netstat on Windows XP 236
Employing a Firewall in a SOHO Environment 239
    Host-Based Firewall Solutions 239
Introducing the SOHO Firewall Case Study 240
    Assessing Needs 240
    Defining the Scope of the Case Study 241
Designing the SOHO Firewall 241
    Determining the Functional Requirements 242
        Determining the Needs of the Family 242
        Talking to Local User Groups 242
    Creating a Site Survey of the Home 243
    Identifying Current Technology
    Options and Constraints .244
    Implementing the SOHO Firewall 245
        Assembling the Components 245
        Installing the Components 245
        Installing the Wireless Cards 246
        Testing the Configuration
        from Various Access Points 249
Summary 250
Solutions Fast Track 251
Frequently Asked Questions .252

Appendix C Glossary of Technology and Terminology 253

Index. 269

Foreword

There's no denying that the personal computer revolution has changed the way we as a society communicate. It's now more common to receive an e-mail message than a postal letter. In fact, computer networks have become an indispensable part of the corporate landscape. With the proliferation of the Internet, both individuals and businesses are realizing more than ever the importance of being able to access the Web and all it has to offer. Every aspect of our existence is or can be touched by the Internet. We can use the Internet to shop for all manner of items; tend to our banking; plan and book excursions and stays; seek advice and reviews; and converse with other users at any time of our choosing and virtually from anywhere. Such convenience, however, does not come without its own set of risks; namely, the hackers and viruses with which we've become all too familiar. You will find this book a reliable resource for the most critical aspects of computer security.

To the newcomer, the Internet may be as alluring and exciting as the Wild West was to many Americans during the mid–1800s. The untapped resources of the West left people open to new discoveries and opportunities. However, like the Wild West, the Internet is largely unregulated; it lacks proper, effective laws for maintaining security and often is full of unpleasant surprises. All individuals and organizations that connect to the Internet are under the risk of an online attack every day, and they need to make and maintain their *own* security.

Although the Internet has become ubiquitous as a communication and research tool, it is important to remember that the Internet is a two-way street—your computer connects to it, and vice versa. The good news is that securing your computer is largely a matter of understanding where you are vulnerable and what tools and techniques are required for security. Luckily, basic computer security is not beyond a nontechnical person's ability to understand. Whether you are using a stand-alone computer or a whole computer network, Tony Bradley will arm you with the knowledge you need to make and keep things secure.

Security is a process, not a product, and computer security is everyone's responsibility. You wouldn't leave the backdoor of your home or business open to intruders, and your computer merits the same prudence. Even Dodge City had a Wyatt Earp to keep order if things got out of hand. In the wild world of the Internet, there *is* no sheriff. With *Essential Computer Security* you can act as your own deputy by arming yourself with fundamental knowledge of the important aspects of computer security.

—Douglas Schweitzer, Sc.D.
Security Expert and Author of
Securing the Network from Malicious Code

Introduction

When you purchase most home appliances, they come with an owner's manual. The owner's manual is the bible of information for that appliance. It tells you what each button does and how to set up and configure your new appliance to get it ready for operation. The owner's manual also includes the actual steps to operate the appliance, and it often contains information on how and where to obtain service and parts, basic troubleshooting tips, and precautions you should be aware of before using the appliance.

This is true for VCRs, microwaves, toasters and vacuum cleaners. All these appliances are commonly found in an average home, and each has an assigned task. When you buy these items you buy them with their specific tasks in mind, and the owner's manual provides all the information you need to accomplish the goal.

Most home users treat their personal computers as an appliance as well. For some users, the PC is a fancy calculator that lets them track and manage their finances. For others, it's a means of communication that lets them send e-mail to their friends and family. For others, it's a high-end game console that lets them play the latest action games. The list goes on and on. The bottom line is that the computer is an "appliance" that has a variety of functions, and it can be different things to different people—sometimes even different things to the same person—depending on what the user wants the computer to do at that moment.

So you would expect the computer to come with a very large owner's manual to encompass every possible task you might use it for, right? Unfortunately, it doesn't. The reality is that the owner's manual for the computer itself is generally quite sparse. Usually a new computer will come with some simple instructions that let you know which cable gets plugged into which hole so that you can set the computer up. It may also provide technical details about the motherboard, the main board on which the processor, memory, and other components are found, or information about configuring the BIOS (basic input/output system, the "brain" that configures and operates the motherboard). However, most computer owner's manuals stop there.

You can't really blame the computer manufacturers, though. Unlike a VCR that is predetermined to record and watch videotapes or a toaster that is designed only to toast bread, the computer has too many potential uses to be comprehensively covered in one owner's manual.

This book is written to give you a manual that covers the system as a whole and teaches you what you need to know to secure it. When you plug your VCR into the wall, nothing special occurs. There is no increased risk of someone getting your personal financial data when you plug your toaster in. Malicious attackers won't be using your vacuum cleaner to launch attacks against other vacuum cleaners throughout the world.

But when you connect your computer to the Internet, you become part of a system of millions of computers and devices that all interact with and possibly affect each other. The computer is unique because it is a household "appliance" with security concerns and implications that go well beyond your home.

You probably know as much about your computer as you do about your VCR or microwave. You know how to use it. You know how to turn it on, log on, surf the Web, send an e-mail, and so on. But you probably can't tell me what speed your processor is, how many megabytes of RAM you have, or whether TCP port 80 is open to external access. You simply don't need to know that stuff to use the computer.

You may not want to be a computer guru or security expert. You may not care how big the hard drive is or how fast your processor is. You just want the computer to do its job with minimal effort on your part. But for you to use the computer safely when sharing the Internet and World Wide Web with others, it's important that you understand the risks involved, how to avoid those risks, and how to protect your computer from malicious threats, such as viruses, worms, and spyware.

The problem with most books about computers and network security is that they are written for people who already understand computer and network security. The average computer user doesn't know enough about network security to even know where to begin. This book is written to provide average computer users or those just getting started in computer or network security with an introductory guide to the different threats and ways to protect your computer from them.

I am neither setting out to teach you everything there is to know nor expecting you to be an expert when all is said and done. I simply hope that reading this book and taking the precautions—or even *some* of the precautions—discussed enables you to have a safer, more enjoyable Internet-surfing experience and ensures that your lack of computer security doesn't affect the rest of us who share the Internet with you. I want this book to be your Internet user's owner's manual that helps you understand the risks you will be exposed to and explains the precautions you should take so that you can get your "appliance" to perform the task(s) you bought it for safely with minimal effort and frustration.

Why This Book?

This book is not intended to be comprehensive. There are hundreds of books on the shelf covering all areas of computer and network security. You can find many books that cover general information security in a much deeper and technical sense than this book will. There are also books that cover specific areas of security, such as encryption, firewalls, backup and recovery, and so on, in much more depth and detail than this book.

This book was written to give security neophytes the information and advice they need to operate this "appliance" securely, both for their own protection and for the protection of the rest of us who share the Internet with them. I have written it in simple terms without too much technical jargon, but if you do come across any acronyms or unfamiliar terms, you can look them up in the glossary in Appendix C.

The goal of this book is to teach you enough about computer and network security for you to understand the potential threats and protect your computer from them. At the end of each chapter you will find a short summary of the key points from the chapter.

This book is focused on security, and the majority of the content will apply to any computer system, but the examples and illustrations will come primarily from Microsoft Windows XP. Details about subjects like firewalls, passwords, and wireless network security go beyond the operating system and can be applied to any system. Don't be concerned if you are not using Windows XP; the fundamental concepts of computer security go beyond the operating system and apply to any platform.

Organization of This Book

This book is divided into four main sections:

- The "Bare Essentials" section provides information about the security concerns that should be addressed immediately. The computer should not be connected to another computer or to the Internet until these areas are taken care of. If you follow the advice in this section you can connect to the Internet with a relative sense of security.

- The section titled "More Essential Security" goes deeper into different security technologies and how to use the computer for e-mail or Web surfing and other activities securely.

- The "Testing and Maintenance" section describes some ways you can test how secure your computer or network is and the different areas you need to monitor and update to maintain your security.

- The "Security Resources" section provides reference material as well as a short primer on the basic concepts of computer networking and the Internet for the readers who want to dig a little deeper.

Chapter Descriptions

In this section I have listed a brief description of the chapters in this book:

- **Chapter 1: Basic Windows Security** This chapter introduces you to basic computer security in the Windows operating system, such as creating and managing user accounts on your computer or network as well as setting permissions on files and folders to secure your data.

- **Chapter 2: Passwords** Passwords are the keys to the gate of your computer. It is essential that you take the time to select passwords that are not easily guessed or cracked and that you treat them with the confidentiality they deserve.

- **Chapter 3: Viruses, Worms, and Other Malware** This chapter discusses how antivirus software works and what sorts of threats it can protect you from. It also covers updating and maintaining your antivirus software to ensure you remain protected.

- **Chapter 4: Patching** This chapter discusses the importance of keeping your computer updated and patched to protect it from having known vulnerabilities exploited. It also includes some steps you can take to protect a freshly installed operating system while you apply the necessary patches.

- **Chapter 5: Perimeter Security** This chapter provides an overview of security technology you can use to build a wall around your computer or network—or protect your perimeter—including firewalls and intrusion detection systems (IDSes).

- **Chapter 6: E-mail Safety** E-mail can be a wonderful tool for communication and increased productivity—if you can get past the spam, hoaxes, and virus-infected file attachments. This chapter is dedicated to helping you eliminate as much of the junk as possible so that you can focus on the e-mail you want to read.

- **Chapter 7: Web Surfing Privacy and Safety** A look at the potential threats and exploits that await you on the Web and what you can do to get the most from your Web-surfing experience while protecting your computer, your network, and your identity.

- **Chapter 8: Wireless Network Security** Wireless networks make connecting to the Internet and other devices easy and convenient. The freedom they provide is very liberating, but that freedom comes at a price when it comes to security, and you need to take extra precautions to keep your wireless data secure.

- **Chapter 9: Spyware and Adware** As you install software and surf the Web, different little programs called spyware or adware might be installed on your computer. Some are legitimate; however, many are not. All are designed to somehow monitor your computer activity and report back to the company or user that planted them. This chapter will help you to guard your machine against spyware/adware and clean it up if it gets on your system.

- **Chapter 10: Keeping Things Secure** You have gone through all of the trouble of installing security products like antivirus and firewall programs and reconfigured your system to make it as secure as possible. Security is a process, though, not a product. There are certain things that you must update and maintain to sustain that security.

- **Chapter 11: When Disaster Strikes** No matter how secure you are, something may eventually happen to your data. It is important to perform regular backups of important data and have a plan in place for how to address security incidents when they arise.

- **Chapter 12: Microsoft Alternatives: Inside the Linux Desktop** Much of the focus of this book is on the Microsoft Windows platform and the built-in Microsoft products, such as Outlook Express and Internet Explorer. This chapter addresses the use of alternative products from other vendors to improve the security of your system.

- **Appendix A: Essential Network Communications** This appendix provides a fair amount of detail about networking and the Internet in general. The scope of this book is simply to provide the essentials of security and not to attempt to teach you everything, but for those who may want some more information, this appendix will help you get a basic grasp of how these things work.

- **Appendix B: Case Study: SOHO (Five Computers Printer, Server, etc.)** Security for the home isn't as well developed as in a corporate environment. Users often do not have the time to become experts while maintaining their businesses or working remotely. This appendix discusses using *netstat* to determine open ports on a system, explains how to use *lsof* to inspect open ports, and includes a case study that shows how a home user designed a SOHO firewall without much hands-on systems or security experience.

- **Appendix C: Glossary** Appendix C provides a glossary of security terms and acronyms that you can use as a resource to refer to when you need to decipher the many foreign terms you may encounter.

Part I:
Bare Essentials

Chapter 1

Basic
Windows Security

Topics in this chapter:

- Why Do You Need to Be Secure?
- Why Are You at Risk?

☑ Summary

☑ Additional Resources

Introduction

The majority of home computers use some version of Microsoft Windows as the operating system. Most of those users, either by purchasing a new computer system in the past couple of years or by upgrading, rely on a version of Windows XP.

Before we go on to the rest of this book and explore how to use different applications securely, such as Web browsers or e-mail clients, you need to understand the fundamental security of the operating system itself. This chapter will explain the following:

- Basic risks of computer use
- Accessing Windows
- User accounts and Security Groups
- File and folder security
- Protecting Windows services
- Dangers of hidden file extensions
- Screen savers as security tools

Why Do You Need to Be Secure?

Do you want your computer to be absolutely, positively, 100-percent secure against all vulnerabilities and exploits, not only those known now, but those yet to be discovered? It's simple: leave your computer in the box, because once you turn the computer on, you begin to walk a tightrope between functionality (or convenience) and security. Unfortunately, many of the features that make your computer easier to use also create various security issues as well.

Some people appreciate that their printer is able to communicate with the computer and alert them with messages when the ink is running low or the paper tray is empty. However, leaving the Windows Messenger Service—the service used for such communication between your printer and your computer—enabled may also leave your computer open to being inundated with unsolicited spam pop-up messages.

One of the points of setting up a network in the first place is to share resources such as data and printers. You may want to share out files or folders so they can be accessed from other computers on the network. Unfortunately, many viruses and worms use these same connections to jump from one computer to the next and infect the whole network.

I assume by reading this book that you do not intend to leave your computer disconnected and sealed in the box. I commend you. There is a vast world of information and productivity awaiting as long as you invest just a little time to do so securely. A little bit of knowledge applied with a little bit of common sense is enough to protect you from most computer threats.

Microsoft has made vast improvements in the security of their operating systems and applications in the last couple of years. Windows XP Service Pack 2 made some dramatic changes aimed at making the operating system even more secure. Sadly though, the operating systems intended for home users, a market that arguably needs the security features the most, are more insecure.

Many users view security from the perspective of "I don't have anything of value worth protecting, so why should I care?" First of all, there is a lot more of value on your computer than you may be aware of. Have you done your own income taxes on your computer and saved the files? Are there any files or documents that contain your full name? Birth date? Social Security Number? All of this information has value to someone that may want to access your financial information or steal your identity.

The other reason to operate your computer securely is "to protect the rest of us," which is a different concept. If you leave your house unlocked and you get robbed, it really only affects you. If you leave your car unlocked and your CD stereo gets stolen, it really only affects you. But, if you leave your computer "unlocked" and it gets "stolen," it can impact other computer systems on the network or the Internet.

Why Are You at Risk?

It has become so common to hear about viruses, worms, identity theft, phishing scams, and other computer attacks that you may actually be wondering "where *isn't* there a threat?" Understanding the importance of computer security is easier, though, if you have some idea of the threats you are defending against.

Malware

Malware is a general term used to refer to a wide variety of malicious programs. It includes threats such as viruses, worms, Trojan horses, spyware, and any other malicious programs.

Even if you believe you have nothing of value to protect on your computer system, leaving it unprotected can leave you vulnerable to hundreds of different malware programs floating around the Internet which could arrive in your e-mail inbox daily. These programs can accomplish a wide variety of malicious activities, including possibly capturing your passwords and credit card numbers, sending out malware to other computers or to e-mail addresses of people you know, using your computer in a denial-of-service attack against a Web site, and more.

Weak Passwords

Passwords are the primary method most users are familiar with for gaining access to a computer system or program. If you have a weak password and an attacker manages to guess or crack it, he or she can access your private information, steal your identity, install and execute programs using your account, and more. Even worse, some of this can be done without ever knowing your password—by using remote threats.

Physical Security

Physical security is admittedly less of an issue in a home environment. Generally, you aren't concerned with someone in your home sitting down at your computer and hacking into it. Nevertheless, your computer could still be stolen or lost.

The bottom line when it comes to physical security is that once someone has physical access to your computer, the gloves are off. There are ways that an attacker sitting at your computer and using your keyboard and disk drives can bypass the various security measures you have put in place to gain access to your data.

Network "Neighbors"

Computers that are connected to the same network as yours or within the same range of IP addresses are able to communicate with your computer more freely and gather information easier than other computers.

If you are using a cable modem to access the Internet, you are sharing the network with the other subscribers in your area. That means it is possible for other cable modem users in your area to view and access your drives and data if you aren't careful about how you share them out and what security measures you implement.

These are just a few of the ways your computer and the data it contains are at risk. The following sections will walk you through securing your computer, limiting the power of users, controlling access to files and folders, and other security measures you should put in place before you start networking with other computers around you or connecting your computer to the Internet.

Logging In

Windows XP has a slick feature called the Welcome screen. The first time the system boots up you will be greeted with the Welcome screen like the one shown in Figure 1.1.

Figure 1.1 The Windows XP Welcome Screen Is Displayed by Default When a Windows XP System Is First Booted

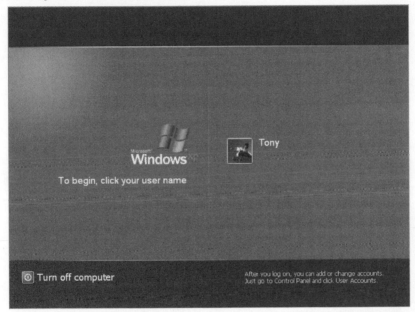

Initially, you will be able to access the system, as an Administrator, simply by clicking the picture next to the username. If you assign a password to a user account, clicking the picture will open a box for you to enter the password before logging in to the system.

On Windows XP Professional machines connected to a domain network, the Welcome screen is replaced with a login screen like Windows 2000. The user is required to press the **Ctrl**, **Alt**, and **Delete** keys simultaneously and then a window appears where you must enter a valid username and password to log in to the system.

User Accounts

A User Account is one of the primary means of controlling access to your data and resources as well as customizing Windows to look and act the way you want it to.

Older versions of Windows, like Windows 95 and Windows 98, have User Profiles which allow each user to customize the look and feel of Windows, but the User Profiles offer no security whatsoever. They give an illusion of security because they are associated with a password, but anyone can simply hit the **Esc** key and log in to the system with the default user profile.

The goal of this book is not necessarily to teach you every detail of User Accounts, but to show you in simple language how to set up your User Accounts in a secure fashion. The bad guys know a thing or two about the User Accounts that are installed by default. By following the advice in this section you can throw most novice hackers off the trail and thwart their attacks.

When Windows XP is first installed, it forces you to create at least one User Account and allows you to create as many as five (see Figure 1.2). Any accounts created at this point are automatically added to the Administrators group for the machine and are created with a blank password. For these reasons, I recommend that you add only one account at this point and add other accounts later when you can control what level of access to grant and assign appropriate passwords.

Figure 1.2 Creating User Accounts with Windows XP

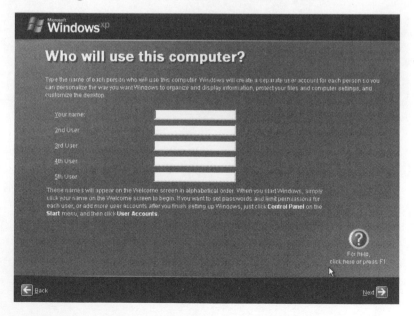

If you are upgrading from a previous Windows version, any existing users will also be automatically added to the Administrators group with a blank password when installing Windows XP. One exception is that if you are installing Windows XP Professional on a system connected to a network domain rather than in a workgroup or as a stand-alone system, the installation will offer you the opportunity to create a password.

NOTE

A quick note before we move on. Most of the advice will require that you log in as the Administrator or that your account is a member of the Administrators group. Based on what I described earlier, that may very well be the case for any accounts that were created during a Windows XP installation. But, if you run into any problems or receive any messages stating that you don't have permission or authority to complete the action, you should check into this and make sure the account you are using to make these changes is a member of the Administrators group.

Limiting the Number of Accounts

In order for different users to have their own customized and personalized configurations of Windows and their own My Documents folder (among other things), they need to have their own User Accounts.

Tools & Traps...

Administrative Tools

Having access to the Administrative Tools will also make life a lot easier when it comes to following the advice in this book and configuring and administering your computer in general. Microsoft does not make these tools visible by default in Windows XP. To get to these tools, follow these steps:

1. Right-click the **Start Bar** at the bottom of the screen and select **Properties**.
2. Click the **Start Menu** tab.
3. Click the **Customize** button.
4. Click the **Advanced** tab.

Continued

www.syngress.com

> **5.** In the **Start Menu Items** box, scroll to the bottom and select an
> option to display the Administrative Tools.

However, the more User Accounts there are, the more targets there are for a potential attacker. Therefore, it is important to limit the number of User Accounts on the system. In a home environment, you may choose to have separate accounts for the adults, but have a single "Kids" account that they share. You definitely want to make sure you remove any duplicate or unused User Accounts.

You can view the User Accounts by clicking **User Accounts** in the **Control Panel**. However, this view only shows you the accounts that are allowed to log in to the computer system locally. There are other hidden accounts used by the operating system or applications. To see the complete list you should view them in the Computer Management module. Unfortunately, in Windows XP Home you can't view the User Accounts in this way. Short of jumping through a ring of fire upside down while chanting Bill Gates (or some risky registry hacking), there isn't much you can do to make some of these changes. Windows XP Home users will have to just stick with making changes through the User Accounts button in the Control Panel.

You can get to the Computer Management module a variety of ways:

- Right-click **My Computer** on the desktop if you have it available and select **Manage**.

- Right-click **My Computer** in the left-hand navigation pane of a Windows Explorer window and select **Manage**.

- Click **Start | All Programs | Administrative Tools**, if you have it available, and select **Computer Management**.

- Click **Start | Run** and enter **compmgmt.msc** to open the Computer Management module.

Using any of these methods will open the Computer Management window (see Figure 1.3). To view the User Accounts, simply click the **plus sign** next to Local Users and Groups and then click **Users**. You will see a window similar to the one in Figure 1.3 that lists all of the User Accounts on the system. Currently disabled accounts will have a red X on them.

Figure 1.3 The Windows XP Computer Management Console Allows You to Manage a Variety of Administrative Tasks

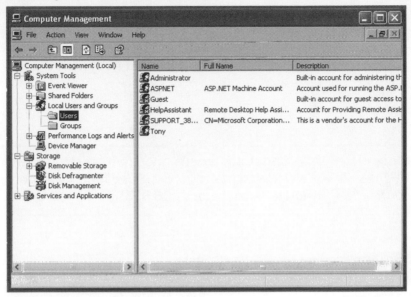

You can right-click any of the User Accounts to rename them, delete them, or change their passwords. You can also select Properties to perform other tasks such as disabling the account, setting the password so that it must be changed at the next login, configuring the password so it can never be changed, and more.

Disabling the Guest Account

Disabling the Guest account has been recommended by security experts since the Guest account was first created. Under previous Windows versions, the Guest account had virtually no real-world purpose and served simply as another means for an attacker to gain access to a system, especially because the Guest account also has no password by default.

In Windows XP, it is another story. The Guest account can still be an easy target for attackers, but in Windows XP Home and in Windows XP Professional systems that are not connected to a network domain, the Guest account is an integral part of sharing resources with other computers on the network. In fact, in Windows XP Home, it is not possible (at least not without the prerequisite jumping through the ring of fire upside down while chanting Bill Gates… you get the idea) to truly delete the Guest account.

By clicking **Control Panel** and going into User Accounts to turn off the Guest account in Windows XP Home, all you've really done is disable the Guest account for local logon. The account won't appear on the Welcome screen and nobody will be able to walk up and log on to the computer using the Guest account; however, the actual credentials and password are still active behind the scenes. Simply put, Windows XP Home relies on the Guest account for its network file and resource sharing. Your best bet to secure the Guest account on a Windows XP Home system is to assign a strong password—a password that is difficult to guess or crack—to the Guest account.

> **NOTE**
>
> For more information about passwords and creating strong passwords, see Chapter 2. See also *Perfect Passwords: Selection, Protection, Authentication* (Syngress Publishing, 2006, ISBN: 1-59749-041-5).

Creating a password for the Guest account is also not an easy task in Windows XP Home. When you open the User Accounts console from the Control Panel in Windows XP Home and select the Guest account, Create a Password is not one of the available options.

To create a password for the Guest account, you will need to open a command-line window (click **Start | All Programs | Accessories | Command Prompt**). Enter the following: **net user guest <password>**.

Leave off the brackets and simply type the password you want to assign at the end of the command line and press **Enter**. Oddly, now that you have created a password for the Guest account, the options for changing or removing the password will now appear in the User Accounts console.

Renaming the Administrator Account

In order for an attacker to gain access to your system, they really only need two things: a valid username and its associated password. It's easy for an attacker to learn what operating system and application vendors do by default when their product is installed. Therefore, everyone knows that Windows sets up a User Account called Administrator, which by default is a member of the Administrators group, and that Windows XP creates these accounts with blank passwords during installation. With this information, an attacker has the keys to the kingdom so to speak.

While there are ways that an attacker can tell which account is *truly* the Administrator account, it is recommended that you rename the Administrator account to make it harder to find. This way, you will at least protect your system from novice or casual hackers.

You should select a name which means something to you, but that doesn't make it obvious it's an Administrator account—in other words, calling it Home or Family or even some variation of your own name (for instance "Chuck" if your name is Charlie, or "Mike" if your name is Michael). If you rename it to Admin or LocalAdmin or anything else, it will still look like an administrative account and you won't be able to throw off an attacker for long.

You can rename the Administrator account by following the steps listed earlier to open the Computer Management console and clicking the **plus sign** next to Local Users and Groups, and then clicking **Users**. You can then right-click the **Administrator** account and select **Rename**. You will have to use a different account with Computer Administrator privileges to make the change, however, because you can't rename the account you're currently logged in under.

Windows XP Home does not create an "Administrator" account per se (it does exist as a hidden account that is only visible if you log in using SafeMode), but you should follow similar logic in deciding what to name accounts given Computer Administrator privileges.

Creating a Dummy Administrator Account

Hand in hand with the preceding advice, you should also create a "dummy" Administrator account. Most users with enough knowledge to try to hack or attack your computer know that Windows 2000 and Windows XP Professional will create an Administrator account by default. If they manage to access your system and see that no Administrator account exists, that will tip them off that one of the other existing accounts must be the "real" Administrator.

Again, there are more sophisticated ways for an advanced hacker to determine which account is truly the Administrator, but that is still no reason to make it easy for the novices. Once you rename the Administrator account by following the previous steps, you should create a new account named **Administrator** and assign it to the Limited account type.

Security Groups

Just like User Accounts, Security Groups help you control access to your data and resources. Where User Accounts allow you to define permissions and grant access on an individual basis, a Security Group allows you to define permissions and grant access on a group basis.

This is more useful in a business network where there are typically more people involved and there is more data that may need to be accessible by one group of employees and inaccessible by others. That is probably why Microsoft only includes the ability to use Security Groups in Windows XP Professional and not in Windows XP Home. If you are using Windows XP Professional on a home network, this information may be helpful, but if you are focused only on Windows XP Home systems, you can safely skip this section.

Using Security Groups can help to make assigning permissions and access privileges more manageable. In situations where a number of users will access a resource, it is much simpler to assign one set of permissions for the parents or managers and a more restrictive set of permissions for the children or regular users. Using Security Groups rather than individual User Accounts will make administering the permissions as users come and go an easier task.

You can use the same steps illustrated earlier under User Accounts to open the Computer Management module, and then just select Groups, instead of Users, from the left pane.

Windows comes with certain Security Groups predefined. Table 1.1 lists the various built-in Security Groups by operating system and includes a brief description of each.

Table 1.1 Windows 2000 and Windows XP Pro Built-in Security Groups

Security Group	Windows 2000	Windows XP Pro	Description
Administrators	X	X	Most powerful Security Group. Members of this group have the power to do just about anything on the computer.
Users	X	X	This group has the ability to use most parts of the system, but has very limited ability to install or change any part of the computer.
Guests	X	X	Guests have very limited access and ability to do anything on the system. In Windows XP, however, the Guest account is integral to the Simple File Sharing system.
HelpServices		X	This group is new in Windows XP and allows support technicians to connect to your computer.

Continued

Table 1.1 continued Windows 2000 and Windows XP Pro Built-in Security Groups

Security Group	Windows 2000	Windows XP Pro	Description
Power Users	X	X	In between Users and Administrators, this group grants users more power and ability to install and configure the system without making them full Administrators.
Backup Operators	X	X	A special group designed to give its members the ability to back up and restore files and folders that they might otherwise not have access to.
Replicator	X	X	Pertinent only in domain-based networks, this group has the ability to manage file replication.
Network Configuration Operators		X	This group grants its members the ability to add, change, or delete network connections, and to change TCP/IP settings.
Remote Desktop Users		X	Members of this group are able to connect to remote computers using the Remote Desktop Connection feature.

If none of these are appropriate for your purposes, you can also create your own custom Security Groups to use in defining access and granting permission to files, folders, or other network resources such as printers.

Windows 2000 and Windows XP Professional users can view these Security Groups and add or remove members from them using Local Users and Groups in the Computer Management console.

Windows XP Home Account Types

The extent of your ability to easily select a Security Group in Windows XP Home is based on what Account Type you select in the User Accounts screen in the Control Panel. You have two choices: Computer Administrator or Limited.

Computer Administrator is equivalent to Administrator with all-powerful access to the whole computer, while the Limited Account Type is more equivalent to the Users Security Group shown earlier. Users assigned to the Limited Account Type will be unable to install or alter programs or computer configurations.

FAT32 versus NTFS

You may never have heard of the terms FAT32 and NTFS, or at least never cared enough to find out what they are, but they are file systems. When you format your hard drive, you can choose whether to format it using FAT32 or NTFS.

They both have pros and cons, but from a security perspective, you should choose NTFS. FAT32 does not offer any sort of file or folder security. NTFS, on the other hand, allows you to secure files at an individual level and specify which users are authorized to access them. You must also use NTFS if you want to use EFS (Encrypting File System) to further secure your data.

When it comes to sharing files and folders with other computers on your network, the underlying file system does not matter. Other computers on your network, whether running Windows XP, Windows NT, Linux or some other operating system, will be able to access the shared data. If you share out files on a drive using FAT32, though, you will be unable to provide security at a file level. Thus, anyone who can access the share will have access to everything in the shared drive or folder.

As a final note, NTFS also offers support for larger file sizes and drive partitions and provides better data compression and less file fragmentation than the FAT32 file systems.

File and Folder Security

One way to secure your data is to set permissions and access restrictions to identify which users or Security Groups are allowed to view, add, change, or delete files. If you set your files up so that only you can access them and a different user on the machine becomes compromised—either through a virus or worm, or by a hacker or some other means—that user's compromised account will not be able to wreak any havoc on your protected data.

To configure the security and permissions for a file or folder, simply right-click it and select the **Sharing and Security** or **Properties** options. Once it opens, you can then select the **Sharing** tab in Windows XP Home or the **Security** tab for Windows 2000 or Windows XP Professional using the classic file and folder security model.

Keeping It Simple

Windows XP Home uses a sharing model called Simple File Sharing. In Windows XP Professional machines that are not connected to a network, Simple File Sharing is an option. Like many "features" designed to make things easier for the user, it also is less configurable and provides less security than the file and folder sharing in Windows XP Professional or Windows 2000.

Simple File Sharing is some sort of Dr. Frankenstein combination of the power inherent in Windows XP combined with the security model (or lack thereof) in Windows 98. With Simple File Sharing, you can choose to share a folder or not to share that folder, but even if you use NTFS, you don't get to take advantage of file-level access or permissions. Essentially, once the folder is shared, anyone on the network will be able to access anything on the share.

TIP

Windows XP Home users are stuck with Simple File Sharing. Users of Windows XP Professional, however, can enable or disable it by clicking **Tools | Folder Options** on the toolbar from within Windows Explorer. Click the **View** tab and then scroll to the bottom of the Advanced Settings to find the Simple File Sharing setting.

This is also a big concern for Windows XP Home users on the Internet. If certain precautions (like blocking the ports Windows uses for file and folder sharing at your firewall) aren't taken, anyone who can see your computer from the Internet will also be able to access the files on the shared folder. If you assigned a strong password to the Guest account, as described earlier in this chapter, the risk of this is even lower.

Windows XP Home and Windows XP Professional systems using Simple File Sharing also offer the opposite end of the spectrum—the option to make a folder "private." When you mark a folder private, the file permissions are set so that only you have the ability to open or view the data they contain (see Figure 1.4).

Figure 1.4 Right-Click a Folder in Windows Explorer and Choose Sharing and Security to Configure Access to the Folder

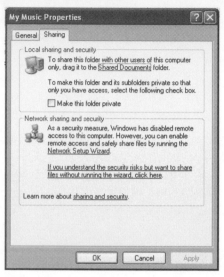

Sharing and Security

If you are using Windows XP Professional, I would advise that you turn off Simple File Sharing and use the standard file and folder security. To turn off Simple File Sharing, open **My Computer** or a **Windows Explorer** window and select **Tools | Folder Options**. Then click the **View** tab and scroll all the way to the bottom of the **Advanced Settings** options and make sure there is no checkmark in the checkbox next to **Use Simple File Sharing**.

Tools & Traps…

XP Password Alert

If you attempt to mark a file or folder as "Private" using a User Account that does not have a password assigned, Windows XP will alert you and offer you an opportunity to create a password.

The alert says:

You do not currently have a password on your User Account. Even though you made this folder private, anyone can log in as you and access this folder.

Do you want to create a password for yourself?

When using the classic file and folder sharing of Windows 2000 or Windows XP Professional with Simple File Sharing disabled, you have a lot of control over the access privileges different users have to your data.

You can add or remove the User Accounts and Security Groups defined for the file or folder you are configuring (remember, it's easier to track and administer permissions using Security Groups if you are dealing with more than just two or three users). For each User Account or Security Group, you can select either Allow or Deny for a variety of actions to customize the level of access granted.

You can choose to Allow or Deny Full Control which would give that User Account or Security Group the ability to do anything they want with the data, including modifying or deleting it entirely or even changing the permissions for other users. If you don't grant Full Control, you can choose to Allow or Deny the ability to Modify, Read & Execute, List Folder Contents, Read, or Write. Table 1.2 includes a brief summary of each of these access levels.

Table 1.2 Access Levels for Windows 2000 or Windows XP Professional

File and Folder Permission	Grants the Ability to
Full Control	Change or configure permissions for other User Accounts and Security Groups, take ownership of the file or folder, delete the folder or any subfolders in the case of Folder permissions, or delete the file in the case of File permissions. Full Control also grants the ability to perform all of the functions of the other file and folder permissions.
Modify	This permission allows users to delete the folder in the case of Folder permissions as well as perform any of the actions permitted by the Write permission and the Read & Execute permission.
Read & Execute	Allows users to read the contents of the folder or file, including viewing the file attributes and permissions. This permission also allows users to execute files or run executable files contained in the folder.

Continued

Table 1.2 continued Access Levels for Windows 2000 or Windows XP
Professional

File and Folder Permission	Grants the Ability to
List Folder Contents	Unique to Folder permissions, this permission allows users to display the directory of names of files and subfolders in the folder.
Read	This permission allows users to view the files and subfolders in a folder in the case of Folder permissions. For file permissions, it grants the ability to read the file in question. Users can also view attributes of the file or folder including ownership, permissions, and attributes (such as Read-only, Hidden, Archive, and System).
Write	The Write permission allows users to add new files to a folder or modify a file or document as the case may be. The Folder permission allows users to also add subfolders to the folder, alter attributes and view folder ownership and permissions. The File permission allows users to perform similar actions on Files, including overwriting the file, altering the file attributes, and viewing file ownership and permissions.

There are two items to note when you are setting permissions. First, permissions can be inherited from parent directories. If you see checkmarks in the boxes but they are grayed out, meaning you can not change them, that is because they are inherited from somewhere else. If you click the **Advanced** button under the **Permissions** settings box, you can view or change the current setup and turn off the inheritance of permissions from parent folders.

On the Permissions tab of the Advanced box, you will see each of the User Accounts and Security Groups with permissions on the object. Next to each it will display their Permission level, where it was inherited from, and what that permission level applies to. At the bottom of this tab are two checkboxes. One is to select whether or not you wish to allow permissions from other directories to be inherited by this object. The second is whether or not you want the permissions from this object to be applied to the files and folders underneath it.

The second item of note is in regards to selecting Deny for any of the permission settings and what the result would be for a user. Deny overrides all other options. So, for example, let's assume Bob is a member of both the Administrators and Users groups. If the Administrators group has Full Control permission, while the Users group only has Read permission, Bob would have Full Control because he would get the cumulative total for both permissions. However, if you also add Bob's individual User Account and select Deny for Full Control, that selection will override his membership in the Administrators and the Users groups and Bob will be unable to access or perform any actions on that object.

In the Advanced options discussed previously, there is also a tab called Effective Permissions. This handy tool will let you enter any User Account or Security Group and it will display for you what the net permissions are for that account on this particular object. This way you can see the effect of different permissions and what level of access the user or group actually has.

You should try to use a designated folder or folders to house your personal and confidential files so that you can easily protect (and back up) that information rather than having to search all over your computer or protect individual files scattered about the hard drive.

WARNING

Any drive or partition that you format using the FAT32 file system will not be able to provide file or folder security. In order to secure your data and apply file and folder permissions as we have discussed here, you must use the NTFS file system.

Windows Services

A Windows "service" is a program that runs in the background on Windows. They aren't programs that will show up on the Start Bar at the bottom of the screen or programs in the sense that you would directly access or interact with them. Windows services generally provide some functionality for the operating system or process actions and requests from other programs.

To see a list of the services installed on your computer and whether or not they are currently enabled, you need to go into the Services Console. You can accomplish this by going into the **Control Panel / Administrative Tools** folder and selecting **Services**.

You will see a number of services listed along with a brief description of what the service does, its current status, its startup configuration, and what access level it logs in under (see Figure 1.5).

Figure 1.5 Select Services from the Administrative Tools Group to Open the Windows Services Console

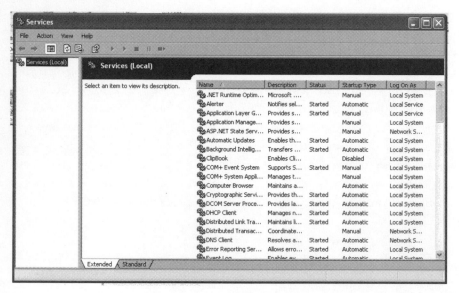

Many of these services are unnecessary or rarely used. Sites such as LabMice.net (http://labmice.techtarget.com/) or TheElderGeek.com (www.theeldergeek.com/services_guide.htm) provide checklists and recommendations for how to configure each of the standard Windows services. For our purposes, we will just talk about the services that directly affect the security of your system.

In general, any service you don't have a need for should be disabled because they simply offer opportunities for someone to possibly exploit a vulnerability or security weakness in that service to gain access to your system.

The following is a list of Windows services that you should disable because they provide an avenue for an attacker to compromise your system while not providing any useful functionality for most users:

- **SSDP Discovery Service** Enables discovery of UPnP (Universal Plug and Play) devices on your home network. This service provides half of the

UPnP functionality which has no real-world purpose but has been proven vulnerable to attack. This service does not affect Windows 2000.

- **Universal Plug and Play Device Host** Provides support to host Universal Plug and Play devices. This is the other half of the UPnP functionality. This service does not affect Windows 2000.

- **NetMeeting Remote Desktop Sharing** Enables an authorized user to access the local computer remotely using the NetMeeting program. Unless you intend to use NetMeeting on a regular basis, leaving this on simply provides a possible way for an attacker to gain access to your system.

- **Remote Registry** Enables remote users to modify Registry settings on the local computer. With rare exception there is no reason that you would want someone to be able to alter your Registry settings remotely. If you leave this service on, you run the risk that an unauthorized user may change your Registry settings remotely.

- **Messenger** Transmits Net Send and Alerter service messages between clients and servers. This service is a security concern from the standpoint that spam pushers have discovered they can use Net Send to transmit spam messages directly to your desktop rather than sending them through your e-mail.

- **Internet Information Services** Internet Information Services (IIS) should not be installed by default on any of these operating systems, but as long as you are in the Services Console you should take a look to make sure the Internet Information Services are not enabled unless you are actually using IIS to host web sites or FTP on your local computer. IIS is prone to vulnerabilities which have allowed viruses such as CodeRed and Nimda to propagate.

If you right-click any of the services in the Services Console, you can start and stop the service. However, stopping a service using this technique will only stop it temporarily. The next time you reboot the computer, or the next time another service tries to call or interact with the service, it will restart.

To disable a service so that it will not start again, right-click the service in the **Services Console** and select **Properties**. In the middle of the screen under the General tab is a drop-down box titled Startup Type. The drop-down box offers three choices: Automatic, Manual, and Disabled (see Figure 1.6).

Figure 1.6 You Can Disable a Windows Service by Right-Clicking the Service in the Windows Services Console and Selecting Properties

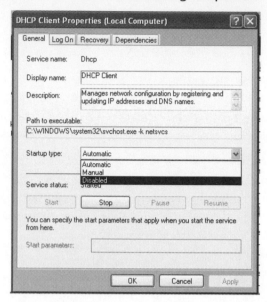

Services configured for Automatic startup will be started each time you boot up the computer and the Windows operating system begins. Services that are configured for Manual startup will only start when another program or service activates them or if you right-click the service and manually start it. Services that are disabled will be unable to start at all.

To secure your operating system and protect it from easy access by hackers, I recommend that you disable all of the services mentioned previously, if they are not already disabled.

Hidden File Extensions

Microsoft created the ability to hide known file extensions so that everyday users would not need to be bothered with too much technical stuff. The icon associated with the file type would show you what sort of file it was so there was no need to inundate users with technical jargon like EXE or VBS or DOC or HTM.

It didn't take long for virus writers and developers of other malware to figure out that you can add more than one extension at the end of the file name and that the last one will be hidden. So a file like mynotes.txt could be replaced with a malicious executable program called mynotes.txt.vbs, and with the file extensions being hidden it would still appear as mynotes.txt.

There are two things to note here. One, an observant user might detect the fact that only the malicious file shows any file extension at all. Using the double file extension hides the true file extension, but it still shows a file extension which gives away the fact that something is different. Two, the hidden file extensions only work in Windows Explorer. If you view the files using the **dir** command at a command prompt window, it will show the complete file name, including both file extensions.

Even with those caveats in mind, though, it is best to simply disable this feature so that any and all file extensions are readily visible. To disable the hiding of file extensions, go into Windows Explorer (**Start | All Programs | Accessories | Windows Explorer**) and select **Tools**, and then **Folder Options**. Click the **View** tab and uncheck the box titled **Hide extensions for known file types** (see Figure 1.7). All that was hidden shall now be revealed unto you, or at least the file extensions of the files on your computer system.

Figure 1.7 Click Tools on the Menu Bar in Windows Explorer and Choose Folder Options to Disable the Hiding of File Extensions in Windows

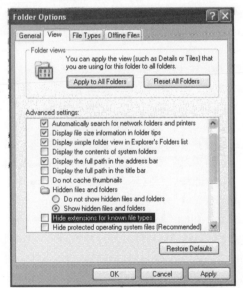

Screen Saver

Screen savers started off as a measure to protect your monitor. The technology used in older monitors was subject to having the image burned into the phosphorous permanently if the same image stayed on the screen for too long. The result of walking away to go to lunch and coming back an hour later might be that the spreadsheet data you were working with would be a permanent ghostly image on your monitor.

Companies sprang up for the sole purpose of developing new and creative screen savers to keep this from happening. Basically, the screen saver program monitors computer activity and if there is no activity for a predefined period of time, the screen saver kicks off sending swirling shapes, flying toasters, swimming fish, or just about anything you can imagine randomly bouncing around the screen so that no single image is left in one place long enough to burn the monitor. Meanwhile, all of your programs and files are kept running in the background just as you left them.

Over time, monitor technology has improved to the point that the screen saver is no longer truly needed to protect the monitor. However, screen savers have taken on a new, arguably more important role. Now when you walk away to go to lunch for an hour the concern is not that your spreadsheet data will be burned into the phosphorous, but that anyone walking by would be able to see your spreadsheet data. Worse yet, anyone walking by could sit at your computer and access any of your files, or files on other computers you have access to, or send e-mail on your behalf, or any number of other things. The bottom line is that walking away from your computer is a huge security risk.

Thankfully, Windows offers an option to require a password to unlock the computer once the screen saver is started. If the user account being used does not have a password assigned, you will still see a message box stating that the system has been locked and that a password is needed. However, anyone can still get into the system by just hitting **Enter** if there is no password in place.

To configure your screen saver in Windows, you can right-click anywhere on the desktop and select **Properties**. Click the **Screen Saver** tab and check the box that says **On resume, password protect**.

You can also set the amount of time you want the system to wait before automatically starting the screen saver. You should set it for a short enough time to provide protection for your computer and your data should you leave your computer system, but long enough that the screen saver won't automatically start while you're trying to read your e-mail and become more of an annoyance than a benefit (see Figure 1.8).

Figure 1.8 You Can Open the Windows Display Properties by Right-Clicking the Desktop and Selecting Properties

Summary

This chapter provided some fundamental knowledge about how to use and configure the basic Windows XP security features. You learned about how Windows controls access to the system, and how User Accounts and Security Groups can be used, together with file and folder security, to restrict access and protect your system.

You also gained some knowledge about Windows services and how to disable those you aren't using, as well as the danger of hidden file extensions and how they can be used against you. Lastly, you learned that the screensaver is more than a frivolous toy to fill your screen while you're away. It can also be used as a security system for your computer.

Armed with this basic knowledge of how to protect and secure the Windows XP operating system, you can proceed through the book and learn how to use other applications more securely.

Additional Resources

The following resources provide more information on Windows security:

- *Description of the Guest Account in Windows XP.* Microsoft's Help and Support Web Page (http://support.microsoft.com/kb/300489/en-us).

- *How to Configure File Sharing in Windows XP.* Microsoft's Help and Support Web Page (http://support.microsoft.com/kb/304040/en-us).

- *How to Create and Configure User Accounts in Windows XP.* Microsoft's Help and Support Web Page (http://support.microsoft.com/kb/279783/en-us).

- *How to Use Convert.exe to Convert a Partition to the NTFS File System.* Microsoft's Help and Support Web Page (http://support.microsoft.com/kb/314097/en-us).

- *Limitations of the FAT32 File System in Windows XP.* Microsoft's Help and Support Web Page (http://support.microsoft.com/kb/314463/en-us).

- *User Accounts That You Create During Setup Are Administrator Account Types.* Microsoft's Help and Support Web Page (http://support.microsoft.com/kb/293834/en-us).

Chapter 2

Passwords

Topics in this chapter:

- Password Power
- Password Cracking
- Storing Your Passwords
- One Super-Powerful Password

- ☑ Summary
- ☑ Additional Resources

Introduction

Passwords are the primary means of security for most home computer users. People have passwords to access their bank account, pay utility bills online, check their investments, and even to log on to their MySpace.com accounts.

It is important that passwords be complex, or strong enough to provide adequate protection, and that they are managed properly. In this chapter you will learn about the basics of passwords. After reading this chapter, you'll know how to choose strong passwords, how to create passwords from phrases, how to crack passwords, and how to set passwords in a BIOS.

Password Power

A password is just a shared secret code or word that proves to the computer or application that you are authorized access. Just as with Ali Baba's "Open, Sesame" or the secret knock children use to gain access to the neighborhood clubhouse, computer passwords enable users to "prove" that they are allowed to use a particular computer, a Web site, or their own bank account.

Your passwords can be quite powerful. Consider what could happen if someone stole them from you. They might be able to do any of the following:

- Access your personal files including e-mail and financial data

- Impersonate you and send e-mail that appears to be from you

- Access your bank account and initiate transactions

- Gain access to information that may provide them with other confidential data, such as other log-on information and passwords

Are You Owned?

Passwords for Cash

In May of 2006, a Trojan horse was discovered (PSW.Win32.WOW.x) that was designed to steal usernames and passwords for World of Warcraft (WoW) accounts.

Continued

WoW is a very popular online adventure game, but the attacker probably was not trying to steal game access. WoW is so big that Virtual Gold from the game is actually bought and sold with real cash by other players.

You may not think you need a strong password for a game, but compromised WoW accounts can be converted to cash by selling Virtual Gold and other items of value from the game to other players

Passwords are used for a wide variety of access controls, including the computer operating system, different software programs, company networks, Web sites and more. There are also different types of passwords used in other areas of your life such as PIN numbers for your bank ATM card, access codes to check your voicemail, and the code to open your garage door, to name a few. These are all different forms of passwords and it is important that you create passwords that are difficult for others to guess and that you keep them secret.

The trick is to make each password unique and original enough that unauthorized parties won't be able to guess it or figure out what it is, while making it something that you can remember. If you can't remember your own password it won't do you much good.

RSA Security, provider of various authentication and identification technologies, conducted a survey of users in late 2005 that shows how insecure passwords can be. Here are some of the key results from this survey:

- The Survey found that 58% of users have more than six passwords. Almost half of those have more than 13 passwords to manage.

- Many users keep track of their passwords using insecure methods such as storing them on a PDA or other handheld device (22%) or writing them down on paper stored in their desk (15%).

- Asked about having a single, master password that would unlock all their systems and applications, 98% of respondents stated that an extra layer of protection would then be required for security.

This survey highlights some of the issues that still plague computer security. Users are inundated with usernames and passwords and many of them choose passwords that are easy to determine or guess because they are trying to select passwords that will also be easy for them to remember.

Many users will also resort to recording their usernames and passwords somewhere—either on sticky notes on their monitor or on a scratch pad in their desk drawer or in a planner that they carry with them. Recording the passwords in a place that they can refer to might make it easier on the user, but it will also make it that much easier on any would-be attacker who might come into possession of this list.

The Keys to Your Data

If you think about the password as the key to your computer or data you can better understand why simple passwords are less secure than complex passwords and why any password, no matter how complex, may eventually be cracked.

Although your life might be easier if the lock on your house, the lock on your car, the lock on your desk at work, and the lock on your locker at the gym could all be opened with the same key, if that one key fell into the wrong hands they would be able to open all of those locks as well.

The same is true for your passwords. The online store where you purchased new ink cartridges for your printer may not guard their customer database with quite the same level of protection that your bank will. Some applications or Web sites may be less secure than others and you never know if your password is being stored in an encrypted form in a secure location or if it is just saved as plain text in an Excel spreadsheet somewhere.

Tools & Traps...

Brief Tips on Password Care

The analogy that compares passwords to underwear has been used in numerous security awareness campaigns, particularly at colleges and universities. Passwords are like underwear because you must:

- Change them often (especially if asked to)
- Only use your own
- Keep them hidden
- Not share them with your friends
- Not leave them lying around

If an attacker manages to get your password from hacking into the ink cartridge merchant's customer database, they can view your profile on the site and probably your purchase history. Your purchase history might reveal your bank name. The attacker might go to the bank Web site on a whim and try to log on using the same password. Now they have access to all your money. They can also view your recent transactions, which might provide them clues as to who your Internet service provider is or who your cell phone provider is or which brokerage manages your investment funds. If you use the same password at all these sites and locations, an attacker gaining access to your password at one location would hold the key to the entire kingdom.

You can use some discretion when it comes to password diversity. You might have one password that you use for all sites and applications that have no confidential or sensitive information such as your bank account number or credit card number or social security number. Your account on an online recipe site or the one you use to access message boards about golfing probably don't need to have exceptionally strong passwords nor would it be the end of the world if one password could get into all of those sites and applications.

However, any site where your personal, confidential, or financial information may be stored in your profile or in a database should receive more attention on your part to take the extra time to give them unique passwords.

Selecting Strong Passwords

So what's a person to do? You can't even remember what you had for dinner last night or what time your son's soccer practice is. How are you going to remember what your password is?

The first thing that most users try is to simply use a word that is familiar to them. Many users will choose things like their own name, their children's names, or the name of a pet.

Going back to the key analogy—if your password is like your key to unlock your computer, then choosing a password based on easily obtainable personal facts is like locking your door and placing the key under the doormat. It is better than nothing, but not by much. Through simple research or just conversation over coffee, an attacker can pick up personal information about you such as your spouse's name, children's names, birth dates, and more.

It is important that you choose a strong password. What makes a password strong? Length is one factor. Another is to use a variety of character types. Passwords are generally case sensitive, so "password" is different from "Password." Of course, capitalizing the first letter might be the first thing someone would try if they were guessing, so using something like "pasSword" or "pasSwoRd" would be even stronger.

When you create a password in Windows XP, you are also asked to enter a word or phrase (see Figure 2.1) to act as a password hint. If you have issues remembering your password, Windows XP can display the hint to try to trigger your memory so you can recall it. Click **Control Panel | User Accounts | Change an Account**, and then select a user and click **Change Password** to create a new password in Windows XP (see Figure 2.1).

Figure 2.1 Creating a new password in Windows XP

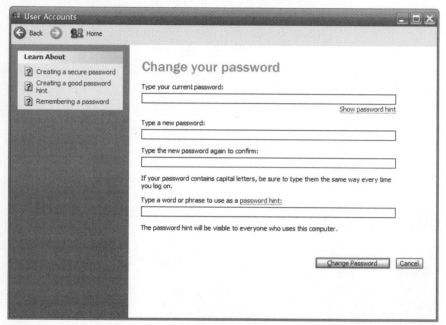

Aside from avoiding the use of personal data or information as your password, you should also avoid all dictionary words. One trick is to substitute numbers or special characters that look similar to letters. This is common in hacker lingo where "elite" becomes "l33t" and "hacker" becomes "h4x0r". Using this method it is possible to still choose a password that might be easy for you to remember, but writing it in a creative way using a variety of character types that will make it harder to guess or crack.

You can also take a phrase or sentence and boil it down to an acronym of sorts. For instance, you might find it easy to remember the phrase, "My birthday is on June 16." However, instead of typing the whole thing, you could use "mbioj16" as your password or scramble it a bit more with alternative characters as discussed above so that it becomes something like "mbi0j16." The net result is that you end up with a password that is more secure and harder to guess or break, but one that is easier for you to remember than just selecting a random grouping of various character types.

If you aren't sure how to transpose the normal characters in a word to alternate characters that look similar, you can use a tool like *L33t-5p34K G3n3r@t0r* available from a number of sites if you simply search for it on Google. You can also visit www.transl8it.com, but the translations are not as consistently good as those created with L33t-5p34K G3n3r@t0r.

If you can't come up with a good phrase or password on your own, you can use a tool like the Secure Password Generator on the winguides.com Web site (www.winguides.com/security/password.php). The Secure Password Generator (see Figure 2.2) has check boxes to let you select the number of characters in your password, whether to use uppercase letters, numbers, or punctuation, and whether to allow a character to repeat. You can also tell it to create up to 50 passwords at one time and then select the one you prefer from the list in case you are concerned that winguides.com will know your password.

Figure 2.2 The Secure Password Generator

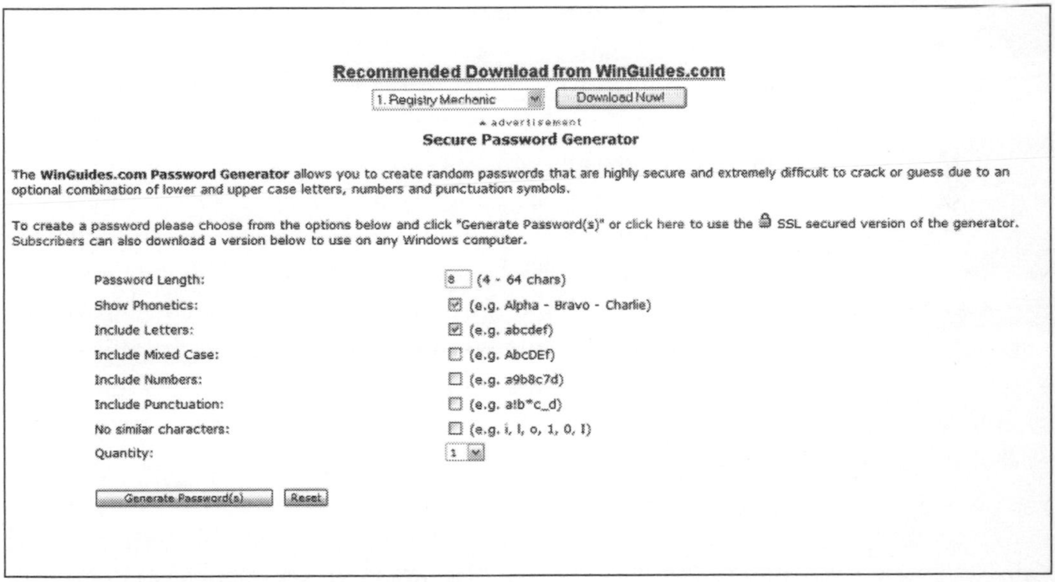

Password Cracking

Password-cracking utilities use three methods for attempting to break a password. The simplest and the fastest—assuming that your password is a word that might be found in a dictionary—is called the Dictionary Attack. The Dictionary Attack tries every word in the dictionary until it finds the right one for the username trying to be accessed.

The second method used to break passwords is called a Brute Force Attack. The Brute Force Attack will try literally every possible combination sequentially until it finds the right combination to authenticate the username trying to be accessed. The Brute Force Attack will attempt to use lowercase letters, uppercase letters, numbers, and special characters until it eventually stumbles onto the correct password.

The third method is called a Hybrid Attack. The Hybrid Attack combines the Dictionary Attack and the Brute Force Attack. Many users will choose a password that is in fact a dictionary word, but add a special character or number at the end. For instance, they might use "password1" instead of "password." A Dictionary Attack would fail because "password1" isn't in the dictionary, but a Brute Force Attack might take days depending on the processing power of the computer being used. By combining a Dictionary Attack with a Brute Force Attack, the Hybrid Attack would be able to crack this password much faster.

Given enough time and resources, no password is 100% unbreakable. Some password-recovery utilities may have success where others fail, and a lot depends on the processing horsepower of the machine attempting to crack the password (see the sidebar on p. 38).

Just like the lock on your home or car door—the idea is to make it difficult to get in, not impossible. A professional thief can probably still pick your lock in under a couple minutes, but the average person will be deterred by a lock and even thieves of moderate skill may be dissuaded by more complex or intricate lock systems.

The goal isn't to come up with a password that is unbreakable—although that would be nice as well. The goal is to create a password that you can remember but that the average person won't be able to guess based on knowing a few details about your life and that would take so long to crack using a password-recovery utility that a hacker of moderate skill would be dissuaded. In the end, someone skilled or dedicated enough could still find a way to break or go around your password, which is one of the reasons this is not the only defense mechanism you will use.

Aside from coming up with strong passwords, it is also important to change your passwords on a regular basis. Even if you have done everything possible to protect your passwords, it is still possible that through a security breach on a server or by an attacker intercepting network traffic, that your password could be intercepted or cracked. I would recommend that you change your passwords every 30 days at a minimum.

Storing Your Passwords

Obviously, having 70, 20, or even 5 different passwords at a given time can be difficult to keep track of. It becomes more complex when different Web sites or programs restrict the number and types of characters that you can use for your passwords, or require that you change your password very frequently. These are some of the reasons why so many people resort to tracking their usernames and passwords in a text file (.txt) using Notepad or a small spreadsheet file (.xls) using Excel.

In spite of the energy that security experts expend to convince people not to write down their passwords or store them in files on their computer, their advice goes largely unheeded. So, if you find that you're not going to be able to remember all the passwords you create, at least try to store them as securely as possible. To that end, I recommend using a free software package such as Password Safe (http://passwordsafe.sourceforge.net/) or Roboform (www.roboform.com/), to help you maintain your passwords more securely. Password Safe, an open-source password-management utility (shown in Figure 2.3), is available for free from Sourceforge.net.

Figure 2.3 Store Passwords Securely in Password Safe

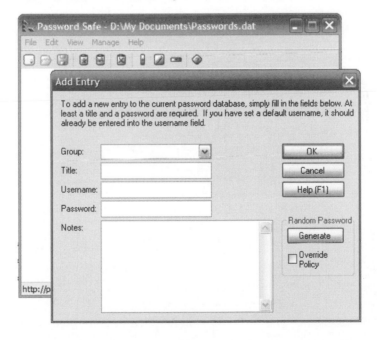

One Super-Powerful Password

Do you want to prevent people from even starting up your computer? You can password protect your entire computer by setting a password in the BIOS. What is the BIOS? The operating system, such as Windows XP, enables your different programs and applications to work on the computer. The BIOS, or Basic Input/Output System, is the brain of the motherboard that controls the inner workings of the computer. The BIOS is typically contained in a chip on the motherboard.

Tools & Traps...

Cain & Abel Version 2.5

Using a freely available password recovery utility called Cain & Abel Version 2.5, I was able to discover the passwords shown in Table 2.1 in the following time-frames using an AMD 2500+ CPU with 512 MB of memory.

Table 2.1 Results of a Password Search Using Cain & Abel Version 2.5

Password	Attack	Time
john	Dictionary	<1 minute
john4376	Dictionary	attack failed
	Brute	>12 hours
j0hN4376%$$	Dictionary	attack failed
	Brute	attack failed

Once you set a BIOS password, the computer will be completely useless to anyone who does not first enter the correct password. They won't even be able to begin trying to guess or crack your operating system or file passwords, because without the BIOS the computer cannot even start loading the operating system.

To configure the BIOS you typically press the F1 or DEL keys while the computer is booting up. The exact key to press varies from computer to computer. You should see a message when the computer first begins to boot, letting you know which key to press to enter the "Setup" screen. For details about accessing the BIOS and how to configure it, check your computer owner's manual.

Summary

Passwords are one of the most essential tools for protecting your data. In this chapter you learned about the important role that passwords play and some of the adverse affects that can occur if someone obtains your password.

To prevent an attacker from being able to guess or crack your passwords, you learned how to create stronger, more complex passwords, and how to use passphrases to generate even more complex passwords that you can still remember.

Lastly, this chapter covered some tools that you can use to securely store and track your passwords when remembering them all just seems too difficult, and how to lock access to your computer entirely by using a BIOS password.

Additional Resources

The following resources provide more information on passwords and password management:

- Bradley, Tony. *Creating Secure Passwords.* About.com (http://netsecurity.about.com/cs/generalsecurity/a/aa112103b.htm).

- *Creating Strong Passwords.* Microsoft Windows XP Professional Product Documentation (www.microsoft.com/resources/documentation/windows/xp/all/proddocs/en-us/windows_password_tips.mspx?mfr=true).

- *RSA Security Survey Reveals Multiple Passwords Creating Security Risks and End User Frustration.* RSA Security, Inc. Press Release. September 27, 2005 (www.rsasecurity.com/press_release.asp?doc_id=6095).

- *Strong Passwords.* Microsoft Windows Server TechCenter. January 21, 2005 (http://technet2.microsoft.com/WindowsServer/en/Library/d406b824-857c-4c2a-8de2-9b7ecbfa6e511033.mspx?mfr=true).

- *To Manage Passwords Stored on the Computer* Microsoft Windows XP Professional Product Documentation (www.microsoft.com/resources/documentation/windows/xp/all/proddocs/en-us/usercpl_manage_passwords.mspx?mfr=true).

Chapter 3

Viruses, Worms, and Other Malware

Topics in this chapter:

- **Malware Terms**
- **The History of Malware**

☑ **Summary**

☑ **Additional Resources**

Introduction

There are more than 200,000 reasons for you to learn the information in this chapter. McAfee, maker of security and antivirus software, recently announced that it has identified and created protection for its 200,000th threat. It took almost 18 years to reach the 100,000 mark, but that number doubled in only two years. Fortunately for computer users, McAfee's growth rate for identifying threats has slowed now.

Viruses rank with spam as one of the most well-known threats to computer security. Notorious threats—such as Slammer, Nimda, and MyDoom—even make headline news. Just about everyone knows that a computer virus is something to be actively avoided. This chapter will show you how to do that, by teaching you:

- Common malware terms
- The threat of malware
- How to install and configure antivirus software
- How to keep your antivirus software up-to-date
- How not to get infected
- What to do if you think you're infected

Malware Terms

Viruses and worms are two well-known types of malicious software. Many threats combine elements from different types of malicious software together, These blended threats don't fit into any one class, so the term malware, short for *malicious software*, is used as a catch-all term to describe a number of malicious threats, including viruses, worms, and more. Malware presents arguably the largest security threat to computer users. It can be confusing to understand what the difference is between a virus and a Trojan, but these explanations should help:

- **Virus** A virus is malicious code that replicates itself. New viruses are discovered daily. Some exist simply to replicate themselves. Others can do serious damage such as erasing files or even rendering the computer itself inoperable.

- **Worm** A worm is similar to a virus. They replicate themselves like viruses, but do not alter files like viruses do. The main difference is that worms reside in memory and usually remain unnoticed until the rate of replication reduces system resources to the point that it becomes noticeable.

- **Trojan** A Trojan horse got its name from the story of the Trojan horse in Greek legend. It is a malicious program disguised as a normal application. Trojan horse programs do not replicate themselves like a virus, but they can be propagated as attachments to a virus.

- **Rootkit** A rootkit is a set of tools and utilities that a hacker can use to maintain access once they have hacked a system. The rootkit tools allow them to seek out usernames and passwords, launch attacks against remote systems, and conceal their actions by hiding their files and processes and erasing their activity from system logs and a plethora of other malicious stealth tools.

- **Bot/Zombie** A *bot* is a type of malware which allows an attacker to gain complete control over the affected computer. Computers that are infected with a bot are generally referred to as *zombies*.

The History of Malware

Every year seems to mark a new record for the most new malware introduced, as well as the most systems impacted by malware. The year 2003 was not only a record-setting year for malware but also the 20th anniversary of computer viruses.

In 1983, graduate student Fred Cohen first used the term *virus* in a paper describing a program that can spread by infecting other computers with copies of itself. There were a handful of viruses discovered over the next 15 years, but it wasn't until 1999, when the Melissa virus stormed the Internet, that viruses became common knowledge.

Since then, there have been a number of high-profile viruses and worms which have spread rapidly around the world. Code Red, Nimda, Slammer, and MyDoom are virtually household words today. The number of new malware threats and the speed at which the threats spread across the Internet has grown each year.

The Brain virus was the first virus designed to infect personal computer systems. It was introduced in 1986, at a time when the general public didn't know what the Internet was and the World Wide Web had not even been created. It could only spread to other computers by infecting floppy disks that were passed between users and therefore had much less impact. Compare that with more recent threats such as *SQL Slammer* which, by spreading through the Internet to the millions of computers now connected to it, was able to infect hundreds of thousands of computers and cripple the Internet in less than 30 minutes.

Are You Owned?

SQL Slammer

In January 2003, the SQL Slammer worm stunned the world with its raw speed. Exploiting a vulnerability that had been identified more than six months earlier, the worm was able to infect more than 75,000 systems in less than ten minutes.

The sheer volume of traffic generated by this worm, as it replicated and continued to seek out other vulnerable systems, crippled the Internet by overwhelming routers and servers to the point that they could no longer communicate.

The effects of SQL Slammer went as far as impacting personal banking in some cases. ATM machines require network communications to process transactions. With the impact of SQL Slammer, the network was unavailable and the ATM system for some banks was effectively shut down.

Gone are the days when new threats were few and far between and had no simple means of propagating from system to system. The explosion of the Internet and the advent of broadband Internet service mean that there are millions of computers with high-speed connections linked to the Internet at any given moment. With millions of potential targets, it is almost a guarantee that at least a few thousand will fall victim to a new threat.

As we discussed earlier in the book, when you are on the Internet you are a part of a worldwide network of computers. You have a responsibility to the rest of us sharing the network with you to make sure your computer system is not infected and spreading malware to everyone else. It is much less of a headache and a lot easier in the long run to proactively make sure your system is secure and to protect yourself by installing antivirus software to detect and remove threats such as these before they infect your computer system.

Protect Yourself with Antivirus Software

The term *antivirus* is a misnomer of sorts. Antivirus software has evolved to include many other security components. Depending on the vendor, the antivirus software may also contain anti-spyware tools, anti-spam filtering, a personal firewall, and more. In fact, recently the major security vendors such as McAfee and Trend Micro have moved to marketing their products as a security suite, rather than simply antivirus software.

Typically, antivirus software will detect and protect you from viruses, worms, Trojan horse programs, and backdoors, as well as blended threats which combine aspects of different threats. Some antivirus programs will also help block well-known joke or hoax e-mail messages, spyware programs, and program exploits. As you can see in Figure 3.1, the Trend Micro PC-cillin software includes scanning for a variety of threats. You should take the time to understand what your security software does and does not protect your computer against.

Figure 3.1 Trend Micro PC-cillin Internet Security Software

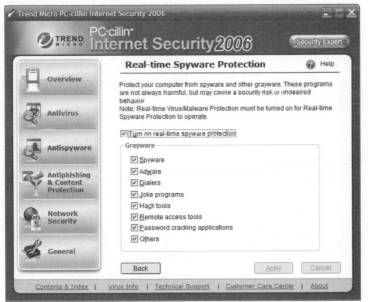

Most antivirus software includes three basic types of scanning: real-time, manual, and heuristic. Real-time scanning is the main line of defense that will keep your computer system clean as you access the Internet and surf the Web. This is the scanning that is done on-the-fly while you are using the computer. Antivirus software real-time scanning typically scans all inbound Web traffic for signs of malicious code, as well as inspects all incoming e-mail and e-mail file attachments. Antivirus products like McAfee VirusScan (see Figure 3.2) also include the ability to scan instant messaging or chat sessions and file attachments from those applications. Often, you can also enable outbound scanning to try and catch any malicious code which might be coming from your computer.

Figure 3.2 McAfee VirusScan Options

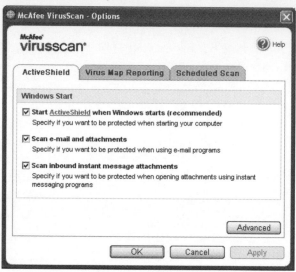

The manual scan is a scan run on your computer to check the files that are already on it and make sure none of them are infected. These scans can be initiated by you if something suspicious seems to be going on, but they should also be run periodically to make sure that no malware got past the real-time scanners. It is also possible that an infected file may make its way onto your computer before your antivirus software vendor updated their software to detect it. Performing a periodic manual scan can help identify and remove these threats.

Products like Trend Micro's PC-cillin Internet Security Suite lets you choose just how aggressive you want to scan your system (see Figure 3.3). You can choose to scan all files, or only those recommended by Trend Micro, which limits the scan to only the file types more likely to contain malware. You can also configure how you want the software to handle cleaning or removing any threats it finds.

Most antivirus products allow you to set up a schedule to run the scan automatically. You should configure the scan to run at least once a week, preferably late at night or at some other time when you won't be using your computer. Scanning your entire computer system usually hogs a lot of the computer's processing power and makes using it difficult while the scan is running.

Figure 3.3 Manual Scan Configuration for Trend Micro PC-cillin Internet Security 2006

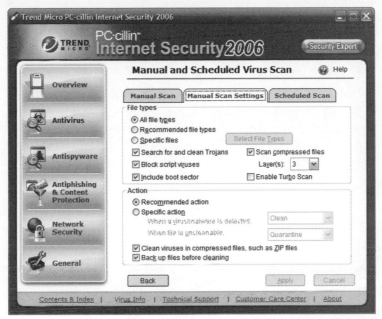

The third form of detection included in most antivirus software is called heuristic detection. The standard malware scanning relies on signatures or pattern files used to identify known threats. However, until a threat is discovered and researchers identify its unique traits that they can use to detect it, your standard malware scanning won't detect the new threat. Heuristic detection doesn't look for specific malware threats. Heuristic detection uses general characteristics of typical malware to identify suspicious network traffic or e-mail behavior. Based on known traits from past threats, heuristic detection attempts to detect similar traits to identify possible threats.

Keep Your Antivirus Software Updated

So, after reading all of this you have decided that viruses, worms, and other malware are bad things to have and that it may be worth a few dollars to spring for some antivirus software to install to protect your computer. Great! Now you can close the book and go back to watching *Everybody Loves Raymond* reruns, right? Unfortunately, no.

Tools & Traps...

Subscription-Based Antivirus Software

It doesn't have to cost a fortune to protect your computer. Generally, antivirus software and personal computer security suites are priced affordably.

It is not a one-time purchase though in most cases. The major antivirus software vendors such as Symantec or McAfee use a subscription-based system. Users are required to continue to pay annually for the privilege of continuing to get updated protection.

There are certainly advantages to buying from established, well-known antivirus software vendors. But, if money is an issue, there are alternatives. Products like Antivir (www.free-av.com/) are available for free for personal use on home computers.

New threats are constant. Securing your computer or network requires maintenance to keep pace with the changing attack methods and techniques. In any given week there may be anywhere from five to twenty new malware threats discovered. If you install antivirus software today and do nothing else, your computer will be vulnerable to dozens of new threats within a couple of weeks.

It used to be that updating your antivirus software on a weekly basis was sufficient in most cases. But, as you can see from looking at the timeline discussed earlier, there were three years between officially defining a virus and the first virus affecting Microsoft systems. Five years later, Code Red spread around the world in a day and infected more than 200,000 systems. Two years after that the SQL Slammer worm spread around the world in 30 minutes and crippled the Internet. The frequency and potency of new threats seems to increase exponentially from year to year. The more users who adopt high-speed broadband Internet connections and leave their computers connected 24/7, the greater the potential for a new threat to spread.

For these reasons, I recommend you update your antivirus software daily. You could try to remember or make a note in your date book reminding you to visit the web site of your antivirus software vendor each day to see if a new update has been released and then download and install it, but I'm sure you have better things to do with your time. Antivirus software can be configured to automatically check with the vendor site for any updates on a scheduled basis. Check your antivirus software instructions for how to configure automatic updates for your application. Keep in mind that the computer needs to be turned on and connected to the Internet in order for the software to be able to connect and download the updates, so pick a time of day that you know the computer will be connected.

How Not to Get Infected

Running up-to-date antivirus software is great, but there is an even better protection against viruses, worms, and other malware threats. A little common sense is the absolute best defense against computer threats of all kinds.

When you receive an e-mail titled "re: your mortgage loan," but you don't recognize the sender and you know that you never sent a message titled "your mortgage loan" in the first place, it's guaranteed to be spam, and may even contain some sort of malware. Fight your curiosity. Don't even bother opening it. Just delete it.

If you follow our advice in Chapter 1, the User Account you use should not have Administrator privileges. If you're using a User Account that does not have the authority to install software or make configuration changes to the operating system, most malware will be unable to infect the system.

You should also avoid suspicious or questionable Web sites. The Web is filled with millions of Web pages, the vast majority of which are just fine. No matter what you're searching for, there is probably a perfectly reputable site where you can find it. But once you venture into the dark and shady side of the Internet, there is no telling what kind of nasty things you can pick up.

Another common source of malware is file sharing. Many of the files and programs that can be found on peer-to-peer file sharing networks, such as Bit Torrent, contain Trojans or other malware. Be cautious when executing files from questionable sources. You should always scan these files with your antivirus software before executing them.

You can get malware infections by surfing the Web, using your e-mail, sharing network resources, or opening Microsoft Office files. It can be scary to think that just about everything you might want to use your computer for exposes you to threats of one kind or another. However, a little common sense and a healthy dose of skepticism should keep you safe.

Do You Think You're Infected?

Is your computer system acting weird? Have you noticed files where there didn't used to be files, or had files suddenly disappear? Does your system seem like it is running slower than normal, or you notice that the hard drive seems to keep on cranking away even when you aren't doing anything on the computer? Does your system freeze up or crash all of a sudden?

All of these are potential signs that your computer system might be infected with some sort of malware. If you have suspicions that your computer may be infected, you should run a manual scan using your antivirus software. First, make sure that your software has the most up-to-date virus information available from your antivirus software vendor, and then initiate the manual scan.

If the manual scan detects and removes the problem, you're all set. But what if it doesn't? What should you do if your antivirus software detects a threat, but is unable to remove it? Or what if your antivirus software says your computer is clean, but you still suspect it's infected? You can dig a little deeper to make sure.

Antivirus and security software vendors often create stand-alone tools that are available for free to help detect and remove some of the more insidious threats (see Figure 3.4). Microsoft, which has recently entered the arena of providing antivirus and other security software products, also offers a Malicious Software Removal Tool which they update monthly to detect and remove some of the more pervasive and tenacious malware threats.

Figure 3.4 McAfee's Free Tools for Removing Malware

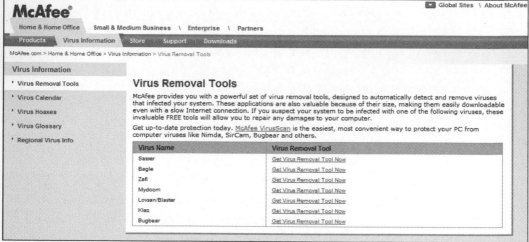

Some malware is written to disable or remove antivirus and other security software in order to prevent the ability to detect or remove it. If your computer system is infected by one of these threats, your antivirus software may be useless.

You can try to find a stand-alone tool like those mentioned earlier, but an alternative is to scan your system with a different antivirus software. Of course, you probably don't have extra antivirus programs on standby that you can just install on a whim. Thankfully, Trend Micro provides a free Web-based scan called HouseCall (see Figure 3.5). If all else fails, you should be able to get your system cleaned up using this service.

Figure 3.5 Trend Micro's HouseCall

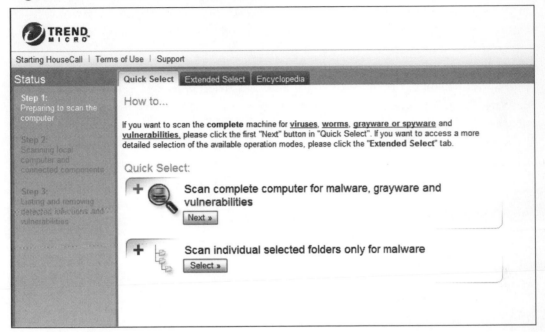

Summary

This is an important chapter. Viruses, worms and other malware are a constant threat and the source of many problems and tremendous frustration for many users. The subject of malware could fill an entire book by itself. In fact, there *are* entire books on the subject. The goal of this chapter was not to make antivirus or malware experts out of you, but to arm you with the knowledge that you need to safely use your computer for your day-to-day tasks.

This chapter provided you with some explanation of the different types of malware and what makes them different, as well as a brief overview of the history of malware. We then talked about how to protect your computer system using antivirus software and how to make sure it is configured properly and kept up-to-date.

You also learned how to exercise some common sense to ensure you don't become a victim of malware, and what to do to clean your system up if you are unfortunate enough to become infected.

Additional Resources

The following resources contain additional information on viruses, worms, and other malware:

- *Experts worry after worm hits ATMs.* MSNBC.com. December 9, 2003 (www.msnbc.msn.com/id/3675891/).

- *HouseCall.* Trend Micro Incorporated's Products Web Page. (http://house-call.trendmicro.com/).

- *Malicious Software Removal Tool.* Microsoft's Security Web Page, January 11, 2005 (www.microsoft.com/security/malwareremove/default.mspx).

- *W32/CodeRed.a.worm.* McAfee, Inc.'s AVERT Labs Threat Library (http://vil.nai.com/vil/content/v_99142.htm).

- *W32/Mydoom@MM.* McAfee, Inc.'s AVERT Labs Threat Library (http://vil.nai.com/vil/content/v_100983.htm).

- *W32/Nimda.gen@MM.* McAfee, Inc.'s AVERT Labs Threat Library (http://vil.nai.com/vil/content/v_99209.htm).

- *W32/SQLSlammer.worm.* McAfee, Inc.'s AVERT Labs Threat Library (http://vil.nai.com/vil/content/v_99992.htm).

- *Virus Removal Tools.* McAfee, Inc.'s Virus Information Web Page (http://us.mcafee.com/virusInfo/default.asp?id=vrt).

Chapter 4

Patching

Topics in this chapter:

- Patch Terminology
- Why Should I Patch?
- How Do I Know What to Patch?

☑ Summary

☑ Additional Resources

Introduction

When it comes to maintenance and upkeep, your computer is more like your car than your toaster. Your toaster may not need any attention, but the car requires oil changes, new tires, tune-ups, and more, to keep it running properly.

This chapter covers the information that you need to know to understand patches and updates and what you need to do to maintain your computer and protect it from vulnerabilities. In this chapter, you will learn:

- Terms used to describe patches and updates
- Why you should patch your system
- How to know what patches to install
- Using Automatic Updates and the Microsoft Update Web site
- Using System Restore

Patch Terminology

When I wear a hole in a pair of jeans, I go to the store and buy a new pair. But, I remember when I was growing up that a hole didn't guarantee a new pair of jeans. My mother would just get a patch and apply it to the hole and, presto, jeans were as good as new. Mostly.

With computer software it works pretty much the same way. In between releases of major versions of software, software publishers typically release patches to fix what's broken. They don't want to give you that new pair of jeans just yet; they've got the iron-on patches ready to go—you just have to install them.

There are different kinds of patches and it can help to know the difference between them because some are big fixes and others are small. Don't worry about learning this stuff; just use this list as a reference. And be sure to read the description for the fixes you're planning to install.

Notes from the Underground…

Batches of Patches

Patching comes in a variety of "flavors." You may hear fixes for flaws and vulnerabilities called by different names and that can be confusing if you don't understand that they are all really just patches. The following list will help you know which patch to use when you find vulnerabilities on your network or computer:

- **Patch** This fixes something small and is usually quick to download and install.
- **Rollup** This might include a group of patches for a program.
- **Update** Updates might add or fix features in your program or fix an earlier patch.
- **Cumulative Patch** A cumulative patch typically includes all previously released patches for one application.
- **Service Pack** This is the biggie; the one you read about in the news when Microsoft releases some big service pack. Service packs are generally very large files that typically include lots of patches to all sorts of things.

Why Should I Patch?

Once a month, Microsoft releases their new Security Bulletins identifying new vulnerabilities and providing the links to download the necessary patches. There is typically at least one vulnerability that could result in your computer being controlled remotely by an attacker and enable them to access your personal files and information, or hijack your computer to propagate viruses or mass-distribute spam e-mail. These Security Bulletins are generally rated as Critical by Microsoft because they consider it fairly urgent that you apply the patch to protect your computer system.

If your computer seems to be working just fine, you may wonder "Why bother upsetting the apple cart by applying a patch?" Simple: You should apply the patch as a sort of vaccination for your computer to keep it running smooth. Many viruses, worms, and other malware exploit flaws and vulnerabilities in your system in order to do their dirty work. Your system may seem fine now, but by not applying a patch you might be opening the door for malware or attackers to come in.

For example, the SQL Slammer worm, discussed in Chapter 3, was able to spread around the world in less than 30 minutes and cripple the Internet by exploiting a vulnerability that had a patch available for more than six months. Had users and network administrators been more proactive about applying the patch, SQL Slammer may have fizzled out without being noticed.

Some patches may fix a flaw in some particular service or underlying program that only a relative minority of users actually uses in the first place and which may not be urgent enough for you to bother downloading and installing. However, some flaws may expose your computer to remote attacks that enable the attacker to assume full control of your computer system enabling them to install software, delete files, distribute e-mail in your name, view your personal and confidential data, and more. Obviously, a patch for such a vulnerability has a higher urgency than the first one.

Patches that repair vulnerabilities that can be exploited remotely, in other words, from some other system, rather than requiring the attacker to physically sit down in front of your computer, are even more urgent when you consider that many viruses and worms take advantage of these flaws to exploit systems and propagate to other vulnerable systems.

These vulnerabilities provide a relatively easy method of attack for malware authors, and the time frame between the patch being released and a virus or worm exploiting the vulnerability being released on the Internet is getting shorter and shorter.

How Do I Know What to Patch?

There are often more than 50 new vulnerabilities discovered or announced in a given week. Some of them will affect products you use, but the majority of them will probably affect other products or technologies that don't affect you.

How can you keep up with so many vulnerabilities and filter through to find the ones that matter to you? More than that, how can you sift through the vulnerabilities that affect your system and choose which ones don't really matter and which ones are urgent?

Tools & Traps…

Keeping Up with Vulnerabilities

A number of sources are available to help you stay informed about newly dis-covered vulnerabilities and current patches. You can subscribe to e-mail mailing lists from sources such as Security Focus's Bugtraq. Bugtraq actually offers a wide variety of mailing lists to keep you informed on various subjects related to tech-nology and information security.

You can get similar vulnerability information by subscribing to Secunia's mailing list as well. The problem with both of these solutions is that the amount of information generated is significantly more than the common user needs or can comprehend.

In either case, you can narrow the list of alerts you wish to receive and cus-tomize it as much as possible to only those products that affect you.

- www.securityfocus.com/archive/1
- http://secunia.com/advisories/

Any software you use is a potential source of vulnerabilities that could lead to a compromise of security on your system. However , the more commonly used a pro-gram is the bigger target it represents and the more likely it is that a vulnerability will be exploited through some sort of automated malware or manual attack. Still, for the more obscure programs you might use you should look into whether or not the vendor offers any sort of mailing list you can join to receive news of updates, patches, or vulnerability alerts.

For users of Microsoft Windows operating systems, Microsoft offers a couple of alternatives to stay informed of the latest vulnerabilities and to make sure you have the necessary patches applied. One is passive—automatically checking for and down-loading any new patches—while the other requires some active participation on the part of the user.

Are You Owned?

Bull's Eye on Your Back

When you play darts, the idea generally is to hit the bull's eye in the center of the board. Obviously, if that bull's eye is 10 feet across it will be a lot easier to hit than if it is only 1 inch across. The same logic holds true for attackers who want to exploit vulnerabilities.

Because Microsoft Windows dominates the personal computer operating system market, it is a large target. Because Microsoft Internet Explorer dominates the Web browser market, it is a large target. Attackers may be able to find flaws in the Opera Web browser, but finding the 1% of computers in the world using Opera is much more difficult than finding the 85% using Internet Explorer.

Granted, there are products that are written more securely than Microsoft's products and that are less prone to attack. But, once a product gains significant enough market share to attract attention, it too will become a target. The Apple Mac has generally been regarded as virtually impenetrable. But, the increasing popularity of the Mac OS X operating system has made it the target of more frequent attacks.

To be precise, it is up to you to choose just how passive you want the Windows Automatic Update feature to be. You can opt to be notified of any existing updates before downloading them; you can configure Automatic Update to automatically download any updates and notify you when they are ready to be installed; or you can configure it to simply download and install the updates on a schedule of your choosing.

To enable Automatic Update in Windows XP, click **System** in the **Control Panel**, and then select the **Automatic Updates** tab (in Windows 2000, click **Automatic Updates** in the Control Panel).

The Automatic Updates tab offers four radio buttons to choose how to configure it. If you leave your computer on during the night and opt for automatically downloading and installing the updates, you may want to choose a time while you are sleeping so that any downloading and installing activity won't bog down the computer while you are trying to use it (see Figure 4.1).

Figure 4.1 Windows XP Automatic Updates Tab

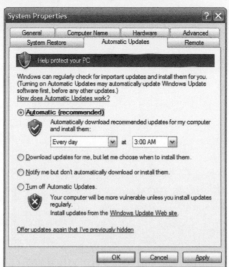

You can also opt to have the updates downloaded to your computer, but not be installed until you manually initiate it, or you can choose to simply receive a notification when new updates are available, but download and install them manually. These configuration options may be helpful for users who don't want their computing interrupted by patches being installed or who have limited Internet connectivity and want more control over when patches are downloaded. In general though, home users should stick with the recommended setting of Automatic.

When new patches are available, or have been downloaded and are pending installation on your system, the Windows Security Center shield icon will appear yellow in the Systray. By clicking on the icon you can view the Details of the updates and then choose whether or not you want to install them.

If you choose not to install updates that have already been downloaded to your system, the files are deleted from your computer. You can still apply the update at a later time by clicking **System** in the Control Panel and selecting the **Automatic Updates** tab. At the bottom you will see a link to "Offer updates again that I've previously hidden," which you can click to re-download updates you previously declined.

The Automatic Updates feature of Windows is a great way to stay current with critical security patches—or at least aware of new patches when they become available, depending on how you configure it. However, Automatic Update notifies you or downloads patches only for flaws that affect the security of your system. For patches that affect the functionality of Windows or its underlying programs, but do not affect security, you should periodically check the Microsoft Update Web site.

To open the Microsoft Update site in Windows XP, select **Start | All Programs | Windows Update** (in Windows 2000, click **Start | Windows Update** at the top of the **Start** menu). If you click the **Express button**, a scan of your system will be initiated (see Figure 4.2), and Microsoft Update will identify any high-priority patches that your system is missing.

Clicking the **Custom button** performs a more comprehensive scan. After it has completed scanning, you will be notified if there are any new updates available from three different categories: high-priority updates and service packs, optional software updates, and optional hardware updates (such as device drivers).

Figure 4.2 Microsoft Update Welcome Page

You can view a brief description of each update to learn more about what it does and choose which updates you want to install. After you have selected the updates you want to apply, click **Review and Install Updates** and click **Install Updates** to start the process.

Patching Precautions

Ideally, the software you are using would be flawless in the first place. But, with millions of lines of code in programs such as Microsoft Windows, often written by diverse groups of people scattered around the globe, it seems almost inevitable that a flaw will be discovered eventually. When a flaw or vulnerability is discovered and a patch is created there are some precautions you should bear in mind before simply applying it.

First of all, you should be aware that sometimes the patch introduces new flaws. In their haste to get a patch distributed to users as quickly as possible—especially in the case of a vulnerability with critical security implications—patch code developers may not perform the quality checks and due diligence the patch deserves before they rush it out the door.

Even in a best-case scenario, the vendor can only test the patch under so many different configurations or conditions. It is still always possible that your particular collection of software or services may interact poorly with the patch and cause a problem that was unforeseen by the developers.

A flawed patch might result in a wide variety of issues ranging from quirky bugs or disabled functionality to random system crashes or could even possibly render the system completely unbootable.

Another thing to keep in mind is that a patch may not always fix the flaw it was intended to fix or at least not completely. Sometimes a vendor might discover a flaw and develop a patch that fixes a specific symptom without correcting the underlying flaw that causes the symptom to begin with.

For this scenario there isn't much you can do. Simply be aware that a patch is not always a silver bullet that will magically fix everything and remain aware of the fact that your vendor may re-release a patch or release a new patch to replace that one if more flaws or vulnerabilities are discovered.

There are a couple of things you can do to protect yourself to some degree. First and foremost, you should always run a backup of your computer—or at least your critical data—so that in the event of a catastrophic failure you can rebuild your system and not lose your data.

NOTE

For more information about backing up or restoring your files, see Chapter 11, "When Disaster Strikes."

Windows XP also has a feature designed to let you recover from problems and return your system to a previous state. The Windows System Restore feature automatically saves restore points on a periodic basis so that you can reset your system to that point in time if it becomes necessary (see Figure 4.3).

You should manually create a restore point immediately before applying a patch or doing any other system updates or upgrades so that you will be able to return to the pre-patch system if need be. I recommend that you create a system restore point weekly as a part of general system maintenance as well.

Figure 4.3 Windows System Restore Welcome Page

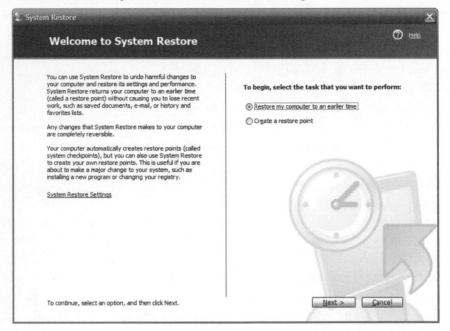

To manually set a restore point, click **Start | All Programs | Accessories | System Tools | System Restore**. Select **Create a restore point**, and click **Next**. Enter a descriptive title for your restore point, and then click **Create**.

In most cases you can also uninstall the patch or update using the Add or Remove Programs function in Control Panel if it causes any problems (see Figure 4.4). It can be a little cryptic, however, to determine which patch to remove after you have applied a number of them. They are listed in Add & Remove Programs by their knowledge base reference—a number which starts with "KB" followed by a six-digit number. Check the **Show Updates** box at the top of the **Add or Remove Programs** console to display Windows patches and updates.

Figure 4.4 Windows Patches and Updates in the Add or Remove Programs
Window

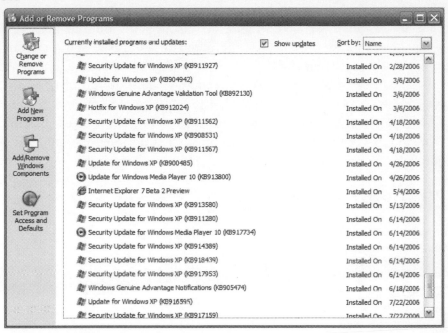

You can typically find the associated knowledge base number at the end of the
title of the applicable Microsoft Security Bulletin. You can also do a search for the
"KB" numbers on the Web using a search engine such as Google to get more details
about them.

If you are unable to locate the exact patch to remove from Add or Remove
Programs or if your system is so unstable or dysfunctional that you can't even get to
Add or Remove Programs, you should simply use your latest backup or the
Windows System Restore feature to restore your system to the way it was before
you applied the patch or update.

Summary

In this chapter you learned that patches or updates for your software may come under a variety of names. We talked about the reasons you should be diligent about applying patches and how you can stay informed and up to date about existing vulnerabilities and the patches available for your operating system and applications.

We also discussed how to use the Automatic Updates feature of Microsoft Windows and how to use the Microsoft Update Web site to identify and download any necessary patches. We wrapped up with a discussion of how to use System Restore or Add or Remove Programs to undo patches if something goes wrong and the importance of regular data backups.

Additional Resources

The following resources provide more information on patching:

- Microsoft Update (www.windowsupdate.com).

- SecurityFocus Bugtraq (www.securityfocus.com/archive/1).

- Secunia Advisories (secunia.com/advisories/).

Part II:
More Essential
Security

Chapter 5

Perimeter Security

Topics in this chapter:

- From Moats and Bridges to Firewalls and Filters
- Firewalls
- Intrusion Detection and Prevention

☑ Summary

☑ Additional Resources

Introduction

Generally, when you think of perimeter security, you think of protecting the outer edges of your network. Hence, the term *perimeter*. Home computers and small office/home office (SOHO) networks typically have some form of firewall in place; this could be a cable router, wireless access point, or switch. Some people think that the perimeter security starts with the Windows Firewall or other firewall located on the computer. If you are thinking that can't be a perimeter security measure, you are wrong. Think about a laptop on a wireless broadband card from Verizon. What is the first point of security? The software on the computer is the right answer.

In this chapter we will take a look at some different aspects of the perimeter security and how they work. We also discuss some ideas that maybe you would have not thought of for security.

From Moats and Bridges to Firewalls and Filters

In ancient civilizations, entire towns or villages were surrounded by some form of protection—possibly a tall wall or a deep moat, or both—to keep unwanted "guests" from entering. Guards would man the entrances and bark out "who goes there?" If the party entering was known or had the right password or sufficient credentials to gain access, the moat bridge or fortress wall was opened up to allow him or her to enter.

If this form of defense were 100 percent effective, there would be no need for any sort of security or law enforcement within the confines of the village or fortress. Ostensibly, you would keep the bad guys outside the walls or moat and everyone inside would behave in a civilized and respectful manner. Of course, this is not typically what happens. Whether it's a malicious intruder who somehow cons his way through the defenses or bypasses them altogether or an internal malcontent who chooses to break the rules, some form of internal law enforcement is generally needed to maintain the peace inside the walls.

Perimeter security in a computer network works in a similar way. A network will generally have a firewall acting as the fortress wall or castle moat for the computer network. If the incoming network traffic doesn't fit the rules defined in the firewall, the traffic is blocked or rejected and does not enter your internal network. Figure 5.1 shows a typical network configuration with an internal firewall and perimeter firewall in place.

Figure 5.1 Perimeter Security

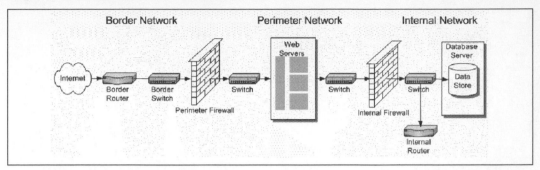

If a firewall were 100 percent effective, and if external traffic entering your network was the only attack vector you needed to be concerned with, there would be no need for any other computer or network security on your internal network or the computers inside of your firewall. But since it's not, you still need internal security measures as well. Running an intrusion detection system (IDS) or intrusion prevention system (IPS) can help you to detect malicious traffic that either slips past the firewall or originates from inside the network in the first place.

Even firewalls and intrusion detection or prevention won't protect you from every possible computer attack, but with one or both of these technologies in place, you can increase your security and greatly reduce your exposure to risk.

Firewalls

In its original form, a firewall is a structural safety mechanism used in buildings. Put simply, it is a wall designed for the purpose of containing a fire. The concept is that if one section of the building catches fire, the firewall will prevent that fire from spreading to other areas of the building or even other buildings.

A network firewall is similar except that rather than surrounding a room or a building, it protects the entry and exit points of your computer network, and rather than trying to contain the fire or keep it inside, the firewall ensures that the "fire" stays outside the network.

Tools & Traps…

NAT

Using NAT, or Network Address Translation, it is actually possible for more than one device on your internal network to connect to the Internet even though you have only one unique public IP address. Home cable/DSL routers and the Windows Internet Connection Sharing (ICS) feature both use NAT.

The devices on the internal network still must have unique IP addresses, though. They are just unique to your internal network and cannot communicate directly with the Internet.

The NAT program or device intercepts all outbound network requests from the computers on your network and communicates with the public Internet. It then receives all network traffic coming in and directs it to the appropriate destination within the internal network.

Think of it like sending mail to an apartment building. The IP address of the NAT device will get it to the right "building," but it is up to the NAT device to make sure it gets to the right "apartment" or internal computer.

To understand how a firewall works or why you should have one to protect your network or computer, it helps to have a basic knowledge of how the network traffic works in the first place.

Network Traffic Flow

Network traffic gets from point A to point B based on an address and a port. Every device on the Internet or even on an internal network must have a unique IP address. Picture a computer's IP address as the computer networking equivalent of your street or mailing address.

In Figure 5.2 you can see that for 10.10.10.1 to reach its mail server it must know the IP address of the mail server, which is 1.1.1.2.

For mail to get to a specific individual, it is first sorted by its ZIP code. The ZIP code enables the postal service to know where that individual is located in a broad sense by narrowing the location down to a particular city and state and possibly even a small portion of the city. After the ZIP code, the postal service can look at the street name to further narrow the destination and then the postal delivery person will ensure that the mail gets to the appropriate building number on the given street.

Figure 5.2 Network IP Flow

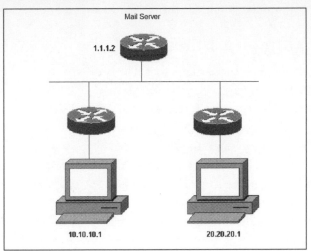

Routers and Ports

Your IP address provides similar information to network routers. The first part of the IP address identifies the network the device is located on and is similar to the ZIP code of a mailing address. This information helps to narrow the destination to a given Internet service provider (ISP) or even a smaller region within the ISP. The second part of the IP address identifies the unique host and is similar to the street address of a mailing address. This portion narrows it to a specific segment of the network and then down to the exact device that owns the given IP address.

Network communications also use ports. Ports are similar in some ways to TV channels or radio stations. There are roughly 65,000 possible ports for network traffic to use. Many of the ports, particularly those in the range from 0 through 1023, have a specific purpose. However, a vast majority of the ports are available for use for any purpose.

For example, if you want to listen to a specific radio station, there is a specific frequency or station you must tune your radio to in order to receive the signal. If you want to watch a particular TV show, there is a particular frequency or channel you must tune your television to in order to receive the signal. In both cases there are also a number of frequencies that are not used for a designated station or channel and could conceivably be used by someone else to broadcast on.

Similarly, certain service or types of communications occur on designated network ports. For example, e-mail uses port 25 for SMTP (Simple Mail Transfer Protocol) or port 110 for POP3. Surfing the Web uses port 80 for normal sites and port 443 for secure or encrypted sites. It is possible to use these services on other ports, but these are the default standards that the Internet operates on.

Packet Routing and Filtering

Another key aspect of network traffic is that it is broken into small pieces. If you wanted to ship a refrigerator to someone in the mail, it would be too large to handle all at once. But you could take the refrigerator apart and ship each piece in an individual box. Some of the packages might go on a truck and some might go on a plane or a train. There is no guarantee that the packages will arrive together or in the correct order. To make it easier to assemble the refrigerator once it arrives at its destination, you might number the packages: 1 of 150, 2 of 150, 3 of 150, and so on. After all 150 packages arrive, they can then be reassembled in their proper sequence.

Network traffic is handled the same way. It would be too slow or inefficient to try to send a complete 4MB or 5MB file together in one piece. So network traffic is broken into pieces called packets. Different packets may take different routes across the Internet and there is no guarantee that the packets will arrive at the destination together or in the correct order. So, each packet is given a sequence number that lets the destination device know what the proper order is for the packets and tells it when it has received all the packets for a given communication.

Each network packet has a header that contains the necessary details, similar to a shipping invoice. The packet header identifies the source IP address and port as well as the destination IP address and port. It is this information that many firewalls use to restrict or allow traffic.

When you surf to a Web site, your computer will communicate with the Web server on port 80, but the traffic coming back to your computer may be on some other port and will be handled differently by your firewall than unsolicited incoming traffic.

Ideally, your firewall will block all incoming traffic except on the ports that you specifically choose to allow. For most home users it is safe to block all ports for incoming traffic because home users do not generally host services such as an e-mail server. Unless you are hosting a Web site on your computer, you don't need to allow port 80 traffic from the Internet into your computer. If you are not running your own POP3 e-mail server, you don't need to allow incoming port 110 traffic. In most cases, the only traffic that needs to come *in* to your network is a reply to a request your computer has made. There are cases with some online games or peer-to-peer (P2P) networking where your computer does need to act as a server and may need to have certain incoming ports open.

This basic sort of firewall is known as a packet filter. You can use a basic packet filter firewall to deny all traffic from a certain source IP address or to block incoming traffic on certain ports. As we stated earlier in this chapter, the ideal configuration for your firewall is to simply deny all incoming traffic and then create specific rules to allow communications from specific IP addresses or ports as the need arises.

Stateful Inspection

There is a deeper or more advanced form of packet filtering called stateful inspection. Stateful inspection not only looks at the source and destination ports and addresses but also keeps track of the state of the communications. In other words, rather than letting traffic in simply because it is on the right port, it validates that a computer on the network actually asked to receive the traffic.

Stateful inspection also evaluates the context of the communications. If a computer on the network requests a Web page from a Web server, the stateful inspection packet filter will allow the Web page traffic through. However, if the Web site is malicious and also attempts to install some malware, a standard packet filter might allow the traffic because it is in response to a request initiated from your network, but the stateful inspection packet filter will reject it because it is not in the same context as the request. This higher degree of scrutiny for incoming packets helps to protect your network better than a standard packet filter.

As you can see in Figure 5.3, stateful inspections used rules or filters to check the dynamic state table to verify that the packet is part of a valid connection.

Figure 5.3 Stateful Packet Inspections

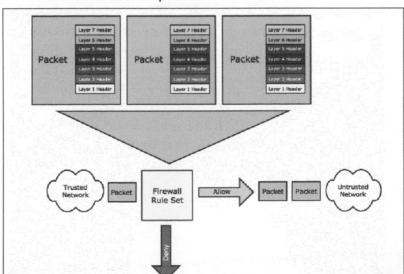

Application Gateways
and Application Proxy Firewalls

For even better protection you can use an application gateway or application proxy firewall. An application proxy mediates the communications between the two devices, such as a computer and server. Essentially, there are two connections—one from the client to the application proxy and one from the application proxy to the server. The application proxy receives the request to start a session such as viewing a Web page. It validates that the request is authentic and allowed and then initiates a Web session with the destination on behalf of the client computer.

This type of firewall offers a significantly greater level of protection and has the added benefit of hiding the client machine's true identity, since the external communications will all appear to originate from the application proxy. The downside is that the application proxy uses a lot more memory and processing power and may slow down network performance. With recent boosts in processing power and with random access memory (RAM) being less expensive, this issue is not as significant any longer.

Personal and Cable/DSL Router Firewalls

There are two different types of firewalls that home or small office users will generally implement: personal firewalls and cable/DSL router firewalls. The two are not mutually exclusive and, in fact, can and should be used in conjunction with each other for added security. In Figure 5.4 you can see that a SOHO firewall sits outside the local switch on which the local computers reside.

Figure 5.4 SOHO Firewall

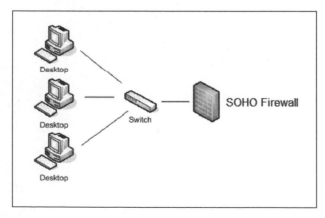

Most home routers designed for use with cable or DSL broadband Internet access come equipped with a basic packet filter firewall, or possibly even a stateful inspection firewall built in. The standard default configuration is generally to Deny All access unless you specifically configure it otherwise, but check the documentation for your router to make sure the firewall is on by default and what the default rule set is.

This sort of firewall can help you provide true perimeter security for your home network. No matter how many computers you connect within your home, all of the network traffic coming from the Internet will have to pass through this device to get in, so all of your computers will be protected. Home routers also typically provide Network Address Translation (NAT), which means that the true IP addresses of any machines on your network are hidden and that external systems see only the IP address of the firewall/router.

There are a couple of key things to remember when using this type of router. First, you should always change the default password as soon as possible. Second, you should change the default IP address used for the internal network. Default passwords are easy for attackers (most attackers will already have them, as they're posted on any number of Web sites) to discover or guess, and most attackers will be aware that the default subnet used by home routers is 192.168.0 and that the administrative screen for the router itself can be accessed at http://192.168.0.1.

One more serious caveat regarding a home router firewall is that they won't provide any protection for users who use a dial-up telephone connection to access the Internet. If you are sharing a single Internet connection, you could conceivably connect other systems on your network through a home router with a firewall, but the actual computer connecting to the Internet over the dial-up connection would still be unprotected.

Whether or not you have a router for your network providing your network with protection through a packet filter or stateful inspection firewall, you can also install a personal firewall application on each individual computer system. Just as the network firewall monitors and restricts the traffic allowed into your network, the personal firewall will monitor and restrict the traffic allowed into your computer.

This can be advantageous for a number of reasons. First of all, if one of your computers participates in online gaming or P2P networking, you may be required to open up ports on your network firewall in order for the communications to work. Although that may be an acceptable risk for the machine using those ports, the other machines on your network still don't need any potentially malicious traffic entering on those ports. Individual machines on your network may also want to protect themselves from suspicious or malicious traffic from other computers in your network.

Windows XP comes with a built-in personal firewall application. The Windows Firewall is a stateful inspection firewall. One advantage of the Windows Firewall over the aforementioned router firewalls is that it can provide security for the computer even on a dial-up connection.

In some ways the Windows Firewall is very robust. It has the capability to detect and defend against certain types of denial-of-service (DoS) attacks (a DoS attack occurs when an attacker is able to disable or overwhelm a device to the point that it no longer responds to requests, thereby denying service to legitimate users) by simply dropping the incoming packets.

If your Windows Firewall is turned off, and you don't have some other third-party firewall running on your computer, the Windows XP Security Center will display a pop-up alert in the systray at the lower right of the screen to let you know your computer may not be secure. To enable the Windows Firewall, click **Start | Control Panel | Security Center**. When the Security Center console comes up, click **Windows Firewall** at the bottom to open the Windows Firewall configuration screen (see Figure 5.5). Just select **On** and click **OK** to turn the firewall on.

Figure 5.5 The Windows Firewall Configuration Screen

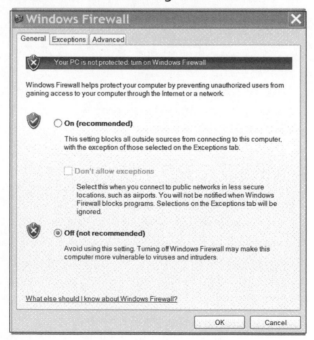

In Figure 5.6 you can see that the **Exceptions Tab** on the Windows Firewall console is selected. Exceptions allow the user to select certain programs or network ports to allow through the firewall. Some programs are added by default by Windows when they are started up and try to access the network. If you need to add a program that is not displayed on the list, you can click **Add Program** and manually select the application. Programs and ports with checks in the box next to them on the Exceptions tab will not be restricted by normal firewall rules and will be allowed to pass through the firewall as if it were not there.

At the bottom of the Exceptions tab is a checkbox to "Display a notification when Windows Firewall blocks a program." This can be very informative or a confusing nuisance depending on how you look at it. If you leave the box checked, you will get a pop-up alert each time a new application tries to communicate through the firewall. You can choose whether to allow the communication or not. Many users do not like to have constant pop-up alerts, though, and generally don't understand what they are about or whether they should approve them. You will probably want to leave this box unchecked, but if you are trying to use a new program and run into issues, always think of the firewall first and remember that without an Exception being added, your program probably cannot communicate freely through the firewall.

Figure 5.6 The Windows Firewall Exceptions

You can select the **Advanced Tab**, to access some settings for more advanced firewall configuration. At the top, it shows the network connections settings (see Figure 5.7), which display a list of all of the network adapters or connections in the computer. The adapters or network connections that have checkmarks in the box next to them have the Windows Firewall protection enabled for them. Those that don't are not protected by the Windows Firewall.

The Advanced tab also allows you to turn logging on and off. If you enable logging, a TXT file will be generated that records information about all the connections made to or from the firewall. It collects the source and destination IP address and source and destination port information as well as the network protocol being used. For an average user, this will probably all appear as gibberish. But the information can be useful for troubleshooting problems or trying to find the root cause of an attack or system compromise.

At the bottom of the Advanced settings tab, you can reset the Windows Firewall to its default settings. After you have customized and tweaked it and added Exceptions and completely reconfigured it, you might find it hard to figure out which setting to change to make things work again. If you are having serious connectivity problems, you might want to return the Windows Firewall to its original configuration and start over.

Figure 5.7 The Advanced Tab of the Windows Firewall Configuration

The Windows Firewall is a great tool, especially for one that is included in the operating system for free. It also works a little too well (which is better than not well enough) in some cases, making it difficult for your computer to even communicate or share resources with other computers on your own network. For these reasons and more we recommend that you leave the Windows Firewall disabled and instead install a third-party firewall product such as ZoneAlarm (see Figure 5.8) or the personal firewall component of a security suite such as Trend Micro PC-cillin. ZoneAlarm is a popular personal firewall program that is very effective and relatively simple to use.

Figure 5.8 Zone Alarm

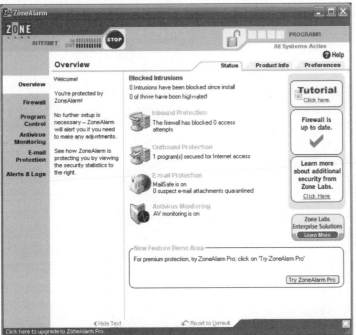

Zone Labs offers the basic ZoneAlarm product free for personal use. ZoneAlarm provides a basic firewall without the bells and whistles that are part of the more advanced ZoneAlarm products. Whereas Windows Firewall only filters or blocks incoming traffic, ZoneAlarm will also watch the outbound traffic. This feature can be helpful in alerting you to any Trojans or spyware that might have compromised your machine and that might try to initiate outbound communications to "call home," so to speak.

ZoneAlarm can be configured to alert you for different types of suspicious traffic so that you can be aware of potential malicious activity as it is happening. As new applications attempt to connect from the computer, ZoneAlarm will ask the user whether or not the connection should be allowed. You can choose whether to allow it for only this occurrence or to allow that program to connect as it needs to. The only problem with these pop-up windows is that the program name might not always be recognizable, and it can be confusing for users to know whether the connection attempt is malicious or benign.

No matter which firewall product you choose, we highly recommend that you use a personal firewall application on each computer in addition to using a cable/DSL router-based firewall if possible. We do offer one caution or word of advice, though: once you install a personal firewall product remember to look there first if you start having any connection problems. Very often a firewall might be blocking traffic or connections that you think should be going through, so take a look at the configuration of the firewall before you get frustrated or spend hours trying to troubleshoot the problem.

Intrusion Detection and Prevention

Having an intrusion detection system (IDS) on your computer or network is like having surveillance cameras or a motion sensor alarm in your home. You hope that the locks on your doors and windows will keep unauthorized intruders out, but should that fail, you want some means of monitoring the intrusion or alerting you that it has occurred. Similarly, you expect that your firewall will keep malicious traffic out of your network, but should something slip past the firewall, your IDS can monitor and alert you.

And that really is all an IDS does, monitor and alert. If your home also had some sort of automated lockdown mechanism to trap the intruder in the home until the authorities could arrive, or if you had armed guards who responded immediately to stop the intrusion, it would be more like an IPS.

An IDS can be networking based (NIDS, or network-based intrusion detection system) or installed on individual computers (HIDS, or host-based intrusion detection system), similar to a firewall. A NIDS examines actual packets traveling the network in real time to look for suspicious activity. A HIDS examines log files like the Windows Event Logs (System, Applications, and Security Event Logs) and looks for entries that suggest suspicious activity. Figure 5.9 shows the Event Viewer in the Computer Management dialog box.

Figure 5.9 Computer Management

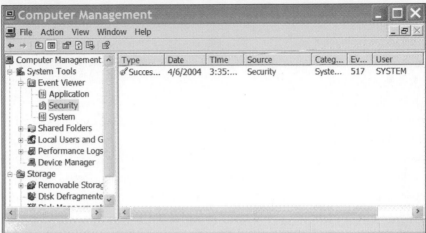

A NIDS has the advantage of detecting attacks in real time. It can also detect even an unsuccessful attack so that you are aware that the attempt occurred and can detect some types of attacks that a HIDS would miss because they can only be identified by looking at the packet headers.

Because a HIDS relies on checking the logs on the host system to identify attacks, it validates that an attack was successful. It can also detect attacks that don't travel the network, such as an attacker sitting at the keyboard of the HIDS. HIDS can also detect attempts to access files or change file permissions, or changes to key system files that a NIDS would not detect.

Neither is necessarily better than the other, and both can be used in conjunction with the other to alert you to all the different types of attacks that might not be caught by just a NIDS or HIDS. Regardless of which you choose, intrusion detection techniques generally fall under one of two categories or a hybrid of both. Signature-based detection works similar to the way most antivirus software does. It attempts to identify suspicious activity by comparing packet headers and other information with a database of known signatures of exploits, attacks, and malicious code.

The downfall of this method is the same as it is with antivirus software; it is reactive. Until a new attack exists, there is no way to develop a signature for it. In essence, someone must get attacked first before the IDS vendors or support groups can develop a signature. Moreover, the time lag between the release of an attack or exploit and receiving a signature you can deploy on your IDS is a time frame during which you won't have protection for that threat.

Anomaly-based detection compares network packets and behavior with a known baseline and looks for patterns or actions that are abnormal. For example, if a certain computer typically does not use FTP, but suddenly tries to initiate an FTP connection with a server, the IDS would detect this as an anomaly and alert you. The downside to anomaly detection is that it can require a lot of intensive "handholding" to define what normal traffic is for your network and establish the baseline. During this initial learning curve, you might get a lot of false-positive alerts or potentially miss malicious activity.

Both detection techniques have their pros and cons, but regardless of how suspicious or malicious activity is detected, the job of the IDS is to alert you. This might be done by sending a console message that pops up on your screen via the Windows Messenger Service or the IDS might send an e-mail or even send an alert to a pager in some cases. It is up to you to configure how you will be alerted. More important, however, it is up to you to respond to the alert. Having an IDS that detects and alerts you to the presence of suspected malicious activity is worthless if you don't have a well-defined incident response plan to address the issue. For details on responding to security incidents go to Chapter 11, "When Disaster Strikes."

One of the best and most popular IDS programs is Snort (see Figure 5.10). Snort is an open-source network intrusion detection (NIDS) application that is available for free. Because of its popularity and the fact that it is an open-source program, there are a number of support forums and mailing lists you can reference to learn about the program or to acquire updated signatures for new threats. Snort analyzes network packets and can detect a wide range of known attacks and malicious activity.

Figure 5.10 Snort

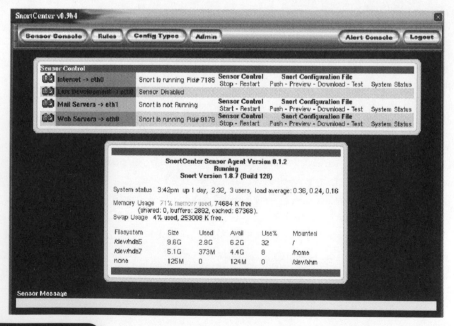

A newer technology exists that will handle that initial response for you. An IPS is somewhat like a hybrid between an IDS and a firewall, or it may work in conjunction with your existing firewall. The primary difference between an IDS and an IPS is that an IPS will do something to respond and attempt to stop the intrusion, whereas the IDS will simply let you know it's going on.

An IPS monitors the network the same way that an IDS does and still uses the same signature and/or anomaly pattern-matching techniques for identifying potentially malicious activity. However, when an IPS detects that there is suspected malicious traffic, it can alter or create firewall rules to simply block all traffic on the target port or block all incoming traffic from the source IP address or any number of custom responses you might configure.

Typically, the IPS will be configured not only to take some immediate action to prevent any further malicious activity but also to alert you like an IDS. Even if your IPS has managed to block the offending traffic, you still need to be made aware of the attack or attempted attack and you might need to respond with a more thorough or long-term solution than the quick-fix measures put in place by the IPS.

Sometimes the line between firewall, intrusion detection, and intrusion prevention gets blurred as applications and devices come out that try to provide all-in-one protection. Small business networks might benefit from implementing intrusion detection or prevention, but for a home network, intrusion detection and prevention are probably more security than you need. However, a router-based firewall and personal firewall application are highly recommended to protect the perimeter of your network and ensure the maximum security for your computer.

Summary

Although it is very hard to say what is right and what is wrong with all the different perimeter security systems from all the different vendors, there is one main philosophy that is right and that is that you need it. No matter what kind of system you have, you need some type of security to protect your data. That is what everyone is after, not your computer and not your mouse. It is better to overdo it, than not do it, as we say. So make sure you have your perimeter security turned on and your host security turned on.

If you are using a cable modem, invest in a good cable router or wireless network router. Both devices, such as equipment from Linksys or Netgear, have good security settings to be used as your perimeter firewall. Read the instructions, set up the firewall on the router as your first line of defense, and then make sure you either turn on your Windows firewall or use a third-party personal firewall on your computer. This will save you in case you have something get by the perimeter firewall. All users should use this for home or SOHO-type installations.

The Windows Firewall is far better than nothing, and the price is right. But most third-party personal firewalls offer more comprehensive protection and provide a more intuitive interface to manage it with.

Additional Resources

The following resources provide more information on firewalls and other topics related to perimeter security:

- Amarasinghe, Saman. *Host-Based IPS Guards Endpoints. Network World.* July 25, 2005. (www.networkworld.com/news/tech/2005/072505techupdate.html).

- Bradley, Tony. *Host-Based Intrusion Prevention.* About.com. (http://netsecurity.about.com/cs/firewallbooks/a/aa050804.htm).

- *Home and Small Office Network Topologies.* Microsoft.com. August 2, 2004. (www.microsoft.com/technet/prodtechnol/winxppro/plan/topology.mspx)

- Tyson, Jeff. *How Firewalls Work.* (www.howstuffworks.com/firewall.htm).

- *Understanding Windows Firewall.* Microsoft.com. August 4, 2004. (www microsoft.com/windowsxp/using/security/internet/sp2_wfintro.mspx).

Chapter 6

E-mail Safety

Topics in this chapter:

- The Evolution of E-mail
- E-mail Security Concerns

☑ Summary

☑ Additional Resources

Introduction

E-mail is one of the most common tasks performed with a computer. With the capability to deliver messages almost instantly anywhere around the globe, it provides speed and efficiency that can't be matched by regular postal mail service.

Unfortunately, as efficient as it is at delivering legitimate messages, electronic mail is also quite efficient at distributing malicious software and filling e-mail inboxes with unsolicited junk mail. The information in this chapter will help you use e-mail productively and safely.

In this chapter, you will learn:

- The history of e-mail
- Precautions to take with e-mail file attachments
- How to use POP3 vs. Web-based e-mail
- How to avoid and block spam
- How to protect yourself from e-mail hoaxes and phishing attacks

The Evolution of E-mail

The concept of e-mail goes back much further than most people would suspect. Computer scientists and engineers were using the ARPANET, the precursor of the Internet as we know it, to send communications back and forth starting in the early 1970s.

From its origins as a command-line program used by a select few to send a handful of communications back and forth, the concept of e-mail evolved slowly into what we use today. Approximately 20 years passed between the first e-mail communications and the large-scale, mainstream adoption of e-mail as a method of communication.

E-mail Security Concerns

Today, e-mail is the primary means of business and personal communications for millions of people. Billions of messages are transmitted back and forth across the Internet on a daily basis. Unfortunately, according to the *MessageLabs Intelligence 2005 Annual Security Report*, almost 70 percent is unsolicited commercial e-mail, commonly referred to as spam, and 1 in every 36 e-mails contains a virus or malware of some sort.

This may not be all that different from your standard postal mailbox. I know that a good portion of the mail I receive is unsolicited commercial advertisements that I generally don't even stop to look at. It may even range between 50 percent and 80 percent just like spam. But, translating the e-mail statistics to your standard mail would mean that if you received ten pieces of mail on a given day, eight of those pieces would be commercial junk mail, one of those pieces would contain anthrax or some other infectious substance, and one would be a legitimate letter from your brother in Kansas with pictures of your niece from her recent dance recital.

Spam and malware are most definitely the bane of e-mail communications, but when you look at the statistics in comparison with the amount of unsolicited marketing on the radio, on television, or in your standard postal mailbox, spam doesn't seem like quite as big a deal. However, even though malware accounts for a much smaller percentage of the total e-mail volume, it can have a significant impact should your computer become infected. For details on viruses and other malware, see Chapter 3, "Viruses, Worms, and Other Malware."

Handwritten letters are wonderful and have a charm and personal touch that are difficult to mirror in an electronic communication, but the capability to communicate virtually instantaneously to anyone around the world makes e-mail perfect for many types of communications. Unfortunately, because of its speed and widespread use it has also become the attack vector of choice for spreading malware. Anyone using e-mail is essentially guaranteed to receive spam and malware, so the key is to make sure you take the right precautions to use this communications medium effectively and safely at the same time.

Opening Attachments

When e-mail first began as a simple text-only command-line application to exchange simple messages between computer engineers it had not occurred to anyone that one day billions of messages would be flying around the globe or that a good percentage of those messages would contain a file attachment of some sort.

When the Internet exploded in the early 1990s and e-mail became a mainstream form of communication, file attachments soon emerged as a standard part of many messages as well. For personal e-mail, users found it a quick and simple way to share pictures of grandchildren with parents across the country or the world. For businesses it became a competitive advantage to be able to send a business proposal or the latest financial figures as a document or spreadsheet file attachment to an e-mail.

It didn't take long for that competitive advantage to become a business necessity and for file attachments to become a requirement for conducting business. Fax machines quickly became glorified paper weights as businesses found e-mail file attachments to be faster and more reliable than faxing.

For personal e-mail messages, the use of file attachments grew rapidly as well. Users found that they could not only attach graphic images such as photographs, but could attach files such as small movies and documents with jokes, and even share entire programs with friends and family.

It is an unfortunate fact when it comes to malware and malicious computer activity that often what was intended as a feature can also be exploited and used against you. If a file attachment can be sent with a program you can click to execute and perform some function, there is nothing stopping a malicious developer from creating one that executes and performs a malicious function.

For the most part, the success of file attachments as a means of propagating malware depends on what is called "social engineering." Basically, the author of the malicious e-mail has to compel the recipient to open the file attachment in some way.

One of the first ways used to persuade recipients to open malicious e-mail attachments was by appealing to the user's curiosity. The Anna Kournikova virus claimed to contain a picture of the photogenic tennis star, but opening the attachment simply infected the computer.

This social engineering was quickly followed by disguising the e-mail to appear to come from someone the user knows. Ostensibly, a user is more likely to trust a message from his Uncle George or a coworker he eats lunch with than he is a message from a complete stranger. Malware developers began by programming their viruses to send themselves out to the addresses in the address book from the e-mail program of the infected computer. Using this method of propagation led to a fairly high rate of success in ensuring that the infected e-mail went to people who personally knew the owner of the infected computer and would therefore be more likely to trust the message.

Eventually users started to get wise to the idea that even a message from a trusted friend might be suspicious. Some companies educated their users and tried to condition them not to open certain types of file attachments because they might execute a malicious program. But, non-executable programs such as a TXT, or text, files were considered to be safe.

Then one day someone received an e-mail from a friend with the Subject line "ILoveYou" and a message attachment called "Love-Letter-For-You.txt"... or so they thought. Without stopping to consider the fact that their Windows operating system was configured not to show known file extensions, therefore the "txt" should not be visible, they double-clicked on the attachment to open it and found themselves infected with the LoveLetter virus.

In actuality, the file attachment was called "Love-Letter-For-You.txt.vbs" which capitalized on the Windows "feature" that hides known file extensions and exploited the acceptance of TXT files as being safe. LoveLetter was an excellent example of both social engineering and using "features" for malicious purposes. For details on hidden file extensions go to Chapter 1, "Basic Windows Security."

Although antivirus software is continually updated to detect these new threats as they are created, it is still a reactive form of defense. Malware still gets past antivirus software and entices users to execute infected file attachments before the antivirus software is updated. To prevent these infections and to try to ensure that users do not even have an opportunity to execute malicious attachments, administrators began filtering certain attachment types regardless of whether they actually contained malicious code or not.

This is one of the most prevalent methods for proactively protecting the network from potentially malicious executable file attachments, or file attachments that will run a program or perform commands if they are opened. As the list of blocked file types grows, malware developers simply find some other executable file types to spread malware and the cycle continues.

Initially, this sort of proactive attachment blocking was reserved for corporate networks with administrators that knew how to build their own custom filters. Eventually, some e-mail client software began to block potentially malicious attachments as well. Starting with Outlook 2003, Microsoft began to block a lengthy list of attachment types that might potentially contain malicious code.

Blocking file attachments that are known to be executable and therefore may pose a risk from a security perspective is a move in the right direction, but it too is somewhat reactive. Although it is more proactive to block a given file attachment type by default, most administrators and mail filters don't add a file type to the list of blocked types until after it has been used by some malware. In my opinion, **all** file attachments should be blocked by default and then the administrator or user should have to designate which types they will allow rather than the other way around.

It has been a fairly common practice in recent years to block all executable file attachments but to allow archive file types, specifically ZIP files from the popular compression program WinZip. The logic was that some users might be tricked through social engineering to double-click an executable file attachment, but surely if they had to first uncompress the archive file and then double-click the executable file it contained, that users would have enough sense not to do so unless they knew exactly what the file attachment was for and trusted the sender of the e-mail message.

Some administrators even went so far as to block ZIP file attachments unless they were password protected to try to ensure that even users who might fall for social engineering requiring them to first open a ZIP file before executing the file attachment would have to go through the additional step of supplying a password to do so. Surely no user would go so far as to not only execute a file attachment they know nothing about and that came from an untrusted source, but to also first extract it from a compressed archive that requires a password.

Tools & Traps...

Filtering ZIP Files

Stripping file attachments that might be malicious or blocking e-mails containing potentially malicious attachments are both good ways to protect your system.

Many network administrators began to block a variety of attachments by default and some even added ZIP files to the list of banned file types.

Some companies were not willing to give up the convenience offered by being able to send ZIP files though, so they came up with other creative workarounds.

For example, files named "file.zip" would be blocked, but files named "file.zzip" would not get caught by the filter. By telling employees and business partners to use the *.zzip designation, a company could continue to benefit from ZIP files without remaining vulnerable to malware spread by them.

Well, early 2004 proved those theories wrong. With a vengeance. New malware dubbed Bagel and Netsky hit the Internet. Rather than trying to overwhelm the user with social engineering in the message, they each had exceptionally short, rather cryptic messages that simply said things like "the details are in the attachment." Both of these malware threats used ZIP file attachments and yet people still opened the ZIP file and executed the enclosed attachment and propagated the viruses. In fact, some versions of these threats even used password-protected ZIP files with the password included in the body of the message and users still opened the attachments and became infected.

Although some users have been told for years to never open a file attachment unless they not only trust the sender, but also know exactly what the file attachment is and why the sender sent it to them, there are a vast number of home users who simply don't know. It's like going to the wrong side of town late at night with no "street smarts" and no concept of the risks and threats that exist.

The "wrong" side of town can be relatively safe as long as you understand the risks and threats and how to avoid them. Using the Internet and e-mail is the same way. Getting a new computer and jumping straight onto the Internet without taking some security precautions is like driving without brakes or skydiving without a parachute. As long as there are file attachments though, the bottom line is that the responsibility falls on you, the user, to exercise an appropriate amount of caution and common sense before choosing to open or execute them.

Web-Based versus POP3 E-mail

Most home users use either a POP3 (Post Office Protocol) e-mail account or Web-based e-mail such as Hotmail or Yahoo. With some ISPs you have the option of doing either. Each type of e-mail has its advantages and security concerns.

One of the biggest issues with Web-based e-mail is that it bypasses many security measures designed for e-mail. Corporate networks often have antivirus scanners at the e-mail server level designed to catch and block any malicious e-mail before it can get to the end user. There are also typically filters that block file attachments that may contain malicious code as well. When e-mail comes through the Web rather than through the pre-defined channels for e-mail, these security measures are useless.

Accessing personal e-mail at all, or at least accessing personal e-mail via the Web on your employer's network is an activity that should be governed by some sort of policy or procedure. You should check to make sure you aren't violating any rules by doing so.

On a positive note, the larger providers of Web-based e-mail; namely, Yahoo and Hotmail, now provide virus protection on their e-mail. It does not replace the need to run antivirus software on your own computer since e-mail is only one means of spreading malware, but it at least significantly reduces the risk of receiving an infected file attachment through Web-based e-mail.

POP3 e-mail is the other standard primarily used by home Internet users. Programs like Outlook Express, Eudora, and Netscape Mail are typically used to download and view e-mail from a POP3 account. When you set up the client software you have to supply information such as your username and password and the incoming and outgoing mail servers so the software can authenticate your account and send and receive e-mail. Rather than simply viewing your e-mail on a Web page, the actual messages are transferred from the e-mail server to your computer.

Whether you use Web-based or POP3 e-mail, there are security concerns you should be aware of. Sending an unencrypted e-mail is the digital equivalent of writing your thoughts on a postcard. Would you write your bank account number, social security number or other personal and confidential information on a postcard to be seen by all as it passes from you to its intended destination? If you wouldn't share the information in public you shouldn't send it in an e-mail. E-mail is not inherently secure. It is convenient and quick, but not secure.

Spoofed Addresses

One of the most confusing things about e-mail for many users these days is spoofed e-mail addresses. Most people by now have experienced receiving an e-mail infected with some type of malware that appears to be from their cousins, best friends, or mothers. But when you contact those people to ask them why they sent you the e-mail or to let them know they are distributing infected e-mail, you discover that they never actually sent you the e-mail to begin with.

Most users have also had the opposite experience as well. You get the e-mail or phone call from your friends asking you why you sent them an infected e-mail message. It is also very common to receive an auto-reply from some mail server either letting you know that the e-mail you sent contained a virus or worm or that the user you allegedly sent the e-mail to does not exist.

All of these are examples of spoofed IP addresses. If I mail a letter to someone I could very easily write any name and address I choose in the return address portion. If I wrote your address in as the return address and the message was undeliverable it would get sent back to you rather than me. It is equally easy to alter or forge the address information on an e-mail.

Using Microsoft Outlook you can enter an address in the From field as well as altering the Reply To address thereby making it appear that the e-mail came from a different source and sending any replies back to that same source. On a corporate network it's not as easy because it will actually check to see if you have permission to send on behalf of the address you are trying to send from. However, you can simply invent a non-existent e-mail address, even if it's on a non-existent domain and that information is all the recipient will see.

Well… almost all the recipient will see. Going back to the postal mail return address example, I may be able to write a return address to make it appear the letter originated from California, but the postmark will bear the mark of the city and state of the post office it actually came from. Similarly, each e-mail message contains information about its true source within the e-mail headers.

In Outlook Express you can right-click on an e-mail message and select Properties to display information about the message. If you choose the Details tab you can click the button labeled Message Source and review information about exactly what server and IP address the message came from. You can view similar information in Microsoft Outlook by right-clicking the e-mail message and selecting Options to look at the Internet Headers.

It would help to stop the confusion and stop clogging users' e-mail inboxes with useless messages if e-mail server antivirus programs were not configured to automatically reply to the sender. Originally it was a good idea. Rather than just blocking or cleaning the e-mail, a courtesy message was also sent to the originator of the message to inform them they had sent an infected message and that perhaps they needed to update their antivirus software or scan their system to make sure they didn't continue propagating the malware.

For the past year or more, however, viruses and worms almost always spoof the source e-mail address. Many malware threats scan deep within infected systems to find addresses to propagate to as well as addresses to use in spoofing the source address. They look not only in the standard address book files, but also scan through temporary Internet files and other such data to find e-mail addresses embedded in Web pages.

That means that the "courtesy" response to the sender ends up at the wrong place and confuses some innocent user into believing their computer might be infected or wondering how or why they even sent an e-mail to that address in the first place.

The primary thing you need to know when it comes to the source address of an e-mail is not to trust it. Almost every part of an e-mail header can be forged with enough knowledge; fields like the Sender or From e-mail address and the Reply-To e-mail address can be changed simply by typing in a new one with some e-mail applications.

Exercise caution and an appropriate amount of common sense before choosing to open an e-mail message. Even if it appears to be from your brother, if the Subject of the message or the message itself seem suspicious or awkward it is better to err on the side of caution and simply delete it. When you receive a misguided response or auto-response to a message that spoofed your e-mail address you should simply delete those as well.

Spam

We have all heard of spam by now. I am not referring to the distinctively flavored spiced ham meat product, but the bane of e-mail. The term has some bizarre link with a classic Monty Python skit based on the Hormel meat product and also owes its origination to a couple of attorneys from Phoenix, AZ who inundated Internet newsgroups with unsolicited marketing in 1994. As much as Hormel might like people to use some other term for unsolicited junk e-mail messages rather than providing a negative connotation to their trademarked meat product name, the term spam has stuck.

Virtually everybody with an e-mail account is accustomed to receiving offers to refinance their home loan; purchase low-priced Vicodin, Viagra, and other pharmaceuticals on the Internet; hook up with an alleged blind date; and any number of other unsolicited commercial marketing.

Most corporations and many e-mail programs now have the capability to filter e-mail to try to block spam messages so that you aren't bothered by them. There are also third-party programs you can use to block spam from getting into your computer. Personal computer security software products such as Norton Internet Security Suite or McAfee Internet Security Suite include spam as one of the threats that they protect against.

Like most of the other security measures we have discussed, such as antivirus software and intrusion detection, the filters to block spam messages are also reactive to some degree. Many of the spam-filtering applications use a point system to determine whether a message is spam or not. They can block source e-mail or IP addresses known to distribute spam and can scan the subject and body of incoming e-mail messages and look for keywords like "Viagra" or "refinance" that tend to appear in spam e-mail messages. The more such keywords appear in a single message, the more likely it is spam and will therefore be blocked.

Spam filtering can still be somewhat messy, though. Legitimate messages you may want to receive may get filtered or quarantined by your spam-blocking software while some spam messages will still make it through. Often you can help to "teach" the spam-filtering software by letting it know when it has a false positive or false negative like this.

The purveyors of spam continue to come up with new ways to try to trick or circumvent spam filters and make sure their message gets to your inbox whether you like it or not. One trick is to include a wide range of meaningless words with the spam message to throw off the point system. The more words there are in the overall message the smaller the percentage of spam trigger words will be so the message will pass the point scale system. The other trick is to use "hacker-speak" in place of real words, substituting alternate characters that look similar to the proper letters. For instance, you will often see spam messages where "Viagra" is spelled "v1@gr@" or something similar. Sometimes other characters might be inserted within the spelling as well like "v-i-a-g-r-a." All of these are tricks are designed to get past spam-filtering software.

Outlook Express does not offer much in the way of spam or junk mail protection. It is possible to block mail from a specific sender or an entire domain, but stopping spam by blocking individual senders is like trying to stop water with a net and blocking the entire domain to stop spam is like demolishing a house to kill a fly.

Outlook, at least Outlook 2003, offers significantly better junk mail filtering. The junk mail filter is enabled by default, but set to Low to avoid having too many false positives and potentially filtering out legitimate messages. As you can see in Figure 6.1, you can add addresses to one of four junk mail filter lists: Safe Senders, Safe Recipients, Blocked Senders, and International. If a message is received from someone on the Safe Senders list it will be delivered even if it might otherwise have failed the spam filter test. You can also provide an extreme level of security for your e-mail by configuring the junk mail filter to allow incoming mail only from addresses that are on your Safe Senders or Safe Recipients lists. In effect, rather than blacklisting one by one all of the addresses you *don't* want to get e-mail from, you create a much shorter list of only the addresses you *do* want e-mail from. Outlook's Junk E-mail options enable you to choose how strict to be with identifying junk e-mail and what to do with it.

Figure 6.1 Outlook's Junk E-mail Options

In 2003, the United States Congress passed the CAN-SPAM Act. CAN-SPAM is a snappy acronym for "Controlling the Assault of Non-Solicited Pornography and Marketing." (Someone in Washington, DC, is probably making a pretty good salary from our tax dollars to make sure that our laws all have names that fit nicely into some fun code word like CAN-SPAM or the USA-PATRIOT Act, which stands for "Uniting and Strengthening America by Providing Appropriate Tools Required to Intercept and Obstruct Terrorism.") Although the law was created ostensibly to reduce or eliminate spam, it actually does as much to legitimize spam as a form of marketing as it does to eliminate it.

What the CAN-SPAM act does do primarily is to provide the rules of engagement, so to speak, for legal marketing via e-mail. CAN-SPAM requires that the purveyors of spam provide some identifiable means for recipients to opt out of receiving any future messages and that no deception is used in transmitting the messages. It requires all e-mail advertising to contain a valid reply-to address, postal mailing address, and a subject line and e-mail headers that are accurate. It provides penalties for any marketer that does not stay within these bounds.

In essence, under this law a company can still inundate the Internet with useless junk mail and as long as they provide a legitimate reply-to e-mail address and postal address and offer a means for the recipient to opt out of receiving future messages, the responsibility falls on the user to basically unsubscribe from the spam. In Europe, the anti-spam law works in reverse, requiring that the user opt-in or choose to receive the commercial advertising before it can be sent.

Tools & Traps…

Spam Zombies

Broadband Internet service provider Comcast has approximately six million subscribers. Spam zombies within those six million subscribers were found responsible for sending out over 700 million spam messages per day.

Although some ISPs such as Earthlink have simply blocked traffic from their customers on port 25, this method may also block some legitimate mail servers within the network.

In 2004, Comcast implemented a slightly different policy. Rather than blocking all traffic on port 25, Comcast opted to identify the source addresses and secretly send their modem a new configuration file that blocked port 25 traffic for them only.

There are three glaring issues with trying to legislate spam in this way. First, so-called legitimate marketers of spam will continue to overwhelm users with spam, just ensuring that they do so within the bounds of the law. Second, the law can only reasonably be applied to companies or individuals within the United States even though a vast majority of spam originates from outside of the United States. Third, trying to control an activity through legislation assumes that the parties involved in the activity have any regard for the law in the first place.

This last issue is evidenced by the explosion of spam zombies. In 2003, the two scourges of e-mail communications, spam and malware, converged as viruses such as Sobig propagated themselves to unprotected computers and, without alerting the owners, millions of computers became spam servers. These Trojan spam servers are commonly referred to as spam "zombies," e-mail servers that are dead until the attacker who controls the Trojan program calls them to life and begins to use them to generate millions of spam messages.

These spam zombies enable the less scrupulous purveyors of spam to continue sending out hundreds of millions of unsolicited commercial message per day without regard for the CAN-SPAM act and with little concern that the messages can be traced back to their true originator. With thousands upon thousands of such compromised machines at their disposal, it also means that these spam pushers have virtually unlimited processing power and network bandwidth to work with.

Aside from using spam filters or third-party spam-blocking software, there are a couple other things you can do to try to prevent spam from overwhelming your inbox. For starters, you should create a separate e-mail account to use for all Internet forms, registrations, and such. Whether your address is bought, stolen, or simply used inappropriately by the company you gave it to, there is a very good chance that once you start using an e-mail address on the Internet you will see an increase in spam. By using a separate e-mail account for those things and always using the same e-mail account you can narrow down where the spam will go to and keep it out of your main personal e-mail account.

Another step you can take is to use the literal word "at" rather than the @ symbol when typing your e-mail address in various places. Much of the e-mail address harvesting done on the Web by spam companies is automated. Since an e-mail addressed to tony(at)computersecurityfornongeeks.com will not actually work it will most likely simply be removed from the spammer's database. Some sites may require you to enter a valid e-mail address, but if you can get away with it you should try the word "at" separated with parentheses or dashes or something.

Of course, the best thing you can do to help control the flood of spam is to never, ever respond to it and never actually purchase anything from a spam message. The cost of advertising in a newspaper or on television can be quite expensive, but the cost of sending out millions of spam e-mails is negligible. As long as even a fraction of a handful of the millions of people respond and make a purchase, it means that the spam campaign was profitable. As long as spamming works and generates profit for the spammers they will continue spamming.

Hoaxes and Phishing

If you have been using e-mail for more than a few weeks, perhaps you have received an e-mail message like the following:

> If you receive an e-mail entitled "Bedtimes" delete it IMMEDIATELY.
> Do not open it. Apparently this one is pretty nasty. It will not only

erase everything on your hard drive, but it will also delete anything on disks within 20 feet of your computer.

It demagnetizes the strips on ALL of your credit cards. It reprograms your ATM access code and screws up the tracking on your VCR and uses subspace field harmonics to scratch any CDs you attempt to play. It will program your phone auto dial to call only 900 numbers. This virus will mix antifreeze into your fish tank.

IT WILL CAUSE YOUR TOILET TO FLUSH WHILE YOU ARE SHOWERING.

It will drink ALL your beer. FOR GOD'S SAKE, ARE YOU LISTENING?? It will leave dirty underwear on the coffee table when you are expecting company! It will replace your shampoo with Nair and your Nair with Rogaine.

If the "Bedtimes" message is opened in a Windows 95/98 environment, it will leave the toilet seat up and leave your hair dryer plugged in dangerously close to a full bathtub.

It will not only remove the forbidden tags from your mattresses and pillows, it will also refill your Skim milk with whole milk.

******* WARN AS MANY PEOPLE AS YOU CAN.

Send to everyone.

The preceding is actually a hoax of a hoax. There is no shortage of hoax e-mail topics, though. Maybe you've heard the one about how Bill Gates is beta testing some secret new e-mail tracking program and will pay you for every address you forward the message to? Or maybe you got the inside tip about the $200 Nieman Marcus cookie recipe?

Any message that implores you to send it to your entire address book or bad luck will befall you and your computer will suffer a catastrophic meltdown is, by definition, a hoax. Just to make sure we've covered all of the bases, here are a few more of the most popular chain letter e-mail hoaxes that you can simply delete and save the rest of us from having to read them yet again:

■ There is no baby food manufacturer issuing checks as a result of a class action law suit.

- Disney is not offering any free vacation for your help in sending their e-mail to everyone you know.

- MTV is not offering backstage passes to anyone who forwards the message to the most people.

- There is no kidney theft ring and people are not waking up in a bathtub full of ice with their kidney mysteriously removed.

- There is no bill pending in Congress to implement a tax on your Internet usage.

The list goes on and on (and on and on) of hoax e-mail chain letters. Some of them have been traveling the globe for years. Small details may change here and there and then off they go around the Internet again. The majority do no harm other than to waste network bandwidth and people's time. One particularly tenacious one causes some minor damage.

The Teddy Bear or JDBGMGR hoax has been around for awhile. The message comes from a friend of a friend to let you know that you may in fact be infected with this dreaded teddy bear virus. There are many variations of the message, but the gist of it reads as follows:

> Hi, everybody: I just received a message today from one of my friends in my Address Book. Their Address Book had been infected by a virus and it was passed on to my computer. My Address Book, in turn, has been infected.
>
> The virus is called jdbgmgr.exe and it propagates automatically through Messenger and through the address book. The virus is not detected by McAfee or Norton and it stays dormant for 14 days before it wipes out the whole system. It can be deleted before it erases your computer files. To delete it, you just have to do the following.

It then goes on to let you know exactly where you can find this insidious file. Lo and behold, there really **IS** a file there with a teddy bear icon. The catch with this hoax is that the jdbgmgr.exe file with the teddy bear icon is a standard file that is installed with many versions of the Microsoft Windows operating system, not an infected virus file.

Inevitably, someone will receive this message and feel compelled to share the information as quickly as possible with everyone they know. One or two of those people will also fall for this hoax and propagate it to their entire address book, and so the domino effect continues.

Here are some things to look for and some precautions to take to try to keep yourself from falling prey to one of these hoaxes and continuing to perpetuate this insanity. First of all, if there are more than ten e-mail addresses in the To: or CC: fields you might want to question it. People don't generally send legitimate messages to such a broad range of addresses.

If the actual message is five levels down because it's a forward of a forward of a forwarded message, it is most likely some form of hoax or chain letter e-mail. If it implores you to forward it quickly or send it to everyone you know, it is most like a hoax or chain letter e-mail. Even if it claims that the information has been authenticated or validated with a reputable source it does not mean that it has. In fact, the simple statement claiming that it has been verified with a reputable source is reason to believe that it has not and also suggests that there is a good likelihood that the message is a hoax or chain letter e-mail.

It is fairly safe to assume that you will never receive a legitimate e-mail message that you actually need to forward to everyone you know. If you ever have any doubts about a message, check it out in one of the many hoax databases like Snopes (www.snopes.com) or the About.com Antivirus Hoax Encyclopedia (http://antivirus.about.com/library/blenhoax.htm) or at an antivirus vendor Web site like McAfee (http://vil.nai.com/vil/hoaxes.asp). Even if you don't find it on one of these hoax reference sites, you should send it to your network administrator or the tech support or customer service from your ISP rather than to the world as you know it.

A phishing scam is a different and more malicious form of e-mail scam. Phishing, an adaptation of the word "fishing," involves sending an e-mail out to a large number of addresses with some bait and seeing how many naïve users you can hook. Typically, the goal of a phishing scam is to acquire usernames and passwords to financial sites such as banking institutions or PayPal in order to get into the accounts and remove the money from them.

Phishing scams are often very sophisticated, with a very professional look and feel designed to mimic the real institution being targeted. In early 2004, the Gartner Group reported a significant spike in phishing scams. By Gartner estimates the number of people who have been victimized by phishing scams is approaching the two million mark.

A phishing scam usually involves creating an elaborate replica of the target company's Web site. Past phishing scams have involved companies like Best Buy, AOL, EBay, PayPal, and Citigroup. An e-mail is then sent out to millions of users designed to look as if it is from the targeted company and using some form of social engineering to convince the user to click on a link that will take them to the malicious replica site. Users may be asked to enter information such as their username, password, account number, and other personal or confidential information. After the attackers have gathered this information, they can then access your account and move or redirect your money to their own account.

Typically, users end up protected and the company or financial institution takes the loss for any money that victims of the phishing scams might lose. There have been suggestions though that perhaps users should just know better or have more common sense and that, in effect, the attacker didn't "steal" anything because the user volunteered the information and gave them the keys to the vault.

It can be very difficult to detect a phishing scam. Both the e-mail bait and the replica Web site are generally very professionally done. The best bet to protect yourself is to remember that no reputable company will ask you to give them your username and password or other confidential and personal information on a Web site.

Under no circumstances should you use the link within the e-mail to connect to the company's Web site. One of the prevailing suggestions for handling phishing scams is to tell users that if they receive an e-mail that they are not sure about, they should close the e-mail and visit the company Web site on their own and figure out how to contact customer service for that company for more information.

This advice falls a little short though. Not only should you not use the link in the e-mail, but you should completely shut down your e-mail client program and close all Web browser windows. The attacker may have somehow executed a script or performed some other malicious magic that might redirect you to a replica site. After you have completely shut down your e-mail client and closed all browser windows, you can then open a new browser window and visit the Web site of the company in question.

Summary

E-mail is a vital function for most personal computer users. This chapter covered the information you need to know to understand the risks associated with e-mail and how to protect yourself and your computer from them.

After discussing a brief history of e-mail, we talked about e-mail file attachments and how to protect yourself from malicious file attachments. We also covered the risk of POP3 versus Web-based e-mail software.

You learned how to filter and block unsolicited e-mails, or spam, and how to recognize e-mail hoax and phishing attack messages and avoid becoming a victim. Having read this chapter, you should be able to recognize the risks associated with e-mail and to effectively protect your computer so that you can use e-mail safely.

Additional Resources

The following resources provide more information on e-mail safety:

- Hu, Jim. "Comcast takes hard line against spam." *ZDNetnews*, June 10, 2004 (http://news.zdnet.com/2100-3513_22-5230615.html).

- Landesman, Mary. *Hoax Encyclopedia*. About.com's Antivirus Software Web Page (http://antivirus.about.com/library/blenhoax.htm).

- *McAfee's Hoax Database* (http://vil.nai.com/vil/hoaxes.asp).

- McAlearney, Shawna. "Dangers of .zip Files." *Techtarget's Security Wire Perspectives*, March 4, 2004 (http://searchsecurity.techtarget.com/qna/0,289202,sid14_gci953548,00. html).

- *MessageLabs Intelligence 2005 Annual Security Report* (www.messagelabs.com/Threat_Watch/Intelligence_Reports/2005_Annual _Security_Report).

- Snopes (www.snopes.com).

Chapter 7

Web Surfing Privacy and Safety

Topics in this chapter:

- **The Revolutionary World Wide Web**
- **Web Security Concerns**

☑ **Summary**

☑ **Additional Resources**

Introduction

Throughout history there have been inventions and discoveries that fundamentally changed the world as we know it. From the wheel to the printing press to the light bulb to airplanes, inventions have often been turning points in history.

In more modern times, the creation of the World Wide Web has proved to be something of a miracle. In one decade it has transformed the way people work, study, shop, and play, and within a generation it has changed the way people interact. It has created entire business models, new streams of revenue, and new fields of employment. The Web has made almost every piece of information you could possibly want available at the click of a button. While the printing press made it possible to mass-produce written works so they could be shared with everyone rather than only an elite few, the Web took the notion a quantum leap farther so that almost every thought that has ever been written can be retrieved in the blink of an eye. In short, the World Wide Web has changed the world. It has created new ways to conduct financial transactions, conduct research, hold an auction, and shop for a car. However, with the advent of the Web and its conveniences, a new type of crime has also emerged: cybercrime. In this chapter, we'll discuss security concerns related to the World Wide Web and show you what you can do to protect your computer while online.

The Revolutionary World Wide Web

The Web has revolutionized shopping: almost anything can be purchased with a few clicks. You can compare prices and review product information from a variety of sources, letting you make informed purchasing decisions and ensuring you get the best price possible. Even items that can't be purchased over the Web per se, such as a car, can still be researched by comparing features, prices, customer feedback, and more before choosing the one that's right for you.

The Web has revolutionized personal finance: You can move money from bank accounts to investment accounts and reconcile your checking account. You can pay bills without licking envelopes or paying postage. You can do research on companies and investment opportunities and buy and sell stocks and mutual funds without a broker.

The Web has revolutionized education: children can use it to play educational games at any number of sites. Adults can take college-level courses via the Web and complete their bachelor's, master's, and even doctorate degrees from their computer. People of all ages can use it for studying and research. What used to take hours pouring through books and magazines at the library can now be done in minutes with a quick search using Google or some other search engine.

The Web has also unfortunately revolutionized crime. The Internet and the World Wide Web have done wonderful things to help bring new services and the access to mountains of information to people. But, just like computer software features that, though helpful to users, can often be used against them, many of the Web's convenient features and services can be exploited by malicious persons to steal users' personal information or harm their computers.

Are You Owned?

The Bloomberg Break-In

One of the most well-known cases of cyber-extortion occurred in 2000 when two hackers from Kazakhstan broke into the Byzantine Bloomberg computer network and demanded $200,000 USD in exchange for not damaging or stealing data from the network.

Thousands of financial institutions and brokers buy and sell billions of dollars worth of investments each day based on data from Bloomberg's computer systems. Having this information damaged, stolen, or altered could have been catastrophic.

While Bloomberg could have easily paid the ransom, there would not be any guarantee that the attackers wouldn't harm the network anyway or come back asking for more money at a later date. Rather than caving to the demands, Michael Bloomberg, the CEO, secretly brought undercover officers from London with him to the meeting where he would hand over the money to the culprits, and they arrested the attackers on the spot.

This cyber-extortion drama had a happy ending, but it remains a growing problem. In addition, it is difficult to know how often it occurs because many companies would rather pay the demands and keep any breaches of their computer network security secret so as not to undermine consumer confidence in their company.

For one thing, the Internet and the World Wide Web have created an entirely new type of extortion: cyber-extortion. By definition, *extortion* means to use illegal force or intimidation to obtain something. Essentially, to extort someone is to threaten them with dire consequences should the demands of the extortionist not be met. Cyber-extortionists typically contact companies and demand money in exchange for not breaking into their networks and causing harm to their data, or exposing or stealing their customers' personal and confidential information. They may also threaten to launch some sort of Denial-of-Service attack, which would effectively render the victim's network useless for an indefinite period if the demands aren't met.

Cyber-extortion doesn't typically directly affect individual users like yourself unless your personal and confidential information happens to be part of the data stolen from the company. However, certain features of the Web, which were designed to make it a richer and more useful medium for users, also provide a means of attack if you're unaware of such weaknesses and don't exercise caution. These features of the Web include the very languages and tools used to create the information you see on the Web page.

HTML (Hypertext Markup Language) is the core language used to create graphic Web pages. HTML can be used to define different fonts and sizes of text, as well as to add color and pictures and configure other attributes of the Web page, but HTML is also static. In order to provide customized information and interactive content, many Web sites use ActiveX controls script languages such as JavaScript or VBScript. These mini-programs allow the Web page to interact with database information and provide more functionality. However, if the Web site can execute a mini-program on your computer in order to customize information for you, a malicious Web site might also be able to execute a mini-program on your computer to install a Trojan or virus of some sort.

In the next sections, we will take a look at some of the security pitfalls of using the Web and how you can get the most out of this great resource without compromising the security of your computer system.

Web Security Concerns

So what are the threats you'll be facing and how do you protect yourself? These threats come in a variety of guises, and over the next few pages we will look at those concerns.

Cookies

Who doesn't like cookies? I love all kinds of cookies. I am particularly fond of homemade chocolate chip cookies or some nice warm snickerdoodles. When Girl Scout Cookie season rolls around I can go broke buying Thin Mints and Tagalongs, but these aren't the kind of cookies we're referring to in this chapter so don't go trying to shove an oatmeal raisin cookie in your CD-ROM drive. The cookies we're referring to here are of a different and much less enjoyable variety.

The basic concept of a Web cookie is not malicious or a security concern in and of itself. Basically, a cookie is a simple text file used by a Web server to store information about a user and the user's activities on a given Web site. The Web server can then retrieve this information to use in customizing future Web pages for that user.

Aside from simply remembering who you are and some of your personal information, cookies help the Web site track how often users visit the site and how long they stay there or what pages they visit so they can work to design the Web site to best meet the needs of their visitors. They can also be used to track information which can used to target advertising that is more likely to interest you or track which ads have been shown to you already.

If you've ever registered with the online retail site Amazon.com, you may have noticed that not only does the site greet you personally upon each return visit, but it remembers items you've shown interest in or purchased in the past and makes recommendations of other items you might like based on your previous activity on the site. It does this through the use of Web cookies.

Cookies are simple text files; they can't actually *do* anything, malicious or otherwise. They can't contain malware or spyware. They can't access your hard drive or compromise your security. The only data that can be passed from a Web server to a cookie is the name of the cookie, the value of the cookie, the path or domain that the cookie is valid for, the expiration date of the cookie and whether or not the cookie requires a secure connection. As such, cookies pose no real security risk.

The main threat from cookies is to your privacy more than your security. You should remember that Web sites and cookies have no way of getting your personal information except by you giving it to them. Many Web sites request that users register for free accounts or provide basic information about themselves before being allowed to use the site. Generally this is because the information and resources on the site are only free because the site is funded by advertising and the advertisers need to know the demographic makeup of the site's visitors so they know whether or not advertising on that site will be worthwhile. It is up to you though to make sure you're comfortable with the privacy policies of the Web site in question and to exercise caution with what sites you choose to provide your information to.

There are a couple different kinds of cookies: session cookies and persistent cookies. A session cookie, as its name implies, exists only for the given Web session. Session cookies are removed from your computer once you close the browser window. The next time you visit that same site it will not retain any information about you or be able to access the information from the previous cookie.

A persistent cookie on the other hand remains on your hard drive until it expires or until you delete it. Cookies like those used on Amazon.com are persistent cookies. They help the site to remember you and your preferences and to customize the information on the site to fit you.

It is possible to control how your Web browser handles cookies or if cookies are allowed at all. In Internet Explorer, you can click Tools on the menu bar and choose Internet Options and then click the Privacy tab. There are six levels to choose from, ranging from Accept All Cookies to Block All Cookies and varying levels in between (see Figure 7.1).

Figure 7.1 Internet Privacy Options

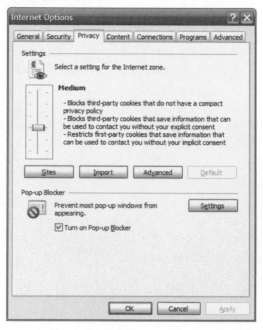

Some personal firewall products also include functionality to protect your privacy while you surf the Web, including restricting cookies. While the base version of ZoneAlarm that is available for free does not have cookie filtering or blocking ability, ZoneAlarm Pro allows you to choose how cookies are handled. You can select whether or not to block session cookies or persistent cookies as well as whether or not to allow third-party cookies. It also lets you remove private header information which prevents sites from seeing information such as your IP address or your computer name or user account login name. You can also choose to override the expiration time frame on persistent cookies and set them to expire when you choose (see Figure 7.2).

Figure 7.2 Custom Privacy Settings

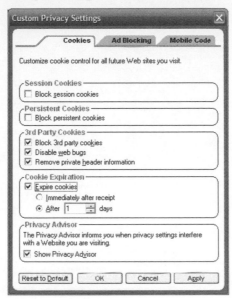

If you're concerned about privacy, it may sound logical enough to simply set your Internet Explorer to Block All Cookies and call it a day. Depending on how you use the Web and the types of sites you visit, this sort of blanket approach may cause more heartache than its worth. Many retail Web sites such as BestBuy.com, HomeDepot.com, or Target.com require cookies in order to provide you customized information about what is available at stores in your area. If you block all cookies, these sites simply won't work.

Internet Explorer does offer the ability to control cookies on a site-by-site basis as well (see Figure 7.3). Even if your cookie settings are set to block all cookies, you can click the Sites button at the bottom of the Internet Options Privacy tab. Here you can override your default cookie restrictions and add domain names to set Internet Explorer to Always Allow or Always Block cookies from a particular domain.

Privacy and Anonymous Surfing

Privacy is a very big issue for some people. It certainly seems you should at least have the right to choose what companies, entities, or individuals get to see your personal and confidential information.

Figure 7.3 Site-by-Site Cookie Control

Unfortunately, that doesn't seem to be the case and hasn't been the case for a very long time. Companies of all sorts collect reams of data on you. It's not that they're trying to spy on you per se, but data has become a commodity of sorts and it's better to have too much than too little as a general rule.

It seems that you can't make a purchase these days without someone asking for your Zip code, phone number, or e-mail address. Why a retail electronics chain would need my life story and a DNA sample from my firstborn to sell me a 9-volt battery is still an enigma to me. I get enough telemarketing calls and spam e-mails as it is without passing my information out at every transaction I make.

When you make a purchase on your credit card or get cash from an ATM machine there is a computer record somewhere marking the date and time you were at that location. Grocery stores have discount clubs with special discounts for members which are primarily a façade for gathering demographic information on their customers and tracking the items they buy for marketing efforts.

Services like the Onstar service offered by General Motors in their vehicles can help you unlock the doors when you leave your keys in the car or summon emergency help if your vehicle is involved in an accident. It also means that there is someone out there tracking the exact location of your vehicle at any given moment.

Just by putting together the pieces of the electronic trail left by people, you can often completely reconstruct their day. Starting from the credit card purchase at Starbucks in the morning, to the cell phone call placed from the dry cleaner, and the gasoline purchased with a credit card on the way to work, straight on through to paying for the pizza delivery on a credit card, you can tell where someone was, what they did and what they ate throughout the day.

None of this data collection is meant to encroach on your privacy. It is all a trade-off of convenience and security for privacy and anonymity. It's convenient to pay by credit card rather than carrying cash. It's convenient to be able to place a phone call virtually any time and any place. There is safety in knowing that even if you are knocked unconscious in a car accident that someone out there will get an alert and dispatch emergency services to your exact location.

A lot of the data collected though does nothing for your safety, security, or convenience. Those inquisitive cashiers asking for your Zip code and those retail discount clubs tracking your purchases are not for your benefit. The information gathered is used for marketing primarily. Almost universally (there might be some less scrupulous company out there that doesn't fit this mold) this information is not tied to any personally identifying information.

By collecting data about how many people from a certain Zip code frequent a given store location, the company can choose how to target its marketing efforts for maximum effectiveness. The more data that can be gathered, the more targeted the marketing can be. By tracking purchasing habits it is possible to correlate information to determine that certain age groups or ethnicities or genders are more likely to purchase a given product or service which allows the company to make the best possible use of their advertising dollars.

This is the same sort of information gathering that goes on while you surf the Web. There is a great deal of seemingly innocuous information about you that can be extracted from the network traffic coming from your computer. When you visit a Web site, it is possible for them in many cases to determine your IP address, your city, state, and country, what Web browser you are using, how many Web pages you have visited since opening the browser window, what Web page you came from to get to the page you are on and even read any information that might be sitting in your Clipboard from the last cut-and-paste operation you performed.

In most cases, this information is harmless. The Web sites that track or collect this data generally do it for the demographic and marketing reasons cited earlier. If they know that the majority of their visitors use Internet Explorer, they can optimize their Web pages for that browser. If a company sees that most of their visitors come from a specific region of the country or the world, they can use that information to target their marketing efforts.

For some, this may not seem like a big deal, but if the legitimate sites can retrieve this information from your computer, so can the malicious sites. Being able to determine your IP address and the Web browser you use is enough information to get an attacker started. They know what address to target and they can research vulnerabilities of the browser being used to find holes they might be able to exploit. If you have copied a credit card number, password, or any other confidential information into your Clipboard, that information may be accessible to an attacker as well.

Some of this information can be blocked or removed fairly easily. By using a DSL/cable modem home router that does NAT (Network Address Translation), you can protect the IP addresses of the individual computers on your network. It will still be possible to find the IP address of the router's Internet connection, but not to identify the individual computers connected to the router. Other personal information is more difficult to block or remove and may require the use of third-party products such as ZoneAlarm Pro or Anonymizer.

Zone Labs states that ZoneAlarm Pro strips or removes your personally identifying information from the packet headers before they leave your computer. Anonymizer is more a service than a product. With Anonymizer, all of your Web access is redirected through Anonymizer servers that hide and protect your identity from the Web servers you are accessing. Anonymizer prevents those Web servers from interacting directly with your computer.

In many cases, having this information available is not harmful in any way, but if privacy is a primary concern of yours, using a product like the two just mentioned will help ensure your personal information is kept personal.

Getting in the Zone

I've mentioned a few times the fact that it is often a program feature designed to make things more convenient or add functionality for the user that is exploited and used against the user. When it comes to surfing the Web, active scripting falls into this category.

Active scripting is a general term which refers to the ability to include a script, or short program, within a Web page that can perform functions or gather information to make the Web page dynamic and "active." Whether it is simple information (like inserting the current date and time on a Web page) or more complicated (such as customizing data on the Web page to fit you personally), these small programs make the Web truly functional rather than simply a repository of static information.

In the following example, document.write is used to load a control dynamically.

```
<!-- HTML File -->
<html>
  <body leftmargin=0 topmargin=0 scroll=no>
```

```
        <script src="sample.js"></script>
    </body>
</html>


// docwrite.js
document.write('<object classid="clsid:6BF52A52-394A-11d3-B153-
00C04F79FAA6">');
document.write('<param name="URL" value="sample2.wmv">');
document.write('<param name="autoStart" value="-1"></object>');
```

By its very nature, though, an active script program is able to interact with your computer. When you visit a Web site and allow an active script to execute, you don't necessarily know if it will just retrieve the current date and time from your computer so it can display it on the Web page, or if it will write a virus to your computer or completely erase your hard drive.

One way of providing at least some protection against this sort of malicious activity is to make sure your User Account does not have administrative privileges. Often, the attack can only perform actions that the current User Account has the authority to do.

A more effective way is to simply disable the ability for active scripting or ActiveX controls to run on your computer. This solution has a serious drawback though. There are sites that require active scripting functionality in order to operate. Internet Explorer uses the concept of "security zones" to let you segregate Web sites and apply a different set of rules to one group than you do to the other.

To get to the security zones configuration, click the **Tools** menu option in Internet Explorer and select the **Internet Options**. Once the **Internet Options** window is open, select the **Security** tab. This window displays the four Internet Explorer Security Zones across the top: Internet, Local Intranet, Trusted Sites, and Restricted Sites (see Figure 7.4).

Each of the zones can be configured using one of the four predefined rule sets in Internet Explorer, or you can create custom security configurations. By default, the Restricted Sites zone is configured for High security, the Internet zone is Medium, the Local Intranet zone is Medium-Low, and the Trusted Sites zone is set for Low.

Figure 7.4 Choose Your Security Levels

Most of the sites you'll visit will fall under the restrictions of the Internet zone. Unless a Web site exists on your local network or has been explicitly placed by you into the Trusted Sites or Restricted Sites zones it is part of the Internet zone by default. If you find a site you know is safe and that needs lower restrictions, you can add it to the Trusted Sites zone. Conversely, if you encounter a site which you determine to be malicious in some way, you can add it to the Restricted Sites zone to protect yourself from it. Any sites that are on your local network fall into the Local Intranet zone.

If you don't like the predefined rule sets or just find you need more security or fewer restrictions, you can customize the security zones as you see fit. You simply select the zone you wish to configure from the four options at the top and then click the **Custom Level** button. From this screen, you can configure just about every aspect of how Internet Explorer interacts with Web pages and what sort of actions are allowed to occur or not to occur (see Figure 7.5).

Figure 7.5 Customize Your Security Settings

You can choose whether or not to allow various types of active scripting. You can either disable them entirely, enable them entirely, or choose to be asked each time one occurs so that you can decide on a case-by-case basis whether to allow it or not. You can select how to handle file downloading from Web sites, whether or not a Web site can open other browser windows, and a variety of other settings.

For the most part, the predefined rule sets will suffice, but for added safety you may want to customize the Internet zone and the active scripting options to Disable or to Prompt so that you can protect yourself from malicious scripts or at least be aware when they are attempting to run.

The Security Zones in Internet Explorer are a fairly effective way of letting you protect yourself from unknown Web sites without having to disable functionality on the sites that you trust. One caveat though is that there have been occasional vulnerabilities which have allowed a malicious Web site to bypass the Security Zones or perform functions under the context of a different Security Zone than the one they were in, so you still need to beware.

So you now have the means of protecting yourself from unknown Web sites, but how do you know a site is what it says it is? That very question is discussed in the next section.

Shopping Safely: SSL and Certificates

My first and best advice when it comes to shopping on the Web is the old Latin maxim *caveat emptor*—Let the buyer beware. I don't mean to scare you away from doing business on the Internet. I do most of my purchasing, banking, and other financial transactions on the Web. But, like most things having to do with the Web and computer security, you have to know a few things and take some basic precautions in order to make it a safe endeavor.

When you go shopping at an actual retail store and make your purchase with your credit card, you obviously know that you are doing business with the store you are standing in. It's a little trickier on the Web. Just because it *looks* like the Web site for the store or company you want to do business with doesn't mean it actually is.

Stores have no way of proving you are who you say you are, though. They don't want to get left with a bad check or a fraudulent credit card purchase because they don't make money that way. Instead, they rely on a third party, preferably a trusted third party, to prove that you are you. In many cases (if they are doing their jobs), the retail clerks will ask to see some form of identification in order to validate that you are the actual owner of the credit card and to match the signatures. Usually the identification is a driver's license or some other form of identification that also has a photo so they can see that you also look like who you say you are.

When you are shopping on the Web, this sort of "prove you are who you say you are" goes the other way. Because anyone can buy a domain name and set up a Web site, and because attackers can sometimes intercept or redirect your attempts to connect with a Web site, you need some way of proving that the Web site is legitimate. Typically, this is done using a digital certificate from a trusted third party. In essence, a company that issues digital certificates vouches for the Web site.

When you try to purchase a digital certificate from companies such as Verisign, Comodo, or Thawte, you are not issued one until you provide proof that authenticates who you are. As consumers, we might be suspicious of whether the site is legitimate, but we accept the "word" of these third parties when we accept the digital certificate.

The major Web browsers today, such as Internet Explorer and Netscape, have the capability to use SSL (Secure Sockets Layer) inherently. SSL is a protocol which not only provides a means for authenticating the Web server but also encrypts the data between your Web browser and the Web server, as well as checks the traffic to ensure it is not tampered with in any way.

If a Web server has a valid digital certificate, your Web browser will automatically connect using an SSL session. If your session is secured via SSL, you will see a locked padlock icon at the bottom of your Web browser window. If the Web server has no digital certificate, your Web browser will establish a normal insecure connection. However, if the Web server has an invalid or expired digital certificate, or if the certificate was issued from a source that your Web browser is not configured to trust, you will typically receive some sort of alert or warning which will allow you to choose whether or not you want to accept or trust that certificate (see Figure 7.6). Unless you are very sure, not only that the company that owns the Web site is a reputable company, but that this is truly their Web server and not a malicious replica, you should not accept the certificate.

Figure 7.6 Accept or Don't Accept the Certificate

There are some caveats even for a seemingly secure SSL connection. SSL relies on keys. The encryption of the data flowing from the Web server to your Web browser is done using the Web server's private key. Many Web servers store the private key in an area that can be accessed by an attacker. If an attacker obtains the private key of a Web server, they can create a spoof replica site and you would be unable to detect it because the digital certificate would match. They also would be able to decode any traffic going to and from that site.

Another thing to consider is that a malicious Web site might have a valid certificate from a trusted third party as well. Your Web browser will establish the SSL connection and display the locked padlock icon, but that just tells you that you have an SSL connection established and that your communications with the Web server are encrypted. It doesn't necessarily mean that the Web server is safe, so you still need to exercise the *caveat emptor* idea and make sure you know who you're connecting to.

Financial Transactions

I have been using financial software such as Intuit's Quicken to track my bank accounts and personal finances pretty much since I have had finances. Initially, it was a great tool but still required a lot more manual effort. I had to enter my transactions out of my checkbook each time I took money from an ATM machine. At the end of each month when my statement would come, I would have to go back line by line to compare the statement to my computer data and make sure they matched exactly.

In recent years, though, more and more banks have gone digital. I can now view my accounts virtually in real time to see how much money is currently in each account as well as what transactions have cleared. I can download all of that information straight into my personal finance software with a single click and reconcile the data on my computer with the information from the bank as I go. I can move money from one account to another with a few clicks of the mouse.

The same digital revolution has occurred with personal investing. Investment sites such as E*Trade and Ameritrade popped up on the Web and soon the traditional brick-and-mortar investment companies like Charles Schwab and Salomon Smith Barney began to establish a presence online as well.

When you establish an account with one of these investment companies, you have many of the same abilities you have with an online bank account. You can view your portfolio of investments and buy or trade stocks, bonds, and mutual funds with a few clicks. These sites also offer a wealth of investment research and resources to help you analyze the various investments and find the ones that work best for your portfolio.

Virtually every type of company you transact money with is now available online. In many cases, you can pay your mortgage payment, car payment, electric bill, gas bill, phone bill, cable bill, and just about any other bill online directly at the company's Web site. Even in cases where the actual company you are conducting business with isn't available online, many banks offer you the ability to pay your bills online directly from the bank Web site as well.

All of these services are tremendously convenient. Without leaving your chair you can move money from your checking account to your savings account and reconcile your bank accounts with your personal finance software. You can sell a few shares of stock and buy a few shares of mutual funds and then pay all your bills without writing a single check or licking a single envelope or stamp. Thousands of dollars whiz back and forth digitally across the Internet in the blink of an eye. Of course, there are security concerns you should be aware of and certain precautions you should take.

In the case of online banking, investing, and bill paying, the security concerns and precautions are pretty much the same as for online shopping. You need to be sure the Web site you're visiting is secure. Banks, investment companies, and other companies that transact money over the Web should have valid digital certificates from a trusted third party. You should check for the locked padlock icon on your

Web browser before conducting any business because that lets you know that the data you send to the Web server is secure.

Most of these Web sites use a unique username and password to authenticate users. The SSL connection and digital certificate are your way of knowing you are talking securely with the correct server. The username and password are the Web server's way of proving that the person accessing the account has the authority to do so. It is important that you choose a good, strong password and that you keep that username and password secure. Anyone who acquires your username and password will be able to access your account and perform any of the same financial transactions you can perform. You should also use a different username and a different password for each site so if your information from one site is compromised, an attacker won't have access to all of your accounts. For more details on using passwords, see Chapter 2.

Another serious security concern when it comes to using financial Web sites is the dramatic rise in phishing scams. It is very important to understand that no reputable company will ask you for your username and password, account number, credit card number, or any other confidential information through e-mail. If you do get an e-mail that claims to be from a financial institution that you do in fact have an account with, you should either contact their customer service by phone or close your e-mail software and all open Web browser windows and then open a new browser window to visit their site. Never click a link in an e-mail to visit a financial Web site. For more details on e-mail phishing, see Chapter 6.

So your financial information is safe. But how about your children?

Content Filtering and Childproofing

The Web is a valuable resource and it can be both entertaining and educational. Almost any piece of information on any subject is available somewhere on the Web if you just know how to look for it. The Web also has a lot of sites of a questionable nature. There are porn sites, sites that push violence or hatred of one sort or another, and malicious sites that will attempt to infect your computer with a virus or compromise your security by installing a Trojan of some sort.

If you stick to visiting well-known, brand-name sites like cnn.com, espn.com, disney.com, bestbuy.com, and so on, you can be fairly sure you won't run into these questionable or malicious sites. But, if you start trying to find information using a search engine like Google or Yahoo, there is no guarantee that the sites that come up on your search will be as clean.

Children seem to be at a higher risk of accidentally landing on sites like these. As a rule they use the Internet and the Web differently than adults. Sites that children tend to frequent more often, such as gaming sites and music sites, seem to have a much higher chance of leading to unscrupulous sites.

If you somehow access a distasteful or inappropriate Web site, you can simply ignore it and shut down the browser window or visit another site. With children though, it is important that such sites not be allowed to be displayed in the first place. You need some means of blocking these sites and shielding your children so that they can use the Web safely.

A variety of products are available to filter the Web content before it's allowed to be displayed on your screen. Some products are available for free, such as the content filter software available at we-blocker.com, while commercial products to filter Web content include such items as Net Nanny.

These products generally work in one of two ways. Some will maintain a database of Web sites that are known to fall into the various categories you might want to block. It will then block access to any Web sites that are in its database based on how you configure the content filter. The other method is to actually examine the Web content in real time and search for key words or phrases or other clues that the site should be blocked. Some products may use a combination of these two methods.

Regardless of which content filtering product you choose it will be up to you to configure it how you wish. Some people may want significantly more or less restrictions than others. You should also ensure that the software cannot be disabled or bypassed in any way by your children. Usually there is a password required to access the master or parent account and other users will not be able to configure or disable the software.

If you are still unsure of what your children are doing on the computer or you want a little extra assurance you can install a monitoring program such as Spector Pro. Spector Pro from Spectorsoft records all e-mail, instant message chatting, keystrokes typed, Web sites visited, programs used, and peer-to-peer network files accessed. Additionally it will block access to Internet Web sites based on your configuration just like the content monitoring programs mentioned above. You can also configure Spector Pro to send an e-mail message to you instantly if the computer is being used in some inappropriate manner, and you can install it in such a way that other users— namely, the children using the computer—are not even aware that the software exists.

A good percentage of your time on your personal computer will probably be spent surfing the Web for one reason or another. There is a seemingly endless supply of news, information, advice, entertainment and education on the Web. If you exercise these basic precautions and use some old-fashioned common sense you can enjoy this vast resource safely and securely.

Summary

So, in this chapter you have learned that while the Web has made advancements possible in online shopping, personal finance, education, and of personal communication, there are dangers lurking out there for the unaware and unprotected. There are ways, however, to protect one's self and with a little effort you can defend yourself and your family from those dangers.

Additional Resources

The following resources provide more information on Web surfing privacy and safety:

- *Do Cookies Compromise Security?* Webopedia.com (www.webopedia.com/DidYouKnow/Internet/2002/Cookies.asp).

- Moulds, Richard. *Whose Site is it Anyway?* Help Net Security. March 29, 2004 (www.net-security.org/article.php?id=669).

- *Safe Internet. Anonymous Surfing and Privacy.* Settings Internet Explorer 6.0. Home.zonenet.com (www.home.zonnet.nl/roberthoenselaar/a)SettingsInternetExplorer.html).

- Salkever, Alex. "Cyber-Extortion: When Data Is Held Hostage." *BusinessWeek Online.* August 22, 2000 (www.businessweek.com/bwdaily/dnflash/aug2000/nf20000822_308.htm).

- *The All-New Netscape Browser 8.12.* Netscape.com (http://wp.netscape.com/security/techbriefs/servercerts/index.html).

- Weiss, Todd. "New Explorer 6 Active Scripting Flaw Reported." *Computerworld.* November 26, 2003 (www.computerworld.com/security-topics/security/holes/story/0,10801,87582,00.html).

Chapter 8

Wireless
Network Security

Topics in this chapter:

- The Basics of Wireless Networks
- Basic Wireless Network Security Measures
- Additional Hotspot Security Measures

☑ Summary

☑ Additional Resources

Introduction

I have a wireless network in my home. I am no "Mr. Fix-it" when it comes to home projects, so when I had to figure out how to run network cable from the router in the kitchen to my kids' rooms, going through walls and floors and around cinder blocks, I sprang for the wireless equipment instead. At first, it was primarily so that I could use my laptop from any room in the house, but as time went by we eventually switched almost every computer in the house to a wireless connection.

Wireless networks provide a great deal of convenience and flexibility, and are relatively easy to set up. Actually, they may be too easy to set up. Some pieces of wireless equipment are almost plug-and-play devices, which might explain why so many people don't read the manual or do their homework to figure out how to secure the network airwaves.

I took my laptop out with me today to work on this book. I had no particular need for a network connection since I was just using my word processor on my computer, but as I drove through the subdivision I watched as my wireless network adapter detected network after network completely insecure and announcing their presence to the world. Unfortunately, this seems to be the norm rather than the exception.

This chapter will take a look at wireless network security from two perspectives, and the steps you must take to use it securely in both. We will start with a brief overview of the wireless protocols and technology, and then look at what's required to secure your own home wireless network to keep unauthorized users out of your network. Lastly, we will examine the security precautions you should take to securely use a public wireless network.

The Basics of Wireless Networks

Think about how a wireless network affects the security of your network and your computers. When you have a wired network, you have only one way in more or less. If you put a firewall on the network cable between your computers and the public Internet, your computers are shielded from most unauthorized access. The firewall acts as a traffic cop, limiting and restricting access into your network through that single access point. Now you throw a wireless device on your network. It doesn't matter if it's one computer with a wireless network adapter or a wireless router or access point, the results are the same: you are now broadcasting data through the air. Your "access point" is now all around you. Rather than a single point of access that can be easily protected, your access point is now three dimensional, all around you, at various ranges, from the next room to the house next door to the roadside in front of your home.

Are You Owned?

Wardriving

The practice of cruising around in search of available wireless networks is known as "wardriving." The term derives from a similar activity to search for available modem connections by "wardialing," or automatically dialing phone numbers to identify which ones result in a dial-up modem connection.

Armed with a wireless device and antenna, wardrivers patrol city streets and neighborhoods and catalog the wireless networks they discover. Some sophisticated wardrivers also tie their wireless network discovery to a GPS to identify the exact coordinates of each wireless network.

For years, a group dedicated to demonstrating how insecure most wireless networks are and increasing awareness of wireless network security issues has organized something called the WorldWide WarDrive (WWWD). After four years, they have decided that the WWWD has done all it can to raise awareness and have moved on to other projects, but their efforts helped to spotlight the issues with insecure wireless networks.

For more information about wardriving and wireless network security in general, you can check out the book *WarDriving and Wireless Penetration Testing*.

Wireless equipment often boasts of ranges over 1,000 feet. The reality is that unless there are no obstructions, the temperature is above 75 and less than 78, the moon is in retrograde and it's the third Tuesday of the month, the range will be more like 100 feet. But if your wireless data can make it the 75 feet from your wireless router in the basement to where you are checking your e-mail while watching a baseball game as you sit on the couch in your living room, it can also make it the 60 feet over to your neighbor's house or the 45 feet out to the curb in front of your home. Although standard off-the-shelf equipment doesn't generally have tremendous range, the wardrivers, a term used to describe actively scouting areas specifically looking for insecure wireless networks to connect to, have homegrown super antennas made with Pringles cans and common household items from their garage that can help them detect your wireless network from a much greater range.

It is important that you take the time to understand the security features of your wireless equipment and make sure you take the appropriate steps to secure your network so that unauthorized users can't just jump onto your connection. Not only are your own computers exposed to hacking if an attacker can join your network, but they may initiate attacks or other malicious activity from your Internet connection which might have the local police or the FBI knocking on your door to ask some questions.

A wireless network uses radio or microwave frequencies to transmit data through the air. Without the need for cables, it is very convenient and offers the flexibility for you to put a computer in any room you choose without having to wire network connections. It also offers you the ability to roam through your home freely without losing your network connection.

In order to connect to the Internet, you will still need a standard connection with an ISP. Whether you use dial-up or a broadband connection like DSL or a cable modem, the data has to get to you some way before you can beam it into the air. Typically, you would connect your DSL or cable modem to a wireless router and from there the data is sent out into the airwaves. If you already have a wired router on your network and want to add wireless networking, you can attach a wireless access point to your router. Any computers that you wish to connect to the wireless network will need to have a wireless network adapter that uses a wireless protocol compatible with your router or access point.

A variety of wireless network protocols are currently in use. The most common equipment for home users tends to be either 802.11b or 802.11g with 802.11a equipment coming in a distant third. The most common protocol, particularly for home users, has been 802.11b; however, 802.11g is becoming the default standard because of its increased speed and compatibility with existing 802.11b networks. The following is a brief overview of the different protocols:

802.11b

Wireless network equipment built on the 802.11b protocol was the first to really take off commercially. 802.11b offers transmission speeds up to 11 mbps, which compares favorably with standard Ethernet networks—plus, the equipment is relatively inexpensive. One problem for this protocol is that it uses the unregulated 2.4GHz frequency range, which is also used by many other common household items such as cordless phones and baby monitors. Interference from other home electronics devices may degrade or prevent a wireless connection.

802.11a

The 802.11a protocol uses a regulated 5GHz frequency range, which is one con-tributing factor for why 802.11a wireless equipment is significantly more expensive than its counterparts. 802.11a offers the advantage of transmission speeds of up to 54 mbps; however, the increased speed comes with a much shorter range and more dif-ficulty traversing obstructions, such as walls, due to the higher frequency range.

802.11g

The 802.11g protocol has emerged as the new standard at this time. It combines the best aspects of both 802.11b and 802.11a. It has the increased transmission speed of 54 mbps like 802.11a, but uses the unregulated 2.4GHz frequency range, which gives it more range and a greater ability to go through walls and floors, and also helps keep the cost of the equipment down. 802.11g is also backwards–compatible with 802.11b, so computers with 802.11b wireless network adapters are still able to connect with 802.11g routers or access points.

Next-Generation Protocols

Wireless networking is relatively new and constantly evolving. A number of new protocols are currently being developed by the wireless industry, such as WiMax, 802.16e, 802.11n, and Ultrawideband. These protocols promise everything from exponentially increasing home wireless network speeds to allowing you to use a wireless connection to your ISP and even maintain a wireless network connection while in a moving vehicle.

Some of these concepts may not appear in the immediate future, but others are already in use in one form or another. Most wireless network equipment vendors have already begun producing Pre-N or Draft-N devices. These devices are based off of the 802.11n protocol, but have been produced before the 802.11n protocol has actually been finalized. They promise speeds 12 times faster than 802.11g, and a range up to four times that of 802.11g.

The major mobile phone carriers, such as Verizon, Cingular, and TMobile, all offer some sort of broadband wireless access which can be used virtually anywhere their cellular phone network can reach. Using a service like this can give you wire-less access almost anywhere, any time, without restriction to any specific site.

Basic Wireless Network Security Measures

Regardless of what protocol your wireless equipment uses, some basic steps should be taken to make sure other users are not able to connect to your wireless network and access your systems or hijack your Internet connection for their own use.

Secure Your Home Wireless Network

To begin with, change the username and password required to access the administrative and configuration screens for your wireless router. Most home wireless routers come with a Web-based administrative interface. The default IP address the device uses on the internal network is almost always 192.168.0.1. Finding out what the default username and password are for a given manufacturer is not difficult. The equipment usually comes configured with something like "admin" for the username, and "password" for the password. Even without any prior knowledge about the device or the manufacturer defaults, an attacker could just blindly guess the username and password in fewer than ten tries. With a default IP address and default administrative username and password, your wireless router can be hacked into even by novices. Figure 8.1 shows the administration screen from a Linksys wireless router. This screen allows you to change the password for accessing the router management console.

Figure 8.1 The Administration Screen from a Linksys Wireless Router

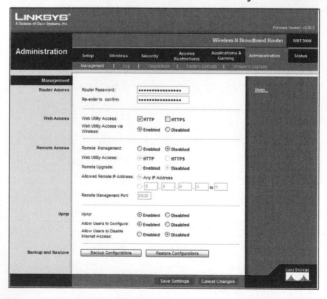

Make sure you change the username to something that only you would think of. Just like renaming the Administrator account on your computer, you want to choose a username that won't be just as easy to guess as "admin" or whatever the default username was. You also want to choose a strong password that won't be easily guessed or cracked. Lastly, you should change the internal IP subnet if possible. The 192.168.x.x address range is for internal use only. A large percentage of those who use this address range use 192.168.0.x as their subnet, which makes it easy to guess. You can use any number from 0 to 254 for the third octet, so choose something like 192.168.71.x so potential attackers will have to work a little harder. For details on user accounts and administrator privileges, see Chapter 1.

Remember, the goal is to make it difficult for attackers or malware to penetrate your system. Nothing you do will make your network 100-percent impenetrable to a dedicated and knowledgeable attacker. But, by putting various layers of defense in place such as complex passwords, personal firewalls, antivirus software, and other security measures, you can make it sufficiently hard enough that no casual attacker will want to bother.

Change the SSID

Another big step in securing your home wireless network is not to announce that you have one. Public or corporate wireless networks may need to broadcast their existence so that new wireless devices can detect and connect to them. However, for your home, you are trying to prevent rogue wireless devices from detecting and connecting to your network.

The wireless router or access point has a Service Set Identifier (SSID). Basically, the SSID is the name of the wireless network. By default, wireless routers and access points will broadcast a beacon signal about every 1/10 of a second, which contains the SSID among other things. It is this beacon which wireless devices detect and which provides them with the information they need to connect to the network.

Your wireless network will most likely only have a handful of devices. Rather than relying on this beacon signal, you can simply manually enter the SSID and other pertinent information into each client to allow them to connect to your wireless network. Check the product manual that came with your wireless equipment to determine how to disable the broadcasting of the SSID.

Your device will come with a default SSID which is often simply the name of the manufacturer, such as Linksys or Netgear. Even with the SSID broadcasting turned off, it is important that you not use the default SSID. There are only a handful of manufacturers of home wireless equipment, so it wouldn't take long to guess at the possible SSIDs if you leave it set for the default. Therefore, you need to change this, and preferably not to something equally easy to guess, like your last name.

Configure Your Home Wireless Network

Next, you should configure your wireless network and any wireless network devices for infrastructure mode only. Two types of wireless networks are available for set up: infrastructure and ad hoc. In an infrastructure mode network, a router or access point is required, and all of the devices communicate with the network and with each other through that central point.

An ad hoc network, on the other hand, allows each device to connect to each other in an "ad hoc" fashion (hence the name). Since you are going through all of this effort to make your router or access point more secure, you also need to make sure that the wireless devices on your network are not configured for ad hoc mode and might be providing another means for rogue wireless devices to gain unauthorized access to your network.

By accessing the Properties for your wireless connection, you can click the **Advanced button** at the bottom of the Wireless Networks tab to configure whether your wireless adapter will connect to infrastructure, ad hoc, or both wireless network types (see Figure 8.2).

Figure 8.2 Configuring Connections for Your Wireless Adapter

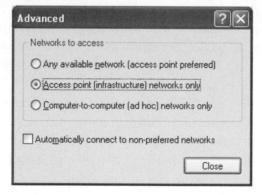

Restrict Access to Your Home Wireless Network

To restrict access to your wireless network even further, you can filter access based on the MAC (Media Access Code) addresses of your wireless devices. Each network adapter has a unique MAC address that identifies it. As stated earlier in this chapter, your network will most likely consist of only a handful of devices, so it wouldn't require too much effort to enter the MAC address of each device into your wireless router or access point and configure it to reject connections from any other MAC addresses.

Even after you do all of these things, you're not completely secure. You're obscure, but not secure. Using tools freely available on the Internet, a war-driver could still intercept your wireless data packets as they fly through the air. They would be doing so blindly because your wireless access point is no longer broadcasting its presence, but it can still be done. Intercepting the traffic in this way can provide an attacker with both the SSID and a valid MAC address from your network so that they could gain access.

By adding the MAC addresses of the devices that you know you want to connect to your wireless network, you can block access by other unknown devices and protect your wireless network (see Figure 8.3).

Figure 8.3 Adding MAC Addresses to Your Wireless Router

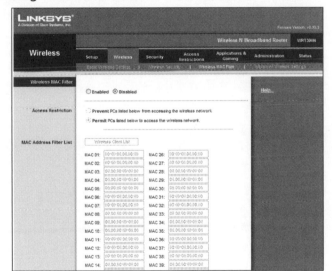

Use Encryption in Your Home Wireless Network

To further protect your wireless communications, you should enable some form of encryption. Wireless manufacturers, in their haste to start selling equipment, rushed to create WEP (Wired Equivalent Privacy) encryption to provide some level of security while waiting for the official 802.1x security protocol to be standardized. It was quickly discovered that the underlying technology of WEP has a number of flaws which make it relatively easy to crack.

The wireless industry has since migrated to the newer WPA (Wi-Fi Protected Access) encryption, which offers a number of significant improvements over WEP yet remains backwards-compatible with WEP devices. In order to use WPA though, all devices on the network must be WPA-capable. If one device uses WEP, the network will not be able to use some of the improved security features of WPA and your network may still be vulnerable to being exploited by the weaknesses found in WEP.

WPA2 has recently emerged to replace even WPA. Devices that are WPA2-compliant meet stricter security requirements. Windows XP with Service Pack 2 (SP2) fully supports the features and functions of WPA2, allowing a higher level of wireless network security as long as all of your wireless network clients are capable of the same security level.

While a knowledgeable and dedicated attacker with the right tools can still crack the encryption and access your wireless data, this should not discourage you from enabling it. It would be unusual for someone to dedicate that much time and effort to get into your wireless network when they can probably find five more unprotected wireless networks on the next block. It isn't practical to think you will be 100-percent secure, but turning on some form of encryption combined with the other precautions listed previously will deter the casual hacker and curious passerby.

The more complex encryption schemes require more processing power to encode and decode, so you may consider sticking with the 40-bit (64-bit on some devices) WEP encryption rather than the stronger 128-bit, or even the WPA encryption, if you notice any performance issues. It is the difference between locking your house with a normal lock or using a deadbolt. Since an attacker can get past both with about the same effort, you may as well use the one that is easier for you but that still prevents most users from accessing your wireless network.

Review Your Logs

Most wireless routers keep logs of the devices that attach to them. Even if you have taken all of the preceding steps to secure your wireless network, it is a good idea to periodically review the logs from your wireless router and check for any rogue devices that may have gained access.

The other major points to consider regarding a secure home wireless network are the same as they are for a wired network or computer security in general. You should make sure you are using strong passwords that can't be easily guessed or cracked on all of your devices, and protect your computers with personal firewall software.

One final word of advice when it comes to securing your wireless network: a device that is not connected to the Internet can't be attacked or compromised *from* the Internet. You may want to consider turning off your wireless router or access point overnight or when you know that it won't be used for extended periods. If there are too many users trying to access the Internet and use their computers at varying hours, it may be impractical to turn off the wireless router, but you can still turn off any computers when not in use so that they are not exposed to any threats whatsoever.

Use Public Wireless Networks Safely

Public wireless networks, often referred to as hotspots, are springing up all over. National chains such as Starbucks Coffee, Borders Books, and McDonalds' have started adding wireless network access to their establishments through services provided by companies like TMobile or Boingo. Major hotel chains have gone from no access to dial-up access to broadband access, and now many are offering wireless network access. Many airports and college campuses have wireless networks as well. It seems like every week someplace new pops up where you can surf the Web while you're out and about.

It is perilous enough jumping onto the Internet using your own network in the comfort of your home, but sharing an unknown network and not knowing if the network or the other computers are secure adds some new concerns. Some of the things you must do to use a public wireless network securely are just simple rules of computer security no matter what network you're connecting to, while others are unique to accessing a public wireless network.

Install Up-to-Date Antivirus Software

For starters, you should make sure you have antivirus software installed and that it is up-to-date. You don't know what, if any, protection the network perimeter offers against malware or exploits, or whether or not the other computers on the network with you are trying to propagate some malware. You also need to make sure that your operating system and applications are patched against known vulnerabilities to help protect you from attack. For details on protecting your computer from malware, see Chapter 3.

Install a Personal Firewall

Your computer should have personal firewall software installed. Again, you have no way of knowing offhand if the network you are joining is protected by any sort of firewall or perimeter security at all. Even if it is, you need the personal firewall to protect you not only from external attacks, but also from attacks that may come from the other computers sharing the network with you. For details on personal firewalls, see Chapter 5.

As a standard rule of computer security, you should make sure that your critical, confidential, and sensitive files are password protected. In the event that any attacker or casual hacker happens to infiltrate your computer system, it is even more important that you protect these files when joining a public wireless network. Make sure you restrict access to only the User Accounts that you want to access those files and use a strong password that won't be easily guessed or cracked.

Tools & Traps...

AirSnarf

AirSnarf, a Linux-based program created to demonstrate inherent weaknesses in public wireless hotspots, can be used to trick users into giving up their usernames and passwords.

The AirSnarf program can interrupt wireless communications, forcing the computer to disconnect from the wireless network. Immediately following the service interruption, AirSnarf will broadcast a replica of the hotspot login page to lure the disconnected user to enter their username and password to reconnect.

The person sitting at the table next to you or sipping an iced latte in the parking lot could be running the program and it would be very difficult for you to realize what was going on. You should monitor your hotspot bill closely for excess usage or charges, and change your password frequently.

More importantly, it is vital that you disable file and folder sharing. This is even more critical if you happen to be using Windows XP Home edition because of the way Windows XP Home manages file and folder sharing and uses the Guest account with a blank password for default access to shared files and folders. Some attackers or malware may still find their way into your system, but that is no reason to leave the door unlocked and a big neon sign welcoming visitors.

Additional Hotspot Security Measures

All of the things I have mentioned so far are basic security measures that apply whether you are at home, at work, or connecting to a public wireless network while browsing books at Borders. Now let's take a look at some extra things you need to do or consider when connecting to a hotspot.

Verify Your Hotspot Connection

To begin with, you need to make sure you *are* connecting to a hotspot and not a malicious rogue access point. When you are connecting to a public wireless network, it will broadcast the SSID, or network name, along with other information your wireless adapter needs to know in order to connect. It is very easy though for an attacker to set up a rogue access point and use the same or similar SSID as the hotspot. They can then create a replica of the hotspot login Web site to lure users into giving up their usernames and passwords or possibly even get credit card numbers and other such information from users who think they are registering for access on the real site.

You should make sure that the location you are at even has a hotspot to begin with. Don't think that just because you happen to be at a coffee shop and a wireless network is available that it must be a free wireless hotspot.

If you are at a confirmed hotspot location and more than one SSID appears for your wireless adapter to connect to, you need to make sure you connect to the right one. Some attackers will set up rogue access points with similar SSIDs to lure unsuspecting users into connecting and entering their login or credit card information.

Watch Your Back

Once you take care of ensuring that you are connecting with a legitimate wireless network, you need to take stock of who may be sitting around you. Before you start entering your username and password to connect to the wireless network or any other usernames and passwords for things like your e-mail, your online bank account, and so on, you want to make sure that no overly curious neighbors will be able to see what you are typing.

After you have determined that nobody can see over your shoulder to monitor your typing and you have established that you are in fact connecting to a legitimate public wireless network, you can begin to use the Internet and surf the Web. You should always be aware though of the fact that your data can very easily be intercepted. Not only can other computers sharing the network with you use packet sniffer programs such as Ethereal to capture and analyze your data, but because your data is flying through the air in all directions even a computer in a nearby parking lot may be able to catch your data using programs like NetStumbler or Kismet.

Use Encryption and Password Protection

To prevent sensitive data or files from being intercepted, you should encrypt or protect them in some way. Compression programs, such as WinZip, offer the ability to password-protect the compressed file, providing you with at least some level of protection. You could also use a program such as PGP to encrypt files for even more security.

Password-protecting or encrypting individual files that you may want to send across the network or attach to an e-mail will protect those specific files, but they won't stop someone from using a packet sniffer to read everything else going back and forth on the airwaves from your computer. Even things such as passwords that obviously should be encrypted or protected in some way often are not. Someone who intercepts your data may be able to clearly read your password and other personal or sensitive information.

Don't Linger

One suggestion is to limit your activity while connected to a public wireless network. You should access only Web sites that have digital certificates and establish secure, encrypted connections using SSL (typically evidenced by the locked padlock icon and the URL beginning with "https:").

Use a VPN

For even greater security, you should use a VPN (virtual private network). By establishing a VPN connection with the computer or network on the other end, you create a secure tunnel between the two endpoints. All of the data within the tunnel is encrypted, and only the two ends of the VPN can read the information. If someone intercepts the packets midstream, all they will get is encrypted gibberish.

For SSL-based VPNs, just about any Web browser will do. However, a large percentage of the VPN technology in use relies on IPSec, which requires some form of client software on your computer to establish a connection. It is not important that the VPN software on your computer and that on the other end be the same or even from the same vendor, but it is a requirement that they use the same authentication protocol. Corporations that offer VPN access for their employees typically supply the client software, but you can also get VPN client software from Microsoft or from Boingo.

Use Web-Based E-mail

One final tip for using a public wireless network is to use Web-based e-mail. If you are connecting to a corporate network over an encrypted VPN connection and accessing a corporate mail server like Microsoft Exchange or Lotus Notes, you will be fine. But if you are using a POP3 e-mail account from your ISP or some other e-mail provider, the data is transmitted in clear text for anyone to intercept and read. Web-based e-mail generally uses an encrypted SSL connection to protect your data in transit, and major Web-based mail providers such as Hotmail and Yahoo also scan e-mail file attachments for malware. For details on Web-based e-mail, see Chapter 6.

Summary

Wireless networks represent one of the greatest advances in networking in recent years, particularly for home users who want to share their Internet connection without having to run network cabling through the floors and walls. Unfortunately, if not properly secured, wireless networks also represent one of the biggest security risks in recent years.

In this chapter, you learned about the basic concepts of wireless networking and the key features of the main wireless protocols currently being used. We also covered some fundamental steps you need to do to protect your wireless network, such as changing default passwords and SSIDs, disabling the broadcasting of your SSID, or even filtering access to your wireless network by MAC address.

This chapter also discussed the strengths and weaknesses of the wireless encryption schemes such as WEP and WPA, and why you should ensure that your wireless data is encrypted in some way. You also learned that a layered defense, including components such as a personal firewall and updated antivirus software, is a key component of overall security, particularly when using public wireless hotspots.

The chapter ended by discussing some other security concerns that are unique to public wireless hotspots, such as ensuring that the wireless network you are connecting to is a legitimate one and not a rogue hotspot set up to steal your information. In addition, you learned that using a VPN for communications and utilizing Web-based e-mail can help improve your security and protect your information while using public wireless networks.

Additional Resources

The following resources provide more information on wireless network security:

- Bowman, Barb. *How to Secure Your Wireless Home Network with Windows XP.* Microsoft.com (www.microsoft.com/windowsxp/using/networking/learnmore/bowman_05february10.mspx).

- Bradley, Tony, and Becky Waring. *Complete Guide to Wi-Fi Security.* Jiwire.com, September 20, 2005 (www.jiwire.com/wi-fi-security-traveler-hotspot-1.htm).

- Elliott, Christopher. *Wi-Fi Unplugged: A Buyer's Guide for Small Businesses.* Microsoft.com (www.microsoft.com/smallbusiness/resources/technology/broadband_mobility/wifi_unplugged_a_buyers_guide_for_small_businesses.mspx).

- *PGP Encryption Software* (www.pgp.com/).

- *Wi-Fi Protected Access 2 (WPA2) Overview*. Microsoft TechNet, May 6, 2005 (www.microsoft.com/technet/community/columns/cableguy/ cg0505.mspx).

- *WinZip Compression Software* (www.winzip.com/).

Chapter 9

Spyware and Adware

Topics in this chapter:

- **What Is Adware?**
- **What Is Spyware?**
- **Getting Rid of Spyware**

☑ **Summary**

☑ **Additional Resources**

Introduction

In many ways, the discussion of spyware is really just an extension of the "Privacy and Anonymous Surfing" section of the Chapter 7. At its core, the problem of spyware relates directly to your privacy and how much, if any, information you wish to share with third parties, especially when you are unaware they are gathering the information. Spyware warrants its own chapter because it crosses the line from the ethical gray area of monitoring your activity and gathering your personal information, and heads into the starkly black area of gathering your information without your knowledge or consent, sometimes with malicious intent. Much of what a spyware removal program detects—such as cookies, Registry entries, and programs known to be related to spyware of some sort—are still more of an annoyance than a threat. However, there are still some spyware programs that pose a risk to the security of your system. But even those that don't pose a threat may still affect the performance and stability of your computer system.

This chapter will examine the following:

- The difference between adware and spyware
- The pitfalls of the End User License Agreement (EULA)
- How to protect your system against spyware
- Tools to detect and remove spyware

What Is Adware?

The terms adware and spyware are often lumped together. In truth, there is a fundamental difference between the two, where adware tends to fall into that ethical gray area and stops short of crossing the line. Adware is software that's commonly used to generate ads, hence the name. Spyware often performs much more insidious actions, such as monitoring your keystrokes and capturing your username and password information or credit card numbers.

When you watch standard network television (not cable), it doesn't cost you anything other than the price of the television itself and the electricity to run it. The various television networks make their money from advertising. Companies choose what programs or what time of day to broadcast their commercials based on viewer demographics. If a show is watched primarily by women, they won't waste their money advertising men's shaving gel. If a show is watched primarily by children, they won't run commercials for Lite beer.

Some web sites and free software programs operate on this same business model. In effect, they provide the program or service to you free of charge and rely on advertising support to generate their profits. In order to determine your interests, these programs will often install adware which sits silently in the background. The adware can monitor various aspects of how you use your computer and what sorts of web sites you frequent, and then transmit that data back to the company. Afterward, the information can be used to select pop-up or banner ads that would most likely be of interest to you.

Ironically, in the case of adware, you often agreed to install it and accepted whatever activity the adware is designed to perform when you installed the software. What makes adware legal, if not fully ethical, is that it is generally contained in the End User License Agreement (EULA). The EULA is that thing that comes up while you are installing software that asks whether you have read and agree to the terms as described—you know, that screen where you glance briefly and see that it's a bunch of techno-legal jargon and just click "yes" without actually reading anything?

One well-known service that works in this way is the Kazaa peer-to-peer (P2P) network. P2P networks have come under a great deal of scrutiny as a result of the Recording Industry Association of America's war against users illegally swapping songs that are protected by their members' copyrights. P2P networking, however, is itself perfectly legal. It is possible to pay for the software and get a version that does not run ads, but a vast majority of users still choose to accept the advertising in exchange for getting access to the Kazaa network for free.

Kazaa has over 2.5 million users, many of whom use the adware version of their P2P client software. Kazaa is not shy or secretive about the fact that adware will be installed on your system. In fact, it is clearly stated during the installation process. Step two of the installation lists all of the applications and adware that you agree to install in order to use Kazaa (see Figure 9.1).

In order to proceed to step 3, you must check the box next to the statement "I agree to the Kazaa Media Desktop End User License Agreement and Altnet Peer Points Manager Package End User License Agreements." There is probably a fair chance that 99 percent of the users who click this box never even looked at the EULAs in question, much less actually read every word of them to understand what they were agreeing to. Unfortunately, this is true of all EULAs. People consider them an annoyance and fail to understand that it is a binding legal agreement between you and the software vendor.

Figure 9.1 The Kazaa Media Desktop Installer

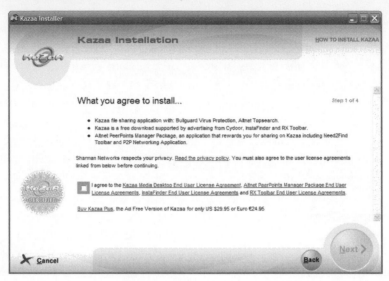

The Kazaa Media Desktop End User License Agreement (EULA) explains that to remove the included adware components or even to attempt to block or impede their functionality is a violation of the agreement (see Figure 9.2). The EULA outlines the terms and conditions you must agree to in order to legally use the product. Many freeware programs contain similar wording in their EULA, and so removing the adware components may in fact disable the free program you are trying to use.

Figure 9.2 The Kazaa EULA

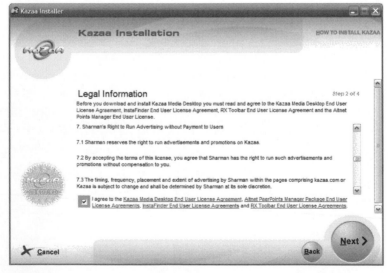

The other EULA Kazaa requires you to agree to is from the third-party adware provider. The programs installed with Kazaa Media Desktop all have some remotely useful function. For example, Gator is used to provide context-sensitive advertising, while PerfectNAV suggests alternate web sites when the site you are searching for can't be found.

The products installed by Kazaa Media Desktop and adware in general may be of value to some. It may seem wrong to force you to install those third-party applications in order to install and use the software, but that is the price for the "free" product. They aren't forcing you to install their software in the first place.

Before you choose to accept installing these programs and agreeing to the EULA that governs them, you should take a look at what you are agreeing to. The EULA for Altnet Peer Points Manager and My Search Toolbar states that you agree that they can update the software at any time without notice and that you agree to accept "all updates" (see Figure 9.3). In effect they could "update" the software with completely new functionality that may perform actions you don't want on your system.

Figure 9.3 The EULA for Altnet Peer Points Manager

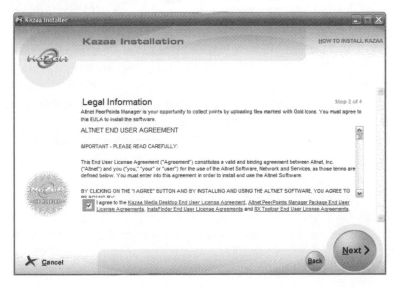

Even if you don't mind the privacy or security implications of running adware on your system and you're willing to accept that as a fair tradeoff for "free" software, you should keep the stability and performance of your system in mind. Adware is constantly running in the background, monitoring and recording your actions so it is using memory and processing power resources that could be put to better use. At some interval, it will have to transmit the accumulated data it has gathered back to its home base, a process which will use some portion of your network bandwidth. On a broadband connection you may not notice it, but on a dial-up connection every byte counts and having adware communicating in the background could bring your already crawling network access to a virtual stop.

What Is Spyware?

While many people call all adware and spyware "spyware," there is a difference. As I just pointed out in the discussion of adware, adware is technically legal, if not always ethically right, and is something that you most likely have unwittingly agreed to install on your system. Spyware, by comparison, is a more covert or stealthy form of adware. In fact, many spyware applications are closer to being Trojan programs than actual adware, due to the fact that they come disguised as something else and install without your knowledge.

Adware tends to stay in that gray area and focus its recording and monitoring efforts on data that is less personal and confidential, such as simply tracking generalities like what types of sites you visit, how often you visit them, how long you stay on each page, and other similar statistical data which can help web sites monitor how the site is used and help advertisers get the most bang for their buck by getting their ads in front of people more likely to be interested in their product or service.

Spyware crosses the line into actual malware by installing itself secretly and without the user's consent, as well as through the data it tracks and reports in many cases. Some spyware actually relies on exploiting known vulnerabilities in your web browser to execute and install without your knowledge or consent.

While adware is, for the most part, up front about the functions it will perform, spyware is covert and tenacious. Many spyware programs not only install without any clear method of uninstalling them, but actually go out of their way to obscure any way of removing them and may even disable some of the configuration and control options of the Web browser to prevent you from tampering with them.

Spyware programs also sometimes spy on a broader scope of information than standard adware. They may even log your every keystroke, allowing them to capture usernames, passwords, account numbers, credit card numbers, and every word you type in your e-mail program, among other things. This obviously crosses the line from simply monitoring your activity for demographic reasons to carrying out pure spying with malicious intent. Still, the majority of spyware consists of Web bugs and tracking cookies designed to track and monitor your activity just like adware, except without your knowledge or consent.

Of course, I keep stating that spyware is bad or malicious because it does these things without the "user's" knowledge. What I should be saying is that spyware is bad and malicious if it does these things without the *owner's* knowledge. There is a whole market segment devoted to legal spyware designed for employers, which they can install on their computers to monitor the activity of their employees, and similar products for parents that can be installed on their computers to monitor the activity of their children.

Products like Spector Pro from Spectorsoft silently sit in the background and monitor and record all Web activity, all incoming and outgoing e-mail messages, all instant-message chat sessions, capture every keystroke typed, and monitor every program used and every file exchanged on peer-to-peer (P2P) networks. In fact, Spector Pro can also be configured to record an actual snapshot image of the screen at set intervals so the contents of the screen can be reviewed as well in case all of the other monitoring and tracking missed something.

Spector Pro CNE (Corporate Network Edition) and similar products such as NetVizor from Employee-Monitoring.com promise to increase employee productivity, eliminate the leaking of trade secrets and confidential company information and aid in the investigation of employees suspected of inappropriate activity among other things.

In a home environment, you aren't typically worried about losing trade secrets (What are your kids going to do? E-mail the secret family recipe for apple pie?) or lack of productivity. But, with so much inappropriate content on the Web and so many unknowns, it provides a tremendous amount of peace of mind to know that you can see every last thing that occurs on the computer when you're not there. With a product like Spector Pro, you can also configure the software to block certain sites or services during specific hours of the day and set it to e-mail you immediately if certain key words occur in e-mails or on the Web sites being viewed.

Getting Rid of Spyware

Eradicating spyware from your system is sometimes much easier said than done. Adware, and simpler spyware that are similar to adware, are fairly easy to remove. Legitimate adware will often have an actual uninstall program. But, to scan your computer for spyware and adware and help remove it, you can use a product such as Ad-aware from Lavasoft (www.lavasoftusa.com) or Spybot Search & Destroy (http://spybot.safer-networking.de/en/) from Patrick Kolla.

Both of these programs are free for personal use and do an excellent job of detecting and removing adware and spyware. They each rely on a database of known spyware, using a method similar to how an antivirus software compares files to a database of known malware. Before running a scan, you should always check for updates from the vendor to make sure your software can catch any new spyware and adware. Both products are excellent, but often one will catch things that the other doesn't, so you may want to run both just to be thorough.

When you run a scan, the product will examine the processes currently running, look for files such as cookies, as well as executable program files, and will scan your system Registry for any entries related to known spyware (see Figure 9.4). Unless you have your cookie security completely locked down, which may make surfing some Web sites difficult or impossible, you will most likely find at least some entries for tracking cookies detected as spyware or adware.

Figure 9.4 Scanning a Computer with Ad-aware

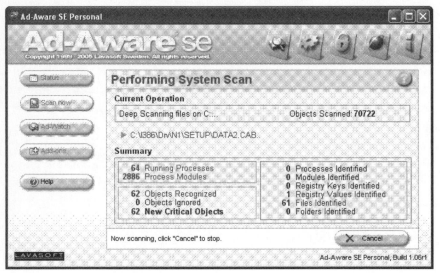

With both products, you will be presented with a list of the files, Registry entries, and processes that were detected and identified as spyware or adware. You can then choose whether or not to remove each of them. Ad-aware allows you to get some clarification about what the object is by double-clicking it to get details such as its size, location, the last time it was accessed and what risk-level Ad-aware has assigned it, as well as a short description of the object (see Figure 9.5). You can also look up the name of the object or the vendor of the object in Google to try and research more details about where the spyware came from and what it is designed to do.

Figure 9.5 Ad-aware's Object Details

I should reiterate that in some cases you agreed to install the adware in exchange for a "free" product or service and that removing or disabling the adware in any way is a violation of your agreement with the EULA. If you opt to remove the adware, you should technically uninstall the software that it came with to remain legal. The spyware removal products will generally warn you of this same thing before moving forward with the cleaning and deleting process.

Ad-aware and Spybot Search & Destroy will both detect and remove the vast majority of spyware and adware in existence. For the money (free) you can't beat them, but they have to be run manually and only remove what they find when you scan your computer after the fact. They don't proactively protect your system from getting spyware and adware installed in the first place.

Antivirus software vendors Symantec (makers of Norton antivirus products) and MacAfee, Inc. have added the capability for their software to detect and block known spyware and adware. Even personal firewall software like Zone Alarm Pro will let you control adware by blocking cookies and alerting you to programs that try to execute without your knowledge. The line between antivirus software, personal firewall software, anti-spyware software, and other security products is constantly being blurred as vendors add functionality to their products.

Lavasoft offers a more advanced version of Ad-aware, Ad-aware Pro, at a reasonable price which provides significantly more security, specifically aimed at protecting your computer from spyware and adware. Ad-aware Pro locks down areas of the memory and Registry targeted by spyware and provides real-time blocking of spyware, adware, and attempts to download software without your knowledge. It also blocks pop-up ads and allows you to scan mapped drives across a network.

Neither Spybot nor Ad-aware will detect or remove commercial spyware products such as Spector Pro or its sibling, eBlaster. Hopefully, if these products exist on your system, they have been installed legitimately by the owner of the computer system to monitor its usage. However, it is possible that someone might install a product like this on your system as a spying tool to stealthily monitor your actions, read your e-mails, collect your passwords, and have it all e-mailed to them without your knowledge. If you feel there may be an unauthorized installation of a program like this installed on your system, you should try scanning it with SpyCop.

SpyCop (http://spycop.com/) will detect not only the typical spyware and adware, but claims to also detect over 400 commercially available snooping programs such as Spector Pro. SpyCop scans every single file on the system to ferret out keystroke loggers, password recorders, e-mail recorders, and all other types of insidious or malicious software. SpyCop boasts the largest database of spying and surveillance software in the world.

If you suspect you might have spyware on your system, or you know that you do but none of the products mentioned can detect or remove it, as a last resort try using HijackThis (www.spywareinfo.com/~merijn/programs.php). This will scan your computer like the other programs, but it will also look for spyware-like traits or activities rather than simply comparing the scan to a database of specific known spyware.

HijackThis is a powerful tool, but analyzing the results can be tricky for novices. When you perform a scan using HijackThis, it quickly generates a log of objects that may or may not be spyware (see Figure 9.6). Some may be programs you've installed intentionally. For most people, the information supplied will look like gibberish. But, thankfully, you can highlight any item on the list and click the program's Info On Selected Item button for a brief description of it. You can also refer to sites such as SpywareInfo.com or WildersSecurity.com for extra assistance. These sites (and many others) offer users an opportunity to submit HijackThis log files, which volunteer experts then help decipher and let you know what is valid and what is potentially spyware or adware.

If the analysis still doesn't make any sense to you or if you're unable to determine if a file or program should be removed or left alone, you can refer to the HijackThis tutorial (it's hosted at a few different sites, but a good place to find it is at www.spywareinfo.com/~merijn/htlogtutorial.html) to learn more about what all of the codes and gibberish mean. The bottom line though is that HijackThis is not a tool for beginners or novices. If you can't find an entry on the forums previously listed that refers to the same object you have a question about, you can click "Save Log" to save the information from your scan and submit it to get some expert help.

Figure 9.6 Results of a Scan with HijackThis

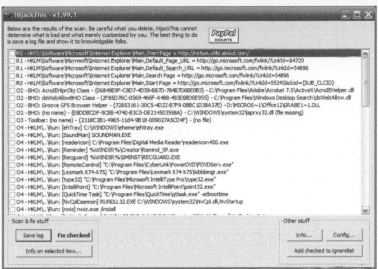

If an item is determined to be safe, you can check the box next to it and click the Add Checked To Ignorelist button so it won't show up again on future scans. If you discover traces of spyware or adware that you want to remove, simply check the boxes for those items and click Fix Checked. You need to be positive that you only check the boxes on items you are sure are related to spyware or malware, however. Once you click Fix Checked, there is no turning back and if you remove the wrong things you may cause legitimate software programs to stop functioning.

Privacy is a serious concern for many, and spyware and adware infringe on your privacy by tracking your actions and habits and reporting that information back to some third party. However, most spyware and adware doesn't infringe on your privacy any more than your credit card company knowing where and when you shopped and what you bought or your cell phone company knowing what phone number you called, where you were when you called it, and how long you talked. It is a personal choice to decide how much information you are comfortable sharing, but remember that spyware and adware also use computer system resources like memory, processing power, and Internet bandwidth, and may cause your system to perform poorly or crash entirely. Using the information and tips from this chapter will help you take back control of just how much information you care to share and with whom.

Summary

Spyware poses a serious threat to computer users and it is important that you understand this threat and how to defend against it. In this chapter, you learned the sometimes subtle differences between adware and spyware, and the way some spyware applications use the EULA to get permission from the user to install themselves.

You learned that many types of adware and spyware are more of a nuisance than a threat, but that there are some very malicious types of spyware out there as well. We then discussed some of the tools and techniques available which you can use to detect and remove spyware applications from your computer. Armed with this information, you should be better prepared to protect your system from the threat of spyware.

Additional Resources

The following resources provide more information about spyware and adware:

- *Ad-aware*
  (www.lavasoftusa.com/default.shtml.en).

- Bradley, Tony. *How to Analyze HijackThis Logs*
  (http://netsecurity.about.com/od/popupsandspyware/a/aahijackthis.htm).

- *HijackThis*
  (www.spywareinfo.com/~merijn/programs.php).

- Kroeker, Kirk. *Beyond File Sharing: An Interview with Sharman Networks CTO Phil Morle.* ECT News Network, Inc.'s TechNewsWorld. January 21, 2004
  (www.technewsworld.com/story/32641.html).

- *So How Did I Get Infected Anyway?*
  (http://forums.spywareinfo.com/index.php?act=SF&f=7).

- Spybot *Search & Destroy*
  (http://spybot.safer-networking.de/en/).

- *SpyCop*
  (http://spycop.com/).

Part III:
Testing and
Maintenance

Chapter 10

Keeping Things Secure

Topics in this chapter:

- **General PC Maintenance**
- **Patches and Updates**
- **Windows XP Security Center**

☑ **Summary**

☑ **Additional Resources**

Introduction

The care and feeding of your computer is an ongoing process, not a product or event. Some people believe that their computer must be secure because it came with antivirus software installed. What they fail to realize is that new vulnerabilities are discovered and exploits created daily.

Your antivirus software, operating system, and other applications are only as strong as their last update. If it has been a week since you last updated, your system is potentially vulnerable to any threat that has been created or discovered in the past seven days.

It is imperative for the security of your computer that you regularly update products such as your antivirus, personal firewall, and anti-spyware software. You should also apply patches and updates for your operating system and applications to make sure they are protected against known vulnerabilities.

Even in the absence of actual threats to the security of your computer system, a computer requires regular maintenance and upkeep. Just like your car needs to have the oil changed, the air filter replaced and the windshield washer fluid refilled periodically, the computer needs some basic cleaning and tuning to keep it running smoothly. Removing unnecessary files and defragmenting your hard drive are two tasks that can speed up your PC and extend its lifespan at the same time.

This chapter will cover the different tasks you need to perform for regular computer maintenance as well as the applications and services that you must keep patched and updated to maintain a secure computer. In this chapter, you will learn how to do the following:

- Maintain your hard drive through Disk Cleanup and Disk Defragmenter.
- Erase your pagefile to protect your personal information.
- Patch and update your computer against new vulnerabilities.
- Use the Windows XP Security Center to monitor security.
- Keep your antivirus and firewall software up to date.

General PC Maintenance

Maintaining your hard drive may not seem like it has much to do with security. In part, this is true. Defragmenting your hard drive will help it run smoother and last longer and increase the overall speed and efficiency of your computer, but it won't do anything to make your PC more secure.

Defragmenting your data will not make it more secure, but it will improve performance and increase the speed of your computer. Slow computer performance is one of the primary indicators of malware infection or computer compromise, so anything that helps keep your hard drive humming along is a good thing and keeps you from being overly paranoid about security.

Disk cleanup may not seem like it has anything to do with security either. However, this general PC maintenance task can help protect your computer system and your personal information. Part of the process of performing Disk Cleanup on a Microsoft Windows XP system is to clean out temporary files and Internet cache files and other data remnants that might be lurking on your computer harboring sensitive or confidential information that an attacker could potentially gain access to.

Disk Cleanup

As you use your computer each day, there are a variety of files that get used or written to your computer that can contain sensitive information. Most of these files are not meant to be kept long term. In fact, they can't even be viewed or accessed like normal files. But, the information is still there and a knowledgeable attacker may be able to locate it and decipher the contents to learn valuable information about you or your computer system.

Files like the temporary Internet files or the temporary files within Windows are two common areas where sensitive information might be lingering. The Recycle Bin may also hold data that you thought you had gotten rid of, but is still hanging around on your hard drive.

To clear out this data and keep your hard drive uncluttered by useless, unnecessary, and possibly damaging data, you should perform Disk Cleanup once a week. To begin Disk Cleanup, click **Start | All Programs | Accessories | System Tools | Disk Cleanup**. You will see a window like the one in Figure 10.1. When you first start Disk Cleanup, you must choose the drive you want to clean.

Figure 10.1 Selecting the Drive You Want to Clean

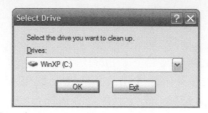

Disk Cleanup works only on hard drives, and it only cleans up one drive at a time. If you have more than one hard drive, or your hard drive is partitioned into multiple drives, you will have to run Disk Cleanup separately for each drive that you want to clean.

After you select the drive you want to clean and click **OK**, Windows will analyze the drive. This can take a minute as Windows checks all the files on the drive to determine which ones should be compressed or deleted. While it is thinking, you will see a window with a progress bar so you can see that things are moving along.

After the analysis is completed, Disk Cleanup will display the results and let you know how much space you can potentially free up on your hard drive by completing Disk Cleanup. The display (see Figure 10.2) begins with statement about the total disk space that can be freed up and lists the different types or areas of data that can be removed along with the total space that you can potentially free up by removing them.

Figure 10.2 Results of Analysis with Disk Cleanup

Check or uncheck the different boxes to choose which data you want to get rid of and which you want to hang on to. You can click on each one to view a short description of it to help you determine what you want to do. After you finish selecting, click **OK** to begin the Disk Cleanup process. This can take some time, particularly if you have selected to compress old files.

Erase the PageFile

Windows uses part of your hard drive space as "virtual memory." It loads what it needs to load into the much faster RAM (random access memory), but creates a swap, or page, file on the hard drive that it uses to swap data in and out of RAM. The pagefile is typically on the root of your C: drive and is called pagefile.sys. Pagefile.sys is a hidden system file, so you won't see it unless you have changed your file viewing settings to show hidden and system files.

Virtual memory enables Windows to open more windows and run more programs simultaneously while keeping only the one being actively used in RAM. The pagefile can be a security risk as well, though. The issue is the fact that information remains in the pagefile even after the program or window is shut down. As you use different programs and perform different functions on your computer, the pagefile may end up containing all sorts of potentially sensitive or confidential information for an attacker to discover.

To reduce the risk presented by storing information in the pagefile, you can configure Windows XP to erase the pagefile each time you shut down Windows. Click **Start | Control Panel**. From the Control Panel, select **Administrative Tools | Local Security Policy** to open the Local Security Settings window (see Figure 10.3). The Local Security Settings window enables you to customize the local security policy settings, including clearing the pagefile on system shutdown. Double-click **Shutdown: Clear Virtual Memory Pagefile**, and then select the **Enabled** radio button. Click **OK** and close the Local Security Settings window. From now on, when you shut down Windows, the pagefile will automatically be cleared as well.

Figure 10.3 The Local Security Settings Window

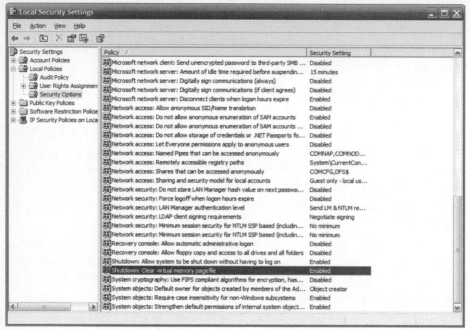

Disk Defragmenter

When you first write a file to your hard drive, your computer does its best to keep all the data together on the disk. However, as data is read, deleted, rewritten, copied, and moved, a single file may end up scattered across the entire drive with a few kilobytes of data here and a sector or two there.

This file fragmentation can degrade performance and reduce the overall longevity of the hard drive. When you access a fragmented file, the hard drive has to work double-time to bounce all over the place and put the pieces of data back together instead of just reading the data in order in one place. To cure this, you should periodically defragment your hard drive.

The Windows Disk Defragmenter utility can be found in System Tools. Click **Start | All Programs | Accessories | System Tools | Disk Defragmenter** (see Figure 10.4).

At the top of the Disk Defragmenter console is a list of the drives available for defragmentation. Initially, you have only two choices for what to do with those drives. After you select a drive, you can simply dive right in and start defragmenting by clicking Defragment, or you can click Analyze to have Disk Defragmenter take a look and let you know just how fragmented your disk is. The Windows Disk

Defragmenter uses a color-coded representation to illustrate how fragmented the selected drive is.

Figure 10.4 The Windows Disk Defragmenter Utility

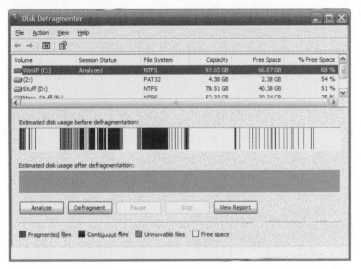

If you do select Analyze, the Disk Defragmenter will take a look and let you know if it is worth your while to defragment the drive at this time. Before you actually start a defragmentation, you should be aware that the process takes a toll on system resources. You can still use your computer, but the drive will be chugging away as fast as it can, moving and juggling pieces of files to get them back in order on the drive. You will probably notice that your computer is much slower and less responsive while it is in the process of defragmenting. It is best to start the defragmenting utility when you are done using the computer for the day or stepping away for a lunch break or something.

Scheduled Tasks

If you leave your computer on overnight, it may be best to simply create a Scheduled Task in Windows to run the Disk Defragmenter automatically while you sleep. Using a Scheduled Task will not only execute the defragmenting when you aren't busy using the computer but also ensure that your hard drive is defragmented on a regular basis without you having to manually initiate it.

To create a scheduled task, click **Start | All Programs | Accessories | System Tools | Scheduled Tasks**. In the Scheduled Tasks console, click **Add Scheduled Task**. You can then follow the wizard to create your task (see Figure

10.5). The wizard displays a list of programs to choose from, but you can also browse
and select virtually any executable to use for your scheduled task. Disk Defragmenter
does not typically show up on the list of programs to choose from in the wizard. You
will need to click the Browse button and find the file manually. The file is called
defrag.exe and is located in the System32 directory under Windows on your hard
drive.

After you select the file to execute, you can provide a name for your scheduled
task and choose the frequency for performing it. I recommend that you schedule
Disk Defragmenter to run at least monthly, or possibly even weekly. You will need to
supply a username and password for an account that has permission to run Disk
Defragmenter.

Figure 10.5 The Add Scheduled Task Wizard

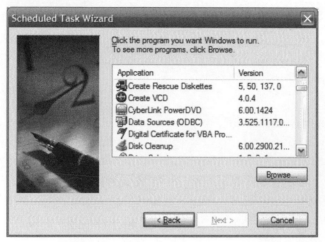

If you click Finish on the next final screen of the wizard, the Disk Defragmenter
utility will run at the scheduled time, but it will just open the utility rather than
actually initiating drive defragmentation. You must specify the drive you want to
defragment in the command line for the scheduled task. If you have multiple drives
or partitions, you will need to create a separate scheduled task to defragment each
one.

On the final screen, make sure you check the box next to **Open advanced
properties for this task when I click Finish**, then click **Finish**. In the **Run** field
of the Advanced Settings, type a space at the end of the command and then add the
drive letter you wish to defragment, such as C: (see Figure 10.6). Click OK to close
Advanced Settings and you are done creating the Scheduled Task to defragment your
drive(s).

Figure 10.6 The Run Field of Advanced Settings

Patches and Updates

When it comes to keeping your computer secure, keeping it patched and updated is arguably the most important thing you can do. Antivirus, anti-spyware, and personal firewall software all contribute to the security of your computer system, but malware and exploits typically take advantage of known vulnerabilities. If your computer was patched so that the vulnerabilities no longer exist, the malware would not be able to function in most cases.

Microsoft provides a number of ways for you to stay informed about the latest vulnerabilities and patches so that you can protect your computer:

- **Automatic Updates** Windows has a feature called Automatic Updates which, as its name implies, automatically checks for new patches that affect the security of your computer system. You can configure Automatic Updates to download and install new updates, just download them, but leave the installation to you, or to simply notify you when new updates are available.

- **Windows Update Site** Automatic updates only works for critical patches or updates that affect security. For patches that affect simple functionality, or updates to device drivers and such, you have to periodically visit the

Windows Update site. Click **Start | All Programs | Windows Update**. Follow the prompts on the site to let Windows Update scan your system and identify the patches or updates that affect your computer. You can choose whether to use Express, and let Windows Update patch your system automatically, or use Custom, which lets you pick and choose which patches you want to apply.

- **Microsoft Security Bulletins** The second Tuesday of each month is Microsoft's "Patch Tuesday." This is the day they release all their Security Bulletins, and related patches, for the month. On rare occasions, if a new vulnerability is discovered and actively being exploited in the wild, Microsoft will release a Security Bulletin out of cycle. But, to stay informed you should mark your calendar or subscribe to receive the notifications from Microsoft when new Security Bulletins are released. Microsoft offers a Microsoft Security Newsletter for Home Users (www.microsoft.com/athome/security/secnews/default.mspx), or you can stay informed using Really Simple Syndication by adding the Security At Home RSS Feed (www.microsoft.com/athome/security/rss/rssfeed.aspx) to your RSS reader.

- **Updating Other Applications** There are far too many vendors and applications for us to cover them all. Many vendors have built-in methods to automatically check for current updates. Where possible, I recommend that you use these features. You can also sign up with vendors to receive notices or alerts when patches or updates are available. You can also use security sites such as Secunia (http://secunia.com) to stay informed of vulnerabilities that affect your operating system or applications.

For more in-depth information, see Chapter 4, "Patching."

Windows XP Security Center

The Windows XP Security Center provides a sort of one-stop shopping information dashboard for the security status of your computer. Using a standard Green/Yellow/Red system, you can tell at a glance if your personal firewall, automatic updates, and antivirus software are up-to-date (see Figure 10.7). To get more information on the status of your computer, click the options in the Windows XP Center.

The Security Center recognizes most personal firewall and antivirus applications, so status will still be reported as Green as long as you have something installed. The

Security Center will report status as Yellow or Red on your antivirus software, though, if the software has not been updated recently.

When the Windows XP Security Center detects an issue that affects the security of your computer, it will also notify you with a pop-up alert from the systray at the lower-right corner of your screen. If your personal firewall or antivirus software is not green, you should check the software to make sure it is running properly and has current information for detecting the latest threats from the vendor.

You can use the links on the left of the screen to access more security information and resources from Microsoft. There is a link to get the latest virus and security information and also a link to access the Windows Update site to get the latest patches and updates for your computer.

Figure 10.7 Options in the Windows XP Security Center

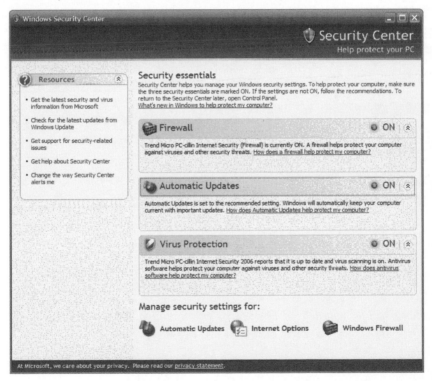

Summary

Installing security software and configuring your computer to be more secure are both valuable accomplishments. However, security is a process, not an event, and it requires ongoing awareness and maintenance to keep your computer secure.

In this chapter you learned about some basic computer maintenance tasks such as Disk Cleanup and Disk Defragmenter and how to erase your pagefile. Some of these tasks are not directly related to security, but they do keep your system running smoothly, which stops you from falsely believing your computer has been infected by malware.

We also talked about ensuring that you keep your computer patched and updated. This applies not only to the operating system, but also to the other applications that you use. You learned that most malware and other malicious attacks use exploits of known vulnerabilities and that by patching your computer you can protect it from those attacks.

Lastly, we had a short overview of the Windows XP Security Center. We discussed how the Security Center is a dashboard for monitoring the current state of security on your computer and that it provides useful information and links to resources that you can use to keep your system secure.

Additional Resources

The following resources provide more information on how to keep your computer secure:

- Bradley, Tony. *Automatically Erase Your Page File.* About.com (http://netsecurity.about.com/od/windowsxp/qt/aa071004.htm).

- *Description of the Disk Cleanup Tool in Windows XP.* Microsoft.com (http://support.microsoft.com/kb/310312/).

- *How to Defragment Your Disk Drive Volumes in Windows XP.* Microsoft.com (http://support.microsoft.com/kb/314848/).

- *How to Schedule Tasks in Windows XP.* Microsoft.com (http://support.microsoft.com/?kbid=308569).

- *Manage Your Computer's Security Settings in One Place.* Microsoft.com. August 4, 2004 (www.microsoft.com/windowsxp/using/security/internet/sp2_wscintro.mspx).

Chapter 11

When Disaster Strikes

Topics in this chapter:

- Check the Event Logs
- Enable Security Auditing
- Review Your Firewall Logs
- Scan Your Computer
- Restore Your System
- Start from Scratch
- Restore Your Data
- Call In the Pros

☑ Summary

☑ Additional Resources

Introduction

No matter how much time, effort, and technology you put into securing your computer or network, it is almost inevitable that something will eventually infect your system or compromise your data. To minimize the impact that such events have on you, it is important to take the proper steps to protect your data.

There are some steps you must take in advance if you want to be able to recover from a security incident, and others that you should take once you think your computer has been compromised in order to clean it up system and to get it back up and running as quickly as possible.

Check the Event Logs

One of the first places you should look if you suspect that something is amiss is the Windows Event Logs. Most users don't even know that the Event Logs exist, and even those who do often forget to use them as a troubleshooting resource.

The Event Logs contain information and alerts regarding virtually any aspect of the Windows operating system. There are different categories of Event Logs. Some applications add their own auditing and logging functionality into the Windows Event Viewer, but by default the categories of logs are Application, Security, and System.

To access the Event Viewer, which lets you see the log entries, click **Start | Control Panel | Administrative Tools | Event Viewer**. If you click **Security** in the left pane, the entries for security events will appear in the right pane of the Event Viewer console (see Figure 11.1). The Event Viewer Console displays the logs for different categories of events, providing information about access, execution, and errors, among other things.

The catch with logging in the Event Viewer, particularly when it comes to events in the Security category, is that Windows will capture log data only for the events it is configured to monitor. By default, none of the security event auditing is enabled in Windows XP Professional, but Windows XP Professional provides control over how event logging is done.

Figure 11.1 The Event Viewer Console

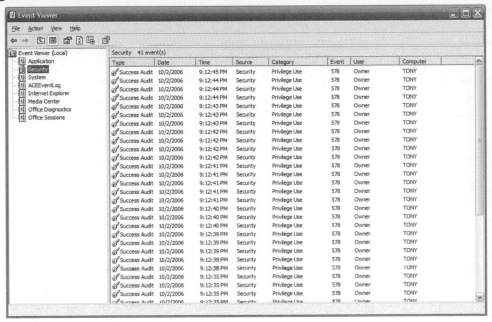

Tools & Traps...

Security Event Log in Windows XP Home

Unlike Windows XP Professional, Windows XP Home does not let you configure what events to monitor for the Security Event logs.

Windows XP Home does audit and log security events, and you can view them in the Event Viewer just as in Windows XP Professional. You just can't customize which events to monitor and log.

Enable Security Auditing

To enable Security event logging in Windows XP Professional, click **Start | Control Panel | Administrative Tools | Local Security Policy**. In the left pane of the Local Security Settings console, click the plus sign (+) next to Local Policies, then click **Audit Policy** (see Figure 11.2). The Local Security Settings Console allows you to specify various security policy options, including which security events to include in auditing and logging.

Figure 11.2 The Local Security Settings Console

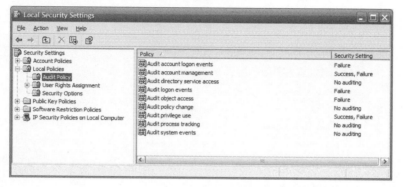

For each of the events listed in the right pane, you can configure Windows to disable event auditing, audit successful events, audit failed events, or audit both success and failure events. For example, if you enable Success for Audit account logon events, a log entry will be created each time an account logs onto the system successfully. If you enable Failure on the same setting, Windows will create a log entry every time an account logon attempt fails.

Tools & Traps…

Control Log File Size

One of the reasons for customizing which events to log is that the log data takes up space. If you log every event possible, you will impact system performance and hard drive space.

You can control how much space the event logs fill and how Windows handles writing events once the log is full by right-clicking the **Event Viewer** category in the left pane of the console and selecting **Properties**.

In the Properties box that appears, under the Log Size section, you can choose a maximum size for the event logs and you can opt to overwrite events once the space is full, overwrite only events older than a specified timeframe, or never overwrite events. If you choose this last option, once the log fills up no events will be written until you manually clear the logs.

After a suspected attack or compromise of your computer, you can review the Event Viewer Security logs for signs of suspicious or malicious behavior. Either Success or Failure alerts could provide useful information depending on the scenario. If you find Successful account logon entries at a time that you know for sure you did not use your computer, it demonstrates that perhaps someone else has gotten your username and password. If you find Failure entries for account logon in the Event Viewer, it shows you that an attacker has been attempting to gain access to your system. These are examples of some entries that you might find suspicious and that could help you determine if your system was compromised, and if so, identify who, when, or how it happened.

At first you might think it makes sense that you would want to audit all events, Success and Failure. You have to keep in mind that the monitoring and logging of each and every event takes its toll on the computer processor and uses memory resources, impacting the overall performance of the computer. Also, the log data takes up space on the hard drive. Logging every single event may cause your log data file to quickly fill up or grow larger than you can effectively manage.

The trick is to find a good balance between monitoring and logging the events that will be most useful in identifying issues without affecting system performance or filling your hard drive. For home users, we recommend that you configure Audit Policy to monitor and log the Security events shown in Table 11.1.

Table 11.1 Security Events

Audit Policy	No Auditing	Success	Failure
Audit account logon events		X	X
Audit account management		X	
Audit directory service access	X		
Audit logon events	X		
Audit object access			X
Audit policy change	X		
Audit privilege use	X		
Audit process tracking	X		
Audit system events		X	X

Review Your Firewall Logs

If you don't find any evidence of suspicious or malicious activity in the Event Viewer logs, you can take a look at the logs for your personal firewall software. Admittedly, the information is more cryptic than most home users will be able to understand, but with a little bit of effort and maybe a few Google searches, you might be able to weed out specific log entries that help identify where or how a problem originated.

If you are using the Windows Firewall, logging will need to be enabled just like the Security event logging. To turn on logging for the Windows Firewall, click **Start | Control Panel | Security Center**, and then click the Windows Firewall link at the bottom of the Security Center console.

In the Windows Firewall properties console, click **Advanced**, then select **Settings** (next to Security Logging) to open the Log Settings window. On the Log Settings window, you can choose to log dropped packets and/or successful connections. You can specify what the log file should be called, where you want it to be located, and what the maximum size is before it begins to overwrite itself (see Figure 11.3).

Figure 11.3 The Windows Firewall Log Settings

The resulting log file generated by the Windows Firewall is simply a TXT file that can be viewed in Notepad or any other text editor program. The information provided includes the time and date of the log entry, source IP address and port, destination IP address and port, the protocol being used, and some advanced information that is typically blank in the logs anyway. Because the information is in a TXT file, the columns don't line up well and it can be difficult to match up the information with the column it belongs in. Other personal firewall software, such as the personal firewall component of Trend Micro's PC-cillin Security Suite (see Figure 11.4), provides a more graphical log viewer that makes it easier to tell which information belongs in which column.

Figure 11.4 The Trend Micro PC-cillin Personal Firewall

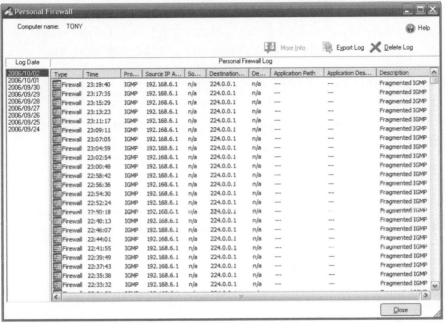

The firewall logs typically show the source and destination IP address and the source and destination port for traffic to or from your computer. Some personal firewalls provide more details, such as what network protocol is being used, the application generating the traffic, or a description of what the potential issue is.

As I stated, this information is more complex and confusing than most home users will be able to handle. However, you may be able to isolate specific traffic that seems suspicious based on the application being used or the time of day the log entries were made; this information may help you determine how or when your computer became infected or compromised.

Scan Your Computer

Scanning through firewall logs or reviewing entries in the Windows Event Viewer may both be too technical for an average user. If analyzing log data seems more involved or complex than you would like, you probably should start by scanning your system using your antivirus and/or antispyware software.

If you notice that your system is acting weird or is unusually slow, or you just have reason to suspect that something isn't quite right, run a manual virus and spyware scan of your computer (see Figure 11.5). You should be aware up front that full system scans generally take quite a while to complete and that they are very memory- and processor-intensive. In other words, you should plan on taking a coffee break or something while the scan is running because it will probably be difficult to do anything productive with the computer during this time.

Figure 11.5 Running a Full Manual Scan of Your Computer with Your Antivirus Software

Before you even start running a virus or spyware scan, verify that you have the most current version of the virus or spyware signatures from your software vendor. There is no point in scanning your system with information from last week if the malware that compromised your machine was just discovered yesterday.

In some cases, you actually may want to reboot the computer into Safe Mode in order to execute the scan. The reason is that some malware can hijack or shut down processes that your antivirus or antispyware software needs to do the scan. There are also some malware threats that are tenacious and can't be removed or cleaned up while they are still running in memory. Booting the computer into Safe Mode allows only the bare minimum processes to run, which blocks malware that is programmed to run at Startup from being able to start.

Restore Your System

Windows XP does provide a very useful feature when it comes to troubleshooting and repairing issues with the computer system. The System Restore feature lets you essentially go back in time to when the computer was still running smooth and happy. If you know approximately when you started noticing issues with your computer or when you think your computer may have become infected, you can simply revert to an earlier system restore point to undo the damage.

Click **Start | All Programs | Accessories | System Tools | System Restore** to open the System Restore console. You can use the System Restore console either to return your system to a previous state or to mark a new system restore point (see Figure 11.6). Installing new software in Windows generally creates a new system restore point automatically, but you can also manually create a system restore point before you make configuration changes as a safety net to let you undo your changes if something goes wrong.

Figure 11.6 The System Restore Console

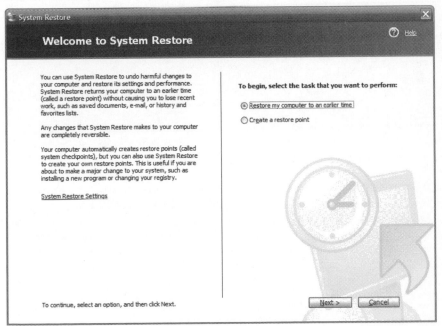

If you click **Restore my computer to an earlier time** and then click **Next**, the System Restore utility will display a calendar. The days that have system restore points saved will be bold. You can click a date, then select the system restore point you want to use and click **Next**.

The final screen warns you that Windows will shut down and reboot as a part of the System Restore process, and that any programs you have installed since the system restore point was created will be lost. It also reassures you that any data files will be retained though, so you won't lose Word documents or Quicken financial data by reverting to a previous system restore point.

Start from Scratch

If your computer is in fact infected or compromised in any way, hopefully your security software, such as antivirus and antispyware applications, will be able to identify and remove the problem. Depending on the threat, though, simply "cleaning up" may not be sufficient.

Are You Owned?

Booting into Safe Mode

Many malware programs embed themselves in Windows to automatically start backing up each time you reboot your computer. Sometimes your security software will be unable to remove a worm or spyware threat that is already running, and because the malware starts itself back up each time you boot the computer, you end up stuck in a vicious circle.

To start Windows without starting the malware process, boot into Safe Mode. To boot your computer into Safe Mode, you should restart the system and press the F8 key repeatedly to bring up the boot menu. Technically, you should press F8 when the screen displays the "Starting Windows…" message, but that appears and disappears so quickly that it is hard to get the timing right.

Select **Safe Mode** from the menu and press **Enter** to complete the boot process. Once you are done working in Safe Mode, just restart and let the computer boot into Windows normally.

For the majority of viruses, worms, and spyware, simply detecting and removing the malware are all that is needed. However, once a system is infiltrated it is sometimes difficult to tell exactly what has or has not been compromised. Your antivirus software may remove the detected malware, but fail to recognize backdoor or rootkit software left behind by the attacker.

If you are not confident that your computer is completely free of malware threats and that no malicious applications are still lingering on your computer, allowing an attacker to access or control your computer, you should consider simply starting over. Make sure you have backed up your personal data, and then simply reinstall the Windows operating system from scratch.

Before you blow away your computer system, you should make sure you have at least Service Pack 2 available on a CD so that you can install it without having to connect to the Internet. Once you reinstall the operating system, you will need to visit the Windows Update Web site or use Automatic Updates to get caught up on vulnerability patching again.

Restore Your Data

As a matter of regular system maintenance and data protection, you should be backing up your personal or critical data on a regular basis. Only you can decide how often is good enough. For a small business, backing up daily to ensure customer data and transactions are protected may make sense. But, if you are a home user who cares about protecting only your personal financial information and you only do your bills monthly, a monthly backup may suffice.

Regardless, it is critical that you back up your data. It is an area where Murphy's Law is almost guaranteed to bite you. If you back up your data, you will probably never need it. But, if you do not back up your data, you are inviting catastrophe to strike and it is only a matter of time before some malware or just a plain, old-fashioned hard drive failure wipes your data out.

For the sake of argument, we'll assume that you have been backing up your data on a regular basis. You might be using a third-party backup product such as Backup For One or WinBackup, or you might be using the built-in backup utility that comes with Windows XP (see Figure 11.7). Whatever method you have used, you will need to follow the vendor instructions for restoring your backed-up data once you complete the fresh installation of your operating system.

Call In the Pros

Between System Restore or simply reinstalling the operating system and restoring your data from backup, most home users ought to be able to remove or undo whatever program or configuration change is causing the problem and get back to using the computer.

www.syngress.com

Figure 11.7 The Built-in Backup Utility in Windows XP

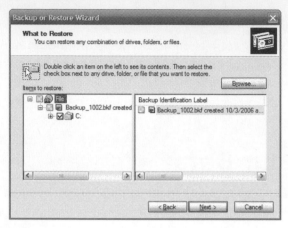

For businesses however, there may be other legal implications involved. Businesses may be governed by a variety of computer security regulatory requirements, which dictate how customer or financial data must be stored and protected and what to do if you suspect that data may have been compromised.

For small office / home office computers that you suspect may be infected or compromised in some way, you should seek professional help to make sure that laws are followed and that all proper steps are taken to clean the system, collect evidence to identify the attacker, and notify any customers whose personal or confidential data may have been compromised.

Summary

If you have followed the advice in the rest of the book, you would hopefully not need to worry about a disaster. But, even with the best of security, it is entirely possible that your computer may someday become infected or compromised by malware or an attack of some sort.

This chapter walked you through some of the steps you can take to identify and remove any threats from your computer when an attack or security breach occurs. You learned how to configure and use the Windows Event Viewer to review Security logs and how to analyze your personal firewall logs for signs of intrusions or suspicious activity.

The chapter also discussed running a manual scan of your computer for viruses, spyware, or other malware, including how to do so in Safe Mode for particularly tenacious threats. You also learned that you can use System Restore to go back in time to undo problems, although sometimes it is best simply to reinstall the operating system and restore your personal data in order to be completely sure that your computer is clean and safe.

Lastly, we talked about calling for professional help, especially in the case of a business where private or personally identifiable customer information may have been compromised. Businesses are governed by a variety of computer security regulations that dictate how security breaches should be handled.

Additional Resources

The following resources provide more information on topics covered in this chapter:

- *Backup for One.* Lockstep Systems, Inc. (www.backup-for-one.com/index.html).

- Bradley, Tony. *How to Configure the Windows XP Firewall.* About.com. (http://netsecurity.about.com/od/securingwindowsxp/qt/aaqtwinfirewall.htm).

- Bradley, Tony. *How to Enable Security Auditing in Windows XP Pro.* About.com (http://netsecurity.about.com/cs/tutorials/ht/ht040503.htm).

- *How to restore the operating system to a previous state in Windows XP.* Microsoft.com. (http://support.microsoft.com/kb/306084/EN–US/).

- *How to use Backup to restore files and folders on your computer in Windows XP.* Microsoft.com. (http://support.microsoft.com/default.aspx?scid=kb;%5Bln%5D;309340).

- *To Start the Computer in Safe Mode.* Microsoft's Windows XP Professional Product Documentation. (www.microsoft.com/resources/documentation/windows/xp/all/proddocs/en-us/boot_failsafe.mspx?mfr=true).

- WinBackup. Uniblue Systems Ltd. (www.liutilities.com/products/winbackup/).

Chapter 12

Microsoft Alternatives: Inside the Linux Desktop

Topics in this chapter:

- **Common Desktop Environments**
- **X Window Servers, and Window Managers**
- **E-Mail and Personal Information Management Clients**
- **Web Browsers**
- **Office Application Suites**
- **Running Windows Applications on Linux**

☑ **Summary**

☑ **Additional Resources**

Introduction

The primary focus of this book has been on how to secure and protect computers that are running Microsoft operating systems, specifically Windows XP. Although you won't typically find them preinstalled on the computer system you buy at the local electronics retail giant, there are alternatives out there. Microsoft has taken a lot of heat for the vulnerabilities and weaknesses in its software security, and it is a favorite target of attackers. Some security experts suggest simply using other products such as a version of the Linux operating system.

When it comes to discussing Linux, most end users are not very interested in what vendors or consultants focus on (i.e., the advantages that appeal to the "propeller head"). The tech set focuses on selling points such as system stability, the possibility of enhanced security, and the fact that Linux can save companies money on licensing.

However, most end users simply care about their desktop experiences. Users state that they want a desktop that is "intuitive" and "easy to understand." What they are implying, however, is that they want a desktop similar to what they already know. One of the things that Microsoft and Apple have done admirably is to convince end users that their interfaces have always been intuitive and easy to use, even though these companies have changed these interfaces radically over the last 10 years.

End users want to know how to access productivity applications once they have logged on. They want to know how to locate files on the hard drive and open them with the proper application. They really tend to care very little about anything else.

So, in this chapter, you will learn about choosing the proper desktop environment and window manager. You will learn which e-mail, personal information management (PIM) and Web browser applications are optimal for to migrating from applications such as Outlook, Outlook Express, and Internet Explorer. Because you want to open Word, PowerPoint, and Excel files, you will need to know the ideal Linux office suite, as well as additional open-source solutions. By the end of this chapter, you will know how to ensure that you will be able to remain productive on your desktop.

Common Desktop Environments

At one time, UNIX versions (like other operating systems of the day) did not have a graphical user interface (GUI). By the time Macintosh and Windows appeared, UNIX systems had become somewhat obscure to the average end user.

With the increasing popularity of Linux, questions such as whether Linux uses the command line are becoming less common. Still, one of the first tasks end users face is choosing the right desktop environment.

You will want to choose a desktop that you consider:

- Easy to use (and easy to learn)
- Easy to customize
- Easy to upgrade

Of course, "easy" is a relative term, but you will have to consider the relative benefits and drawbacks of the most common desktop environments. Remember, with any UNIX-based operating system, there is more than one way to do anything. You should get information from consultants who will provide you with a manageable set of choices. Ask consultants to justify the environments that they recommend to you.

The most common desktop environments are Gnome (www.gnome.org) and KDE (www.kde.org). Additional environments exist, including the Common Desktop Environment (CDE) and Xfce. In the following sections of this chapter, we discuss each of these environments. We have one caveat for you, however: Please do not think that we are partial to any one of these desktops over the other. We prefer an environment provided by the Blackbox window manager, mostly because the interface is cleaner and does not imitate the Windows desktop. Making the "right" choice of a desktop environment depends on various factors.

Avoid becoming a victim of the "Gnome versus KDE" wars. Have a consultant show you various desktop environments. Take a "test drive." Only then will you be able to make a relatively informed choice. So, as you read on, consider the relative strengths and weaknesses of each environment.

Gnome

The Gnome desktop was developed by The GNU Project (www.gnu.org), which is responsible for developing a wide array of software for various platforms, including Windows, Linux, and Macintosh. Figure 12.1 shows the Gnome desktop on a Red Hat Linux system.

Understand, however, that the desktop shown in Figure 12.1 represents default settings. It is possible to customize your desktop so that it appears significantly different. Gnome offers users the following benefits:

- It is associated with The GNU Project (www.gnu.org). Consequently, Gnome is licensed under GNU's General Public License (GPL), which ensures that the code is created by open-source, freely available technology.

Figure 12.1 The Gnome Desktop Environment

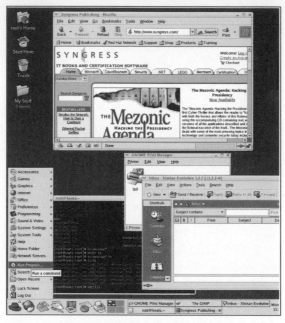

- Many applications are written to Gnome or use Gnome libraries. Gnome prides itself in being the desktop environment that welcomes diverse development environments, including C, C++, Tcl/Tk, and Python. Gnome's use of the GPL is also a contributing factor to the sheer diversity of applications available to Gnome.

- The code is reviewed by the same team that works on projects such as GnuPG (essentially open-source PGP) and many other applications.

- Gnome desktop developers have taken special steps to make sure that Gnome is accessible by the disabled.

- If you want to use applications such as Galeon, Evolution, and GnomeMeeting, you might want to consider using Gnome as the default desktop.

- Gnome is often considered cleaner because, by default, it provides fewer options.

The Gnome desktop often does not appear as tightly integrated as KDE's desktop. Moreover, Gnome applications have traditionally been produced at a slower rate than KDE applications. However, many vendors have adopted Gnome because of its association with GNU, which means that the software is more likely to remain open source. To learn more about Gnome, go to www.gnome.org.

KDE

For many, KDE appears to be the most similar to the Windows environment. Figure 12.2 shows the KDE environment in a Red Hat Linux system.

Figure 12.2 Using KDE

Compare Figure 12.2 with Figure 12.1. As you can see, Red Hat took special pains to make both interfaces look remarkably similar. This does not have to be the case. KDE offers the following benefits:

- Applications are tightly integrated. You can tell that the people who developed KDE set out from the start to design a desktop with a logical flow and a coherent organization. End users often feel that a KDE desktop provides access to more applications more quickly.

- The KDE desktop provides well-written applications that allow you to configure networking easily.

- If you like applications such as KMail and Konqueror, you might want to make KDE the default desktop.

One of the drawbacks of the KDE environment is that it tends not to invite diverse development, as does Gnome. Therefore, you may not find as many KDE-compatible applications as in Gnome. KDE is based on the Qt GUI toolkit, and as a result, it was not based on GNU's GPL. This is no longer the case. Nevertheless, this history caused many developers to adopt Gnome, at least throughout the 1990s. In addition, there is a general perception that KDE runs slower than Gnome. Personally, we have found that both KDE and Gnome run slowly, compared with more Spartan environments, such as Blackbox, which is discussed later in this chapter.

Notes from the Underground...

Avoiding Controversy

In some ways, we wish we hadn't discussed Gnome and KDE in terms of "benefits and drawbacks." Discussing KDE and Gnome tends to make people get quite passionate very quickly. You will have to determine the best environment for your own situation. Make sure that any consultants you speak with are ready to justify their recommendations based on solid business reasons, and not necessarily on their own personal preferences.

Common Features

Both Gnome and KDE have the following priorities:

- Ease of use and customization
- Support for multiple languages

Both Gnome and KDE support Windows-like menus. Experienced Windows users should feel comfortable quite quickly, as long as they know where to access the applications they need. Both KDE and Gnome include their own versions of the "Start" application dialog box, which allows end users to launch applications that do not reside on the menu. Again, the best strategy for you is to experience both environments.

Because both KDE and Gnome pride themselves in providing a full GUI environment, they can run quite slowly. Many people seem to have access to powerful, modern computers, so this is often not an issue.

Install Both, Make One the Default

If disk space permits, install both Gnome and KDE. Then choose the desktop you want to use by default. Consequently, you can have access to both KDE and Gnome applications in either environment. Not every Gnome application is compatible in KDE, and vice versa. However, compatibility problems are increasingly rare.

Conduct research about additional desktop environments and how to choose them. This way, you will be empowered to choose and customize your desktop environment.

Alternative Window Managers

The Xfce desktop environment was designed to run on any UNIX system, including Linux. It is also designed to be compatible with both Gnome and KDE. One of the features special to Xfce is that it supports "drag-and-drop" file management more completely than its competitors do. For more information on Xfce, go to www.xfce.org.

Another alternative desktop environment is the Common Desktop Environment (CDE), which was developed by a team composed of employees from HP, Novell, Sun, and IBM. Sun Solaris systems have traditionally shipped with CDE. It is not a common window manager. For more information about CDE, go to wwws.sun.com/software/solaris/cde/.

The X Window System and Window Managers

The X Window system was designed to provide a standards-based GUI environment. Thus, a developer who wants to create an X Window server simply needs to read common standards. He or she can then create applications that conform to those standards.

The X environment was designed from the beginning to be network compatible, meaning that it is possible to run an X Window session over the network. Consequently, using the X Window environment, you can connect to a remote system's X Window server to control it as if you were sitting directly in front of the remote system.

An X Window server is responsible for making sure that the GUI environment is available. This environment is most often made available to the local system, but it can also be made available to remote systems. Thus, whenever you log on to the

Gnome or KDE environment, you are running an X Window session. The Gnome or KDE environment is simply a client to the local system.

Two primary implementations of the X Window environment exist:

- **X.org** The X Window server used by the majority of Linux distributions, because it conforms to the GPL.

- **XFree86** Until roughly 2002, the default X Window server software for most platforms. However, XFree86 adopted a new license, dropping the GPL. As a result, many vendors and developers began supporting the X.org server.

Figure 12.3 shows the X.org Web site.

Figure 12.3 The X.org Web Site

X Window Servers versus Window Managers

A window manager mediates between the X server and the desktop environment. It is responsible for managing window toolbars and menus. It is also responsible for determining the position of applications as they are launched. Commonly used window managers include:

- **Metacity** The default window manager for Gnome desktops, after version 8.0.

- **Sawfish** The default window manager for Gnome versions 8.0 and older.

- **KWin** The default window manager for KDE.

- **Tab Window Manager (TWB)** An older window manager designed to provide only the necessary elements for a desktop. Often used during remote X sessions to ensure maximum compatibility with systems that may not have more ambitious window managers installed.

- **Enlightenment** At one time, Enlightenment was meant to be an upgrade to FVWM. For some time, however, it has been an independent project. You can learn more about Enlightenment at www.enlightenment.org.

- **FVWM** The latest version of FVWM is FVWM2, available at www.fvwm.org.

- **AfterSTEP** You can learn more about AfterSTEP at www.afterstep.org.

- **WindowMaker** You can learn more about WindowMaker at www.windowmaker.org.

- **Blackbox** Some support for KDE, but does not officially support Gnome. You can obtain Blackbox at http://blackboxwm.sourceforge.net.

At least a dozen window managers exist. Choose a window manager that makes sense to you. If you expect a full KDE environment that most closely imitates Windows, then you will want to use KWin. If you want a simpler desktop, you could use WindowMaker or Blackbox. If you want a desktop that appears exactly like a Macintosh system, then choose Metacity. For more information about window managers, go to www.xwinman.org.

Tools & Traps…

Desktop Environment, X Window Server, Window Manager . . . What's the Difference?

You may not understand the difference between desktop environments, X Window servers, and window managers. Here is a brief discussion of each.

A desktop environment such as Gnome is not the same thing as a window manager. A desktop environment includes many features, such as configuration applications (for example, yast/yast2 for SUSE Linux, or draconf for Mandrake Linux) and default applications (for example, word processors, FTP applications, and calculators). A desktop environment includes a window manager. Without

Continued

the desktop environment, you would have a "bare bones" graphical environment that would alienate most users accustomed to Windows.

An X Window server acts as the foundation of a Linux GUI. It is responsible for providing the fonts, and the networking capability. Without the X Window server, you would not be able to have a GUI.

A window manager is a client to the X Window server (for example, one from X.org, or from the XFree86 organization). It works behind the scenes, and is responsible for the look and feel of desktop windows, including the appearance of toolbars and menus. A window manager controls how menus appear on your desktop, too. If you can access a Linux system, begin an X Window session and then launch any application. Look at the title bar to the application. Notice how the application is launched into a certain portion of the screen (for example, in the center, or to the left). Use your mouse's right and left buttons. These elements are all controlled by your window manager. Without a window manager, the content served up by the X Window server would be incoherent, and would not have a common theme.

Window Managers as Alternative Desktop Environments

You are not limited to Gnome, KDE, CDE, and XFCE. Alternatives to the Blackbox window manager are shown in Figure 12.4. Blackbox is quite different from both Gnome and KDE. For example, it does not have Windows-like menus or taskbars. In addition, Blackbox is a window manager, and not simply a desktop environment.

Figure 12.4 The Blackbox Environment

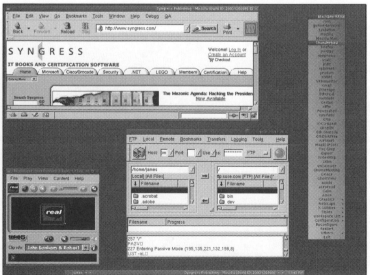

You simply right-click on the desktop to make the menu appear. You can then select the applications you want to run. One of the benefits of an environment like Blackbox is that it is less resource intensive, and thus loads faster. We prefer speed in any case, mostly because we do not have the money to purchase a new system each time a Gnome or KDE developer introduces a new process-hungry GUI feature.

Notes from the Underground...

What Do You Want?

When migrating from Windows to Linux desktops, you need to consider the following points:

1. **Identify your needs**. Determine the services that you want. Create a detailed list of your needs. Present your needs to a consultant and ask him or her to determine right away if an open-source alternative exists. If Linux is not part of that solution, do not let a consultant try to force-fit Linux into your environment. If you do, you will end up a disgruntled customer.

2. **Identify solutions.** Make sure you find a consultant who understands the open-source choices that exist. Be sure the consultant has knowledge about the latest solutions. Frequently visit sites such as Freshmeat (www.freshmeat.net), SourceForge (www.sourceforge.net), and even Slashdot (www.slashdot.org) to remain informed concerning the latest software developments.

3. **Fulfill your needs.** Meet with a consultant who uses Linux-based applications to create feasible, workable solutions that enable you to access the desired services and obtain the desired information with minimal retraining. Make sure that your consultant has run an extensive test deployment to ensure that a solution truly meets your needs. Another step includes conducting a final acceptance test. You will want to have a "grace period" so that you can determine if a solution is working properly. Finally, make sure that you receive proper training from a consultant so that you understand the solution.

Even the most experienced consultants have failed to please their customers at one point or another. Avoid being disappointed by a consultant by making sure you follow the preceding three steps.

E-mail and Personal Information Management Clients

E-mail and PIM have become closely related, because most people communicate their availability through e-mail these days. This section discusses e-mail and PIM software that will help you remain organized, even without Outlook.

It has been our experience that most end users think Outlook *is* e-mail. Many people don't realize that they are simply using an application to send and get their e-mail. So even if you you no longer use Outlook or Outlook Express, you still can use e-mail.

If you aren't sure how e-mail exists outside of Outlook or Outlook Express, read the following sections. There is certainly no shortage of e-mail applications in the Linux space. Commonly used e-mail applications include:

- Evolution
- KDE Suite/KMail
- Mozilla mail/Thunderbird
- Aethera
- Sylpheed

Evolution

Evolution is Gnome's default mail and PIM client. KMail and Evolution will run in any window manager you decide to use. They will also run inside the KDE, Gnome, or Blackbox environments. Figure 12.5 shows the Evolution e-mail interface. From here, you can send and receive e-mail.

Evolution stores its files in the mbox format. If your username is james, look for e-mail in the directory /home/james/evolution/local, which contains directories for all of your mail folders. Inside each folder you will find a file called mbox, which is your mail in mbox format.

Evolution also has PIM features, including the calendaring feature shown in Figure 12.6.

Figure 12.5 Evolution and the E-mail Interface

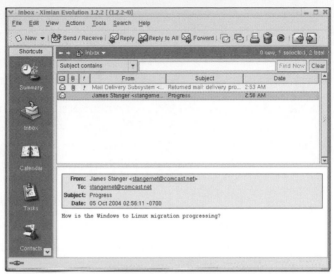

Figure 12.6 Evolution Showing the Calendaring Interface

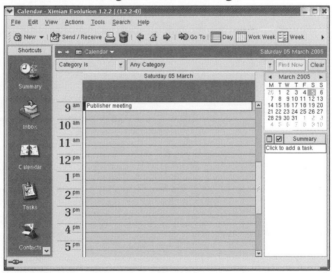

Benefits of using Evolution include:

- It is developed by Novell, a company with a history of developing a solid customer base.

- It will run on any common window manager (for example, KDE or Gnome).

■ It is designed to work with common groupware servers, such as Microsoft Exchange.

Evolution, Microsoft Exchange, Novell GroupWise, and OpenExchange

Evolution is unique in that it works well with servers created by other vendors. For example, Evolution's Connector for Microsoft Exchange allows you to take advantage of all features provided by Exchange. Similarly, plug-ins for Evolution allow it to act as a client for Novell GroupWise and Novell's OpenExchange servers. You can learn more about Evolution at www.novell.com/products/evolution.

KDE Suite/KMail

KDE's default mail client is called KMail. It can either be run by itself or built into Kontact, which makes it look more like Outlook. In KMail and most other mail clients, all your mail will end up in your home directory in a folder called Mail unless you are running IMAP. Inside your /home/user_name/Mail folder are all of your mail files such as inbox, trash, sent, drafts, and so forth. Copy the files over and make sure you set permissions correctly so that you have sole read and write permissions on them. Your Mail folder should look something like this:

```
ls -lh /home/james/Mail
total 11M
-rw------- 1 james james 0 Aug 20 19:51 drafts
-rw------- 1 james james 11M Aug 20 19:51 inbox
-rw------- 1 james james 0 Aug 20 19:51 outbox
-rw------- 1 james james 26K Aug 13 19:04 sent-mail
-rw------- 1 james james 0 May 17 18:32 trash
```

Figure 12.7 shows the KMail application.

Kontact

Kontact is essentially KMail on steroids. It allows you to connect to the following groupware servers:

Figure 12.7 KMail

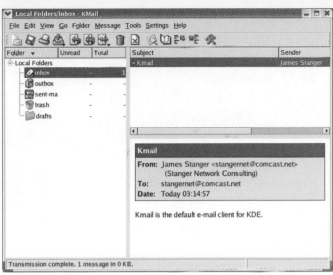

- **Microsoft Exchange** Currently, Kontact supports Microsoft Exchange 2000 only. For more information, go to www.microsoft.com.

- **Novell GroupWise** Currently, Kontact supports version 6.5. For more information, go to www.novell.com.

- **eGroupWare** A PHP-based groupware application designed by and for the open-source community, eGroupWare runs on Linux servers. For more information, go to www.egroupware.org.

- **The Kolab project** Kolab is a groupware server first established by the German government. For more information, go to www.bsi.bund.de.

Thus, KMail is a competitor (or should we say, kompetitor?) to Evolution. You can learn more about Kontact at www.kontact.org.

Aethera

Like Evolution, Aethera is an e-mail application with bundled PIM software, and it is licensed under the GPL. However, Aethera is designed to support only the Kolab groupware server as of this writing. Figure 12.8 shows Aethera's calendaring feature.

Figure 12.8 Aethera's Calendaring Feature

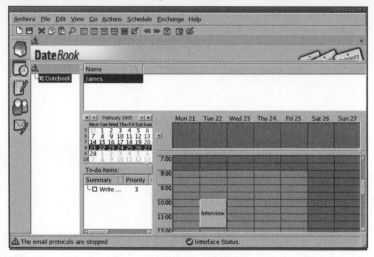

Aethera is a GPL application, and is considered quite reliable. However, its limited groupware support may be a problem for those companies that do not want to migrate to a Kolab server. You can learn more about Aethera at www.thekompany.com/projects/aethera/index.php3.

Mozilla Mail/Thunderbird

Mozilla Mail, shown in Figure 12.9, is bundled in with the Mozilla Web browser and Composer, a GUI HTML editor. Mozilla Mail is a capable e-mail client, and supports SMTP, POP3, and IMAP.

Figure 12.9 Mozilla Mail

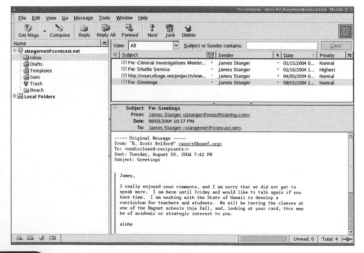

Mozilla Mail is extremely common, and it is a stable product. Because it is bundled with an HTML editor and a browser, it is a perfect recommendation for companies that want an integrated suite. Many companies will find that their end users can take advantage of the HTML editor, and the Web browser. You can learn more about Mozilla Mail at www.mozilla.org. We also discuss Mozilla Mail in the section of this chapter titled "Migrating Mail."

Thunderbird

Even though Thunderbird is also created by the developers at Mozilla.org, it uses different code than Mozilla Mail does. Thus, Thunderbird deserves to be treated as a different application. Figure 12.10 shows the Thunderbird application.

Figure 12.10 Thunderbird Application

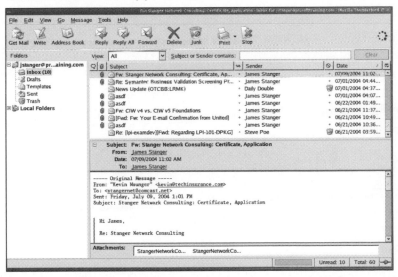

Thunderbird does not support groupware servers, loads fast, and has a small footprint, making it ideal for those who need a stand-alone e-mail application. You can learn more about Thunderbird at www.mozilla.org.

Sylpheed

Sylpheed, shown in Figure 12.11, is one of many e-mail applications that exist in the market. It does not have groupware or scheduling features. However, it does one thing quite well: it supports PGP and GPG. Although many clients say that they support PGP and GPG, few work as well as Sylpheed.

Figure 12.11 Sylpheed

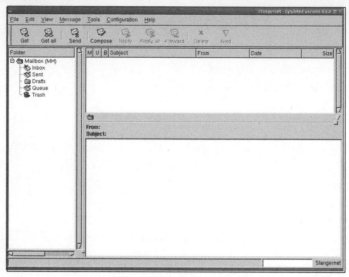

Thus, if you need to use PGP or GPG, consider Sylpheed. To learn more about Sylpheed, go to http://sylpheed.good-day.net. Sylpheed's creators have focused on making sure that it supports IPv6, which is the next version of IP, designed to improve security.

Essential Information

No matter what client you plan to use, you will need the following information:

- The SMTP server name or IP address
- The POP3 or IMAP server name or IP address
- User authentication information (for example, username and password)

Take the time to write down this information so that it is handy. As you conduct a migration, you will not want to repeat this information constantly to those who are helping you.

E-mail and PIM Software

Don't think that you have to receive just one recommendation from a consultant for e-mail or a PIM application. In many cases, you may have to install multiple applications to get what you want. For example, you may need to use Evolution to connect to your company's Exchange server and use your calendars, but use KMail in order to use your Internet e-mail. It is more likely, however, that you will want to standardize to use of one application.

If you preferred Outlook, you will probably prefer Evolution. If you already use the Windows Mozilla/Netscape/Thunderbird variants, you will find it very easy to make a transition over to their Linux counterparts. If you are still using Eudora, you will likely choose KMail, as it has a relatively similar look and feel. All these applications are all quite stable and feature rich.

Migrating Mail

If you are using something other than Outlook for your mail, you may not have to convert your e-mail format, as your mail is most likely already in an mbox format. However, if you are using Outlook, you have to convert the format in which your mail is stored. There are five ways to do this. We will start with the easiest, and move to the "if all else fails" way last. Depending on the version of client that is in use, you might have to upgrade before you can move the mail. This part of the migration can take a long time per person if you need to migrate thousands of e-mails per client.

One of the best ways to ensure that you have time for a proper migration is to plan a staged migration, which involves using multiple applications to convert your e-mail. You may find that you cannot export mail directly from a Windows e-mail application and then import it into a Linux application. You will find that you must first export e-mail into an intermediary e-mail client that can then export your e-mail into the format required by the e-mail application you want to use.

Now, let's look at the steps necessary when migrating from Outlook and Outlook Express.

Migrating from Outlook or Outlook Express

The first step is to back up your e-mail in case you have any problems. In Outlook, you want to export your e-mail messages to a single .pst file. This step is done by clicking on **File | Import and Export** to bring up the Import and Export Wizard dialog box. You then select **Export to a file**, as shown in Figure 12.12.

After clicking **Next**, choose **Personal Folder File (.pst)**. Then, select the top of the tree by clicking on **Personal Folders** and make sure to select the check box **Include all subfolders**. Make sure that you remember where you save the backup.pst file. As you save the file, do not export your backup using any encryption, compression, or password protection. If you do, the import process will fail. You can now import the file into Mozilla.

Figure 12.12 The Microsoft Outlook Import and Export Wizard Window

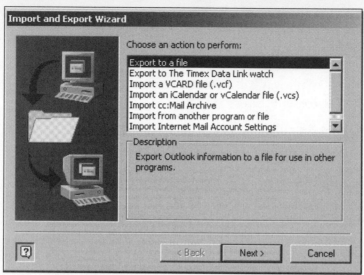

Importing Outlook Mail into Mozilla

Now, install Mozilla on the Windows desktop system. Make sure you select Mozilla and not Firefox or Thunderbird for this step, even if you do not plan to run Mozilla at the end of the process.

First, install Mozilla and select **Complete** when asked which components you want to install. You do not need to tell the system to make Mozilla the default browser or e-mail client. Once it's installed, start Mozilla and click on **Windows | Mail & Newsgroups**. You do not need to fill in the settings in the account wizard that will pop up. You can import these into Mozilla from Outlook if you're so inclined; it will appear as a second account.

Once you have the account set up you need to import the old mail out of Outlook into Mozilla. Now, do the same for the settings and the address book. If you prefer, you can just export the address book in .csv format from Outlook or Outlook Express and import it into Mozilla the same way as the mail.

To do so, click **Tools | Import** on the Import screen, select **Mail**, and select the mail client your importing from; it will do the rest. Once you have completed these steps, you will have your mail converted from a .pst format to a standard mbox mail format. In our case, the imported mail folders end up in C:\Documents and Settings\james\Application Data\Mozilla\Profiles\default\033c70c1.slt\Mail\Local Folders\Outlook Mail.sbd\Inbox.sbd.

Inside this folder are all the folders that existed in the Outlook client. You will notice you have two files for every folder: the mail file itself and an index of what is in the file. If you try to open the file without the .msf extension in something such as Notepad, you will see it's a standard mbox mailfile. Some people have reported that Mozilla does not do the conversion.

Now you can copy all of these files over to the new system in whatever fashion you prefer—burn them to a CD, FTP them to the server, or use winscp to copy them over to the new system.

LibPST

LibPST is a Linux application that converts PST files into Mozilla-compatible mbox files. Therefore, once you have generated a PST file, you simply install and use LibPST on your Linux system to prepare the contents of your PST file for use with Mozilla. You can obtain LibPST from http://sourceforge.net/projects/ol2mbox. LibPST is ideal if you have a particularly large PST file that you need to convert. In many cases, Mozilla will fail to process it using its own conversion utility.

Importing Outlook Mail into Evolution

One way you can import Outlook Mail into Evolution is to use an application called Outport. You can download Outport from http://outport.sourceforge.net. For example, suppose you have a group of e-mail messages named Syngress in Outlook Express, similar to that shown in Figure 12.13.

Figure 12.13 E-mail Messages in Outlook

All you have to do is download Outport, and then double-click the outport.exe application. The Outport main interface will appear, as shown in Figure 12.14.

Figure 12.14 Using Outport to Export Messages from Outlook

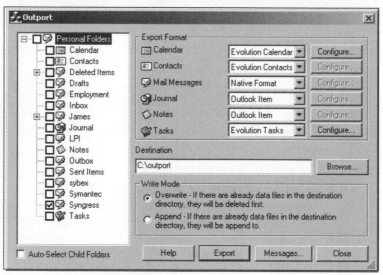

When the Outport interface appears, you can choose various Outlook elements to export, including:

- Outlook Calendar entries

- Contacts

- Mail messages

- Journal entries

- Notes

- Individual tasks

Before clicking the **Export** button, you will need to specify a destination directory. In the preceding example, the C:\outport directory is used. After clicking **Export**, Outport will convert and export the files into the Outport directory, where you can view them in a file manager, such as Windows Explorer, shown in Figure 12.15, or Gentoo, a file manager for Linux (www.obsession.se/gentoo).

Figure 12.15 Viewing Exported Messages in Windows Explorer

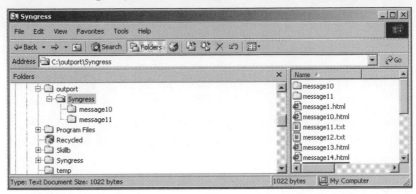

Once you have exported these files, you can then import them into Evolution or into another application so that you can more easily convert them into files that Evolution understands.

Document Standards

As you migrate e-mail and PIM software settings from Windows systems to Linux, you will have to become familiar with the following standards:

- **The Internet Calendaring and Scheduling Core Object Specification (iCalendar) standard** Known as Ical, it is defined in RFC 2445. Apple machines were among the first to adopt this standard. Used for personal calendars.

- **The Vcalendar standard (Vcal)** Used for making appointments.

- **Virtual Card standard (Vcard)** An electronic business card format meant to provide a uniform, textual representation of an event. It is a cross-platform way to represent a calendar event. Outport can export into these formats. This standard is defined in RFC 2426, and is used often used in PIM software.

The Hard Way

The least favorable migration option is to simply forward e-mail from a Windows client to the new Linux system. If you have to resort to this method, perhaps the easiest way is to forward an entire mail folder. Still, forwarding a large number of e-mail messages as one e-mail will probably guarantee that you will never find the e-mails again, unless you work hard to sift through (perhaps) dozens of attachments buried in a folder. Therefore, use your best judgment when forwarding e-mail.

Web Browsers

Web browsers are not just used to "surf the Web"; they can be used to launch embedded applications, check e-mail, and view groupware calendars. As a result, Web browsers are increasingly sophisticated, and must support various authentication and encryption schemes. In this section, we discuss how to choose the appropriate browser(s).

Most end users will expect their Linux systems to offer one (and only one) browser. With Windows, everyone tends to use Internet Explorer. This browser has been on every computer since Windows 98; many end users became accustomed to Internet Explorer on Windows 95 systems.

With Linux, however, there are several choices, including:

- Mozilla

- Firefox

- Galeon

- Konqueror

- Opera

No single Linux Web browser can meet everyone's needs. You will have to become familiar with many of the browsers available. In this section, we discuss the most important GUI-based browsers.

Mozilla

Mozilla, shown in Figure 12.16, is actually a group of applications that includes the Mozilla browser, Mozilla Mail, and Composer.

Mozilla's advantages include:

- **Tabbed browsing** The ability to see multiple pages in one window allows you to browse more efficiently.

- **The Gecko rendering engine** An engine that renders the Web pages quickly and efficiently.

- **Speed** The browser renders pages quickly and loads into memory quite easily.

- **Stability** The code is extensively reviewed, and it can be more stable than many other vendors' browsers.

- **Built-in pop-up blocking** You do not need to download third-party software to block pop-up ads if you are using Mozilla.

- **Built-in applications** You can view newsgroups and can use an Internet Relay Chat (IRC) client.

Figure 12.16 Mozilla

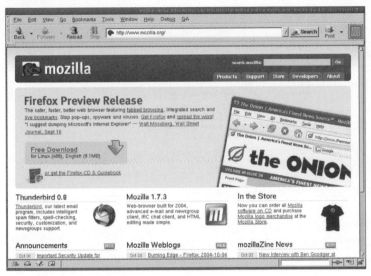

If you need a full-service package and do not want to deal with separate applications, choose Mozilla.

Mozilla and Microsoft CHAP

The Internet Information Services (IIS) Web server uses a special form of the Challenge Handshake Authentication Protocol (CHAP), called MS-CHAP. Microsoft designed IIS this way. The intent was that if an IIS administrator was to enable MS-CHAP, only those using Internet Explorer could authenticate securely.

However, Mozilla.org was able to implement MS-CHAP as of version 1.6. This is an important development, because it eliminates one more reason for remaining with Internet Explorer, which has experienced the most serious security problems.

Firefox

Firefox is a stand-alone browser based on the Gecko engine, just like Mozilla (see Figure 12.17).

Figure 12.17 Firefox

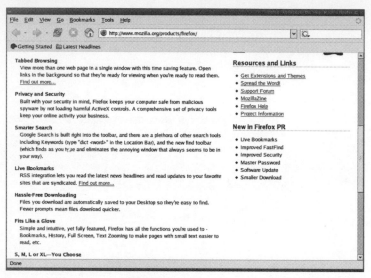

However, Firefox is not simply another form of Mozilla. Firefox has the following features:

- **Improved customization** From font choice to determining which buttons you will see, Firefox is designed to allow more customization.

- **Faster page rendering** Firefox has a more current version of the Gecko engine.

- **Smaller footprint** The Firefox developers have tried to keep the application's size down to roughly 4 MB.

If you do not mind using separate applications (for example, separate Web browsers and e-mail clients), then choose Firefox. Finally, Firefox benefits from MS-CHAP compatibility. You can learn more about Firefox at www.mozilla.org.

Galeon

Galeon is specially designed for the Gnome desktop. However, it uses Mozilla's Gecko rendering engine. Consequently, it is a solid choice if you want the stability and speed of the Gecko engine, and want to take advantage of the Gnome desktop environment. As good as Mozilla and Firefox are, they are not specifically designed to run in Gnome. Therefore, Galeon may load and render faster than any browser in an optimized Gnome environment. For more information about Galeon, go to http://galeon.sourceforge.net.

Konqueror

Konqueror, shown in Figure 12.18, is KDE's default browser. It uses the KHTML rendering engine. Interestingly, the new browser in Mac OS, Safari, uses the same rendering engine. If you are migrating over from Macintosh systems, Konqueror might be the best choice.

Figure 12.18 The Konqueror Web Browser

Of all the browsers profiled in this chapter, Konqueror is the only one meant specifically for Linux/UNIX systems. It is not a cross-vendor browser.

Opera

Opera is the only fee-based browser discussed in this chapter. To some companies, paying for software actually brings a sense of security. Paying for software, many feel, results in a stronger support contract. Opera's developers argue that Opera has the following advantages:

- The fastest rendering of any Web browser
- Tabbed browsing
- The ability to focus and "zoom in" on content
- IRC compatibility

In many ways, Opera offers the same features as Mozilla.

Migrating Bookmarks

You will find that migrating to a Linux browser is relatively easy, because virtually every browser that runs Linux automatically imports the bookmarks exported from Internet Explorer. The exported bookmark data is easily found. However, with recent versions of Internet Explorer, this data is stored in a directory. On our system, the Internet Explorer bookmarks are found in C:\Documents and Settings\james\Favorites.

Once you have installed Mozilla, Firefox, or Opera, this data is easier to get to since it will be stored in a single file. This file can be called bookmark.htm, bookmarks.htm, bookmark.html, or bookmarks.html, depending on the version of the browser. All you have to do is copy this file to the new Linux system when you migrate the operating system. Then, simply find the feature for managing bookmarks. In Firefox, for example, you would go to **Bookmarks | Manage Bookmarks**. When the Bookmarks Manager window opens, go to **File | Import**, and then select the **From File** option button. You can then select the Internet Explorer bookmark file you exported.

Browser Plug-Ins

Windows users are likely aware of dozens of browser plug-ins. In Linux, you will find a more limited set of plug-ins, although most of the essential ones are supported, including:

- Macromedia Flash, and Shockwave/Director
- RealNetworks Realplayer
- Adobe Acrobat Reader

Following is a discussion of each plug-in technology.

Macromedia Flash and Shockwave/Director

Macromedia Flash has been available in Linux for a number of years. It is relatively easy to install. However, Flash does not automatically upgrade itself in Linux as it does in Windows browsers. Make sure you understand that you will have to manually update your Flash plug-ins periodically.

Installing Flash is as simple as downloading it from Macromedia's Web site at www.flash.com. Once you download the file (for example, install_flash_player_7_linux.tar.gz), you simply unzip and untar it and then change to the install_flash_player_7_linux/ directory. You then run the flashplayer-installer script (for example, flashplayer-installer) and follow the onscreen instructions.

As of this writing, Macromedia Shockwave/Director can be installed in Linux only by using the CrossOver Office Plugins bundle, which we discuss later in this chapter. However, this will likely change, as Macromedia has begun demonstrating true interest in Linux, now that its market share has increased. Because there is virtually no business justification for it, though, few people other than graphic artists or home users will need this functionality. In short, if you need Shockwave/Director, install the CrossOver Office Plugins bundle.

RealPlayer

RealPlayer, shown in Figure 12.19, is one of the more essential plug-ins, because it allows you to view streaming media. You can use it for both streaming audio and video.

Figure 12.19 RealPlayer

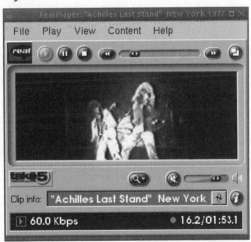

You can run RealPlayer from any of the Web browsers profiled in this chapter. For example, in Konqueror, you will be asked which application you want to use. Simply enter the name of the RealPlayer binary (for example, realplay), and you will be able to see or hear the media you have chosen. You can download the basic version of RealPlayer free of charge at www.realplay.com. You will have to meet with a consultant to discuss which version to use.

You may have to specify RealPlayer as a "helper application" in order to properly run streaming video. To do this, open the **Preferences** in any browser and access the appropriate window that allows you to define file associations. For example, in Konqueror, you would go to **Settings | Configure Konqueror**, and then select the **File Associations** screen. In Mozilla, you would go to **Edit | Preferences**, select **Helper Applications**, and then define the appropriate MIME type. Common MIME types for streaming media include:

- application/x-pn-realaudio (for rm and ram files)

- audio/x-realaudio (for ra files)

- audio/x-wav (for wav files)

Adobe Acrobat Reader

Another essential plug-in is Adobe Acrobat Reader, shown in Figure 12.20.

Figure 12.20 Acrobat Reader

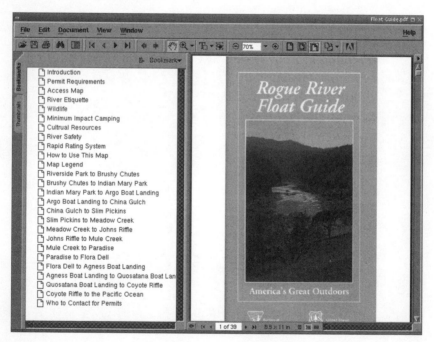

You may have to define the MIME type for PDF on certain browsers. MIME types you can define include:

- application/pdf

- application/x-pdf

- application/acrobat

- text/pdf
- text/x-psdf

We have always found application/pdf to be sufficient. Acrobat Reader is available free of charge at www.adobe.com.

Office Application Suites

You have already learned about migrating workstations to Linux-based e-mail/PIM clients and Web browsers. You will likely find a way to be happy managing e-mail and using browser-based applications. However, you do not simply use e-mail and Web browsers all day; you will need to create documents and presentations. "Where," you will ask, "is Microsoft Word?" You will also want to know where your Excel and PowerPoint applications are. In other words, you will want to know if you will be able to work with your files.

You will want to do your jobs, and you will not want the operating system to "get in the way." Managers will be concerned about lost productivity. You will need to receive assurance from a consultant that even though you will be migrating from Microsoft Office, you will remain productive. You will need to be shown that you will:

- Still be able to work with your .doc, .rtf, .xls, and .ppt files.
- Become comfortable with new applications in an acceptable period of time.
- Be able to exchange files with others who will still be using Microsoft software.

The most common office software suites include:

- OpenOffice,org
- StarOffice
- KOffice
- Hancom Office

The following sections will discuss each suite.

OpenOffice.org

OpenOffice.org quickly became the standard for the Linux office suite when Sun introduced it in 1999. OpenOffice has several applications. The following are the most often used:

- **Star Writer (swriter)** A word processor; the equivalent of Microsoft Word.

- **Star Impress (simpress)** Slide presentation software; the equivalent of Microsoft PowerPoint.

- **Star Calc (scalc)** Spreadsheet software; the equivalent of Microsoft Excel.

- **Star Web (sweb)** Web page creation software; the equivalent of Microsoft FrontPage Express.

Basically, very little needs to be done to OpenOffice once you have it installed. If you share documents outside of your company, as many people do, you can make document sharing easier by telling OpenOffice to save in .doc, .xls, or .ppt format natively. This step is done by clicking **Tools | Options | Load&Save | General**, and in the standard file format section, make sure you select **Always save as Microsoft Word 97/2000/XP for Document type, text document**. Do the same for **Spreadsheet and Presentations**. Make sure you do not select templates, though, as this has to be done differently. You can learn more about OpenOffice at www.openoffice.org.

OpenOffice.org can open any document created in Microsoft Office 2000. For example, the document shown in Figure 12.21 was created in Microsoft Office 2000.

Figure 12.21 Star Writer

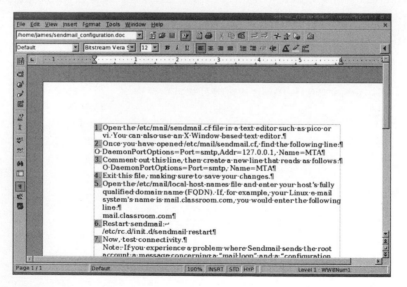

The document shown in Figure 12.21 was also modified by Office 2003. Figure 12.22 shows the Star Impress program. You can see that the interface is quite similar to PowerPoint.

Figure 12.22 Star Impress

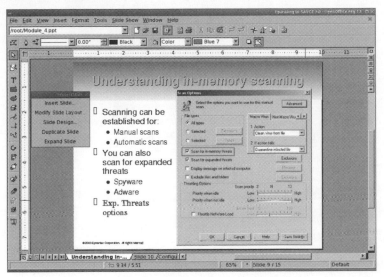

The document shown in Figure 12.22 was created in PowerPoint, and then opened in Star Impress. In fact, the majority of the slides created for this chapter were created in Star Impress. These slides were then sent to several individuals who used nothing but Microsoft PowerPoint. They were completely oblivious that the slides were created on a Linux system.

Figure 12.23 shows the Star Calc application opening a simple spreadsheet.

The spreadsheet in Figure 12.23 is relatively simple. However, most individuals will do little more with a spreadsheet than create rows and columns, and then calculate summaries. Notice also that this particular spreadsheet supports tabbed sheets.

Figure 12.23 Star Calc

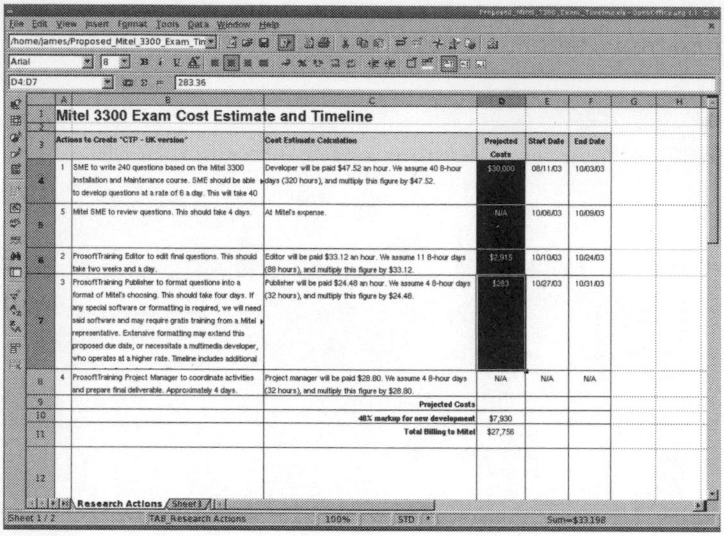

Limitations: Macros and PDF Files

With very few exceptions, PDF files are all easily read, created, or modified by OpenOffice. The exception to this rule is if you're using macros. Although these won't run natively on OpenOffice or any of the other alternatives, there is a way to rewrite your macros to work with OpenOffice, as it contains its own very powerful Macro Writer.

OpenOffice.org has the capability to create PDF files "on the fly." This feature is quite impressive, but is still not completely perfected. It is anticipated that future versions will offer production-quality PDF generation.

We have found that more complex templates do not work well in OpenOffice. This suggests that more complex work, such as that done by desktop publishers, may be too ambitious for OpenOffice.org. However, OpenOffice.org can handle the vast majority of your word processing, slide presentation creation, and spreadsheet development demands.

Nevertheless, the average end user will not encounter any difficulty using OpenOffice. Only those end users who engage in truly advanced word processing and spreadsheet creation will encounter problems. Microsoft Office 2003 has introduced features not supported by OpenOffice.org, as well as Office 2000 and Office XP. For example, Microsoft Office 2003 allows you to create editing restrictions on certain portions of a file. OpenOffice.org does not support this feature. It is important to understand, however, that many people have not upgraded their Office 2000 software to Office 2003, and that they, too, do not take advantage of these features.

One other weakness of OpenOffice.org is macro support. You cannot simply import all of your macros into StarOffice. At its best, recreating macros is never particularly fun. At its worst, it is an enormous time burden. If you require extensive macro support, we suggest that you read about CrossOver Office.

So don't let a consultant leave you with the impression that office suites such as OpenOffice.org will replace Microsoft Office painlessly. In some cases, you will end up disappointed. Make sure that you determine exactly what you need and make sure that any consultant you meet with has thoroughly tested a solution before recommending it.

Future Plans

It is likely that OpenOffice.org will be able to generate Shockwave Flash (SWF) files on the fly. Thus far, no office suite has this capability. OpenOffice.org already uses XML as the basis of its files. Consequently, this suite is capable of handling complex tasks. It is simply going to take time for OpenOffice.org to equal products such as Microsoft Office.

StarOffice

StarOffice is essentially a stable version of OpenOffice.org with the promise of customer support. Perhaps an analogy will help: StarOffice is to OpenOffice.org much like Netscape Navigator is to Mozilla. Just as Netscape takes a stable version of Mozilla and then sells it, Sun takes OpenOffice.org and sells it as StarOffice.

Corporations are becoming increasingly fond of StarOffice, because they can purchase customer support in case of a problem or bug. For a nominal fee, you receive customer support, Internet-based file storage, additional document templates, and increased macro support. You can learn more about StarOffice at www.staroffice.com.

KOffice

A project of the KDE team, KOffice is a fully functional replacement for Microsoft Office. Figure 12.24 shows the KWriter application, the default KDE text editor. Although more powerful than a simple text editor such as Wordpad or Notepad, it is nevertheless not as powerful as Star Writer.

Figure 12.24 KWriter

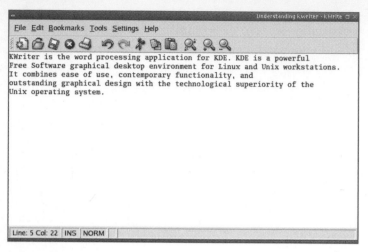

Hancom Office

Hancom Office is sold by a Korean company that has the following goals:

- Create a user-friendly suite that is compatible with Microsoft Office.

- Support a large number of languages. Extensive Unicode support means that Hancom office is also ideal if you need to support offices that process documents in Chinese (both simplified and traditional), Korean, and Arabic.

You can learn more about Hancom Office by going to www.hancom.com. One of the ways in which Hancom Office tries to ensure compatibility with Microsoft Office documents is an automatic update feature. This feature allows you to quickly obtain the latest filters and rendering engines.

One of the limitations of Hancom Office is that it does not support macros written in Visual Basic. Hancom Office does not improve upon OpenOffice.org or StarOffice in this regard.

Running Windows Applications on Linux

Every user in a company will not be able to be ported over to Linux at all times. Rather than concede defeat, you have two alternatives:

- **Use an emulator.** Install software that allows your Linux system to imitate, as it were, a Windows system. Once you get the emulator properly installed, all you have to do is install a Windows application on the Linux system. The emulator will then allow the Windows application to run directly from inside Linux.

- **Use remote desktop administration software.** Simply install a server that allows you to directly access the desktop through a Web browser or specialized application.

We'll now discuss each option.

Compatibility Layer Software

In many ways, the software discussed here is not emulation software. In the strictest sense, emulator software recreates the software application programming interfaces (APIs), and the actual functions of the CPU (for example, a Pentium chip). Wine, CrossOver Office, and Win 4 Lin Workstation do not recreate the architecture of the CPU. Therefore, they are technically not emulators.

Nevertheless, it is still common practice to lump this software into the emulator category, because using applications such as Wine, you can make your Linux system behave as if it were a Windows system. In fact, if you properly configure these applications, certain native Windows applications will run, thinking that they are in a Windows environment. These applications use sets of APIs to help convince native Windows applications that they are, in fact, running on Windows.

So, to avoid controversy, we will not call these applications "emulators," even though that's basically what they are. Taking the lead of the developers of Wine, we are calling these applications "compatibility layer software," because they all create a layer between the Linux operating system and the Windows application.

The benefit of this type of emulator, well, software, is that you can use native Windows applications directly from your Linux desktop. You do not have to rely on a network connection to another system. However, emulators can be somewhat tricky to configure, and the slightest change in the application's configuration can "break" your configuration and force a time-consuming and possibly costly service call.

As you prepare to use an emulator, ask the following questions:

- What version of the Windows operating system does the application require?

- Do you require access to raw data from inside Linux?

- How many people need to access these applications, and the resulting data from them, at one time? In short, what is the expected load on this system?

These questions will help you determine the correct hardware size, and the appropriate software. Now, let's look at some of the common emulators available.

Wine

Wine is an acronym for "Wine is not an emulator." Wine is meant to provide a replacement for Windows; it does not require Windows to run. Therefore, you do not need a Windows license to run a Windows application. You will, however, need a license to run the application. Suppose, for example, that you managed to run Microsoft Word on Wine. You would not need a license for the Microsoft Windows operating system. However, you would need to license Microsoft Word.

It is important to understand that Wine has enjoyed a "work in progress" standing for many years. Many Windows applications do run in Wine. A list of Windows applications verified to run in Wine is available at www.winehq.org/site/supported_applications.

A Web site called "Frank's Corner" (http://frankscorner.org) provides tips to help get various applications going. Applications that Frank has worked with include:

- Microsoft Office 2000
- Macromedia Flash MX
- PhotoShop 7.0

People have had significant success with Wine. However, Wine is not yet a "production quality" tool; it is more of an extended "hack in motion." The fact that your needed application runs today on the latest and greatest version of Wine is no guarantee that it will run properly when you upgrade to the next version. However, there is a much more reliable application: Code Weavers' CrossOver Office.

Code Weavers' CrossOver Office

CrossOver Office is essentially a perfected commercial version of Wine. CrossOver Office allows any Windows application to run smoothly (or, as smoothly as any application can run using compatibility software). As with Wine, if you use CrossOver Office you do not need to purchase a Windows license. You will find that with CrossOver Office, upgrades will not cause existing configurations to fail. In addition, CrossOver Office makes it possible to run all of the Visual Basic macros on which many Microsoft Office users rely.

CrossOver Office makes it relatively easy to install and run Windows applications in Linux. Still, there are drawbacks to this solution. First, CrossOver Office requires significant amounts of memory. In addition, not all of the features of your

Windows applications will be available. Therefore, although you may be able to run a copy of Macromedia Flash MX, you may still find some features missing.

In spite of these drawbacks, you will likely find that between the alternative programs discussed previously and applications such as CrossOver Office, you will be able to migrate any user to Linux. To learn more about CrossOver Office, go to www.codeweavers.com/site/products.

Summary

Choosing the appropriate desktop environment requires several skills. First, you need to know about the options. Second, you need to identify what you want and need. You then need to know how to match current technologies to your needs. In this chapter, you learned about available technologies and how to weigh them against your needs.

From common desktops such as Gnome and KDE to e-mail and Web applications, you learned how to choose solutions that can save you time and money. You also learned how to migrate settings and how to install native applications on Linux that cannot, for some reason, be replaced by their Linux counterparts.

This chapter helped you identify problems, possibilities, and solutions. Now that you are more familiar with Linux desktop solutions, continue your learning process by installing some of the software profiled in this chapter. The only way you can take the next step in your knowledge and ability to solve problems is to go through the process of installing the software.

Additional Resources

The following links provide more information related to alternatives to Microsoft products:

- Eastham, Chuck, and Bryan Hoff. *Moving from Windows to Linux, Second Edition.* Boston: Charles River Media, 2006 (www.charlesriver.com/books/BookDetail.aspx?productID=122989).

- *Fedora Core Linux* (http://fedora.redhat.com/).

- *Firefox Web Browser* (www.mozilla.com/firefox/).

- *Star Office Productivity Suite* (www.sun.com/software/star/staroffice/index.jsp).

Part IV:
Security Resources

Essential Network Communications

Topics in this appendix:

- Computer Protocols
- Communication Ports
- Understanding IP Addresses and DNS
- Managing IP Addresses
- TCP and UDP Protocols
- Firewalls

Introduction

In order to better secure your home computer or home network, it helps if you have some basic knowledge of how it all works so that you can understand what exactly you are securing and why. This appendix will help provide an overview of the terms and technology used and some of the tips, tricks, tools, and techniques you can use to make sure your computer is secure.

This appendix will provide an understanding of what these terms are so that when you read about the latest malicious code spreading through the Internet and how it gets into and infects your computer, you will be able to decipher the techie terms and determine if this affects you or your computer and what steps you can or should take to prevent it.

The information in this appendix is a little more technical than the rest of the book, and is included for those who want to learn a little more and gain a deeper understanding of how computer networking works and the technologies that make it work.

Computer Protocols

In the *Merriam-Webster Dictionary*, protocol is defined in listing 3b as, "A set of conventions governing the treatment and especially the formatting of data in an electronic communications system." I'm not sure that makes things much clearer to a layperson.

Put simply, if you called an orange an apple and I called it a plum we would never be able to communicate. At some point we would have to come to some agreement as to what to call it. For computers and the Internet there were many organizations coming up with their own proprietary way of formatting and transmitting data. To ensure that all computers would be able to talk to each other and not just to their "own kind," protocols were created and agreed to.

TCP/IP, which stands for Transmission Control Protocol/Internet Protocol, is not a single protocol. It is a set of communication standards. TCP and IP are the two main protocols of the bunch. TCP/IP has been accepted as the standard for Internet communications and comes packaged by default with all major operating systems.

To communicate using TCP/IP, each host must have a unique IP address. As we discussed earlier, your IP address is similar to your street address. It identifies your host on the Internet so that communications intended for you reach their destination.

Communication Ports

When you sit down to watch TV, you have to tune your TV to a specific frequency in order to view the Weather Channel. If you want the Disney Channel, you need to change to a different frequency. To view CNN, you need to set your TV to yet another frequency.

Similarly, when you are surfing the Internet, there is a certain port that is used when your computer wants to receive HTTP (Hypertext Transfer Protocol, used for viewing HTML or Web pages) traffic. To download files you might use FTP (File Transfer Protocol), which would be received on a different port. SMTP (Simple Mail Transfer Protocol, used for transmitting e-mail messages) communications would be received on a different port.

There are 65,536 ports available for use in TCP or UDP. They are divided into three ranges. The Internet Assigned Numbers Authority (IANA) manages the first 1,024 ports (0–1,023). This range is known as the well-known port numbers and includes standard default ports such as HTTP (port 80), FTP (port 21), and SMTP (port 25). These port numbers are reserved and should not be used arbitrarily.

The second range is the registered port numbers, which contains ports 1024 through 49151. The Registered Port Numbers can be used by ordinary programs and user processes that are executed by the user. The use of specific port numbers is not carved in stone. These ports are generally used transiently when needed.

The third range is the dynamic or private port numbers, which range from 49152 through 65535. These can be used by applications and processes initiated by the user, but it is uncommon. There are known Trojan horse and backdoor programs that use this extreme upper range so some security administrators are leery of traffic in this range.

TCP and UDP Protocols

One of the protocols that use this block of ports is TCP. TCP enables two hosts on the Internet to establish a connection with each other. One host will initiate the connection by sending a request to the other. That host will respond, agreeing to establish the connection. Finally, the originating host will respond once more to acknowledge receipt of the acceptance and the connection is established.

When data is fed to TCP, TCP breaks it into smaller, more manageable pieces called packets. A header is written for each packet, which specifies the originating IP address, the destination IP address, the sequence number, and some other key identifying information.

When the packets leave to traverse the Internet and get to their destination, they may not take the same path. There are thousands of routers, and complex algorithms help to decide from nanosecond to nanosecond which path is going to be the best path for the next packet. This means that the packets may not arrive at their destination in the same order they were sent out. It is the responsibility of the TCP protocol on the receiving end to look at the sequence number in the packet headers and put the packets back in order.

If there are missing packets, error messages are sent back to let the sending computer know to resend the data. TCP also does flow control by sending messages between the two hosts letting them know to speed up or slow down the rate of sending packets depending on network congestion and how fast the receiving computer can handle processing the incoming packets.

UDP is another protocol that works with IP networks. Unlike TCP, UDP does not establish a connection. UDP does not provide any sort of error protection or flow control. It is primarily used for broadcasting messages. The sending host gets no acknowledgement that the message was successfully received.

Because UDP does not take the time to set up a connection between the two hosts, perform flow control to monitor network congestion, or do the sort of error-checking and receipt acknowledgement that TCP does, it has much less overhead in terms of time and resources. Some services that benefit from this are DNS, SNMP, and streaming multimedia (for example, watching a video clip over the Internet).

Understanding IP Addresses and DNS

The term "host" can be confusing because it has multiple meanings in the computer world. It is used to describe a computer or server that provides Web pages. In this context, it is said that the computer is "hosting" the Web site. Host is also used to describe the companies that allow people to share their server hardware and Internet connection as a service rather than every company or individual having to buy all their own equipment.

A "host" in the context of computers on the Internet is defined as any computer that has a live connection with the Internet. All computers on the Internet are peers to one another. They can all act as servers or as clients. You can run a Web site on your computer just as easily as you can use your computer to view Web sites from other computers. The Internet is nothing more than a global network of hosts communicating back and forth. Looked at in this way, all computers, or hosts, on the Internet are equal.

Each host has a unique address similar to the way street addressing works. It would not work to simply address a letter to Joe Smith. You have to also provide the street address; for example, 1234 Main Street. However, there may be more than one 1234 Main Street in the world, so you must also provide the city: Anytown. Maybe there is a Joe Smith on 1234 Main Street in Anytown in more than one state, so you have to add that to the address as well. In this way, the postal system can work backward to get the mail to the right destination. First they get it to the right state, then to the right city, then to the right delivery person for 1234 Main Street, and finally to Joe Smith.

On the Internet, this is called your IP (Internet Protocol) address. The IP address is made up of four blocks of three numbers between 0 and 255. Different ranges of IP addresses are owned by different companies or ISPs (Internet service providers). By deciphering the IP address, it can be funneled to the right host. First it goes to the owner of that range of addresses; then it can be filtered down to the specific address it's intended for.

I might name my computer "My Computer," but there is no way for me to know how many other people named their computer "My Computer," so it would not work to try to send communications to "My Computer" any more than addressing a letter simply to "Joe Smith" would get delivered properly.

With millions of hosts on the Internet, it is virtually impossible for users to remember the IP addresses of each Web site or host they want to communicate with, so a system was created to enable users access sites using names that are easier to recall.

The Internet uses Domain Name Service (DNS) to translate the name to its true IP address to properly route the communications. For instance, you may simply enter "yahoo.com" into your Web browser. That information is sent to a DNS server, which checks its database and translates the address to something like 64.58.79.230, which the computers can understand and use to get the communication to its intended destination.

DNS servers are scattered all over the Internet, rather than having a single, central database. This helps to protect the Internet by not providing a single point of failure that could take down everything. It also helps speed up processing and reduces the time it takes for translating the names by dividing the workload among many servers and placing those servers around the globe.

In this way, you get your address translated at a DNS server within miles of your location, which you share with a few thousand hosts rather than having to communicate with a central server halfway around the planet that millions of people are trying to use.

Your ISP will most likely have its own DNS servers. Depending on the size of the ISP, it may have more than one DNS server and they may be scattered around the globe as well for the same reasons cited earlier. An ISP has the equipment and owns or leases the telecommunications lines necessary to establish a presence on the Internet. In turn, they offer access through their equipment and telecommunication lines to users for a fee.

The largest ISPs own the major conduits of the Internet referred to as the "backbone." Picture it the way a spinal cord goes through your backbone and acts as the central pipeline for communications on your nervous system. Your nervous system branches off into smaller paths until it gets to the individual nerve endings similar to the way Internet communications branch from the backbone to the smaller ISPs and finally down to your individual host on the network.

If something happens to one of the companies that provide the telecommunications lines that make up the backbone, it can affect huge portions of the Internet because a great many smaller ISPs that utilize that portion of the backbone will be affected as well.

Managing IP Addresses

Originally, IP addresses were manually coded to each computer. As the Internet exploded and millions of hosts were added, it became an overwhelming task to track which IP addresses were already in use or which ones were freed up when a computer was removed from the network.

DHCP (Dynamic Host Configuration Protocol) was created to automate this process. A DHCP server is given a block of addresses that it controls. Hosts that are configured to use DHCP will contact the DHCP server when they are turned on to request an IP address. The DHCP server will check its database of addresses and find one that is not in use to assign to the host. When the host is turned off or removed from the network, that IP address is released and the DHCP server can use it for a new host.

The exponential growth of the Internet caused a shortage in the available IP addresses similar to the way the growth of cell phones, pagers, and the like have caused a shortage of phone numbers. Unlike the phone system though, the Internet could not simply add a new prefix to the mix to create new phone numbers.

While the current version of the IP protocol (IPv6) is designed to allow for an exponential increase in the number of available addresses, the IPv4 protocol is still the primary version in use, and it was running dry fast.

NAT (Network Address Translation) can be used to expand the potential number of addresses. NAT essentially uses only one IP address to communicate on the Internet and a completely separate block of IP addresses on the local network. The local network addresses need to be unique from each other, but since the outside world will not see the local network addresses, they don't need to be unique to the world.

Without NAT, a company with 100 computers that wanted all 100 to connect to the Internet would need to have 100 separate public IP addresses. That same company using NAT would only need one public IP address and would assign the computers on the local network internal IP addresses.

This "hiding" of the internal IP addresses works not only to allow for more hosts to share the Internet, but also to provide a layer of security. By not allowing the outside world to know the precise IP addresses of your internal hosts, you take away a key piece of information that hackers could use to break into your network.

Firewalls

Now that we have covered TCP, UDP, and ports we can move on to discussing firewalls. A basic firewall is designed to block or control what traffic is allowed into or out of your computer or network. One way to do this is to simply block all incoming TCP and UDP traffic on all ports. For many home users this will work just fine. The firewall will still allow a response using the TCP or UDP ports through as long as the connection was initiated by your computer, but blocking in this manner will make sure no external computers can initiate a session with your computer.

If you do want to host a Web site or enable files to be downloaded from your computer using FTP, or enable other computers to connect to yours for online gaming, you will need to open the respective port. For example, to host a Web server, you would configure your firewall to block all incoming UDP and TCP traffic on all ports except port 80. On most basic home cable/DSL routers, the port-blocking firewall can be configured to allow traffic through a port to a specific host so that your other computers are still protected from this sort of traffic, but external hosts are able to access your Web server or game connection or whatever else you want.

This sort of basic firewall has some issues that can be exploited by hackers and malicious programmers to sneak through, which is why there are more advanced firewall systems. I mentioned that with this sort of port blocking, communications in response to connections initiated by your computer would be allowed through even on ports you were blocking. Using this knowledge, a hacker can forge the packet to make it look like it is a reply rather than an initiation of a connection and the firewall will allow it through.

Even on connections that are initiated by your computer, a malicious programmer can still exploit weaknesses in the system to sneak packets through. To guard against some of these weaknesses there are other types of firewalls: stateful inspection packet filters, circuit-level gateways, and application-level gateways to name a few.

Another consideration for firewalls is that it is not always enough to monitor or block inbound traffic. You may get a virus or Trojan horse program through a connection you initiated, thereby bypassing the firewall, or through e-mail. These malicious programs can open ports and initiate connections *from* your computer once they are planted there. Most software-based firewalls like Zone Alarm or Sygate, as well as more advanced hardware-based firewalls, will monitor outbound connections.

Case Study: SOHO (Five Computers, Printer, Servers, etc.)

Topics in this chapter:

- Introducing the SOHO Firewall Case Study
- Designing the SOHO Firewall
- Implementing the SOHO Firewall

☑ Summary

☑ Solutions Fast Track

☑ Frequently Asked Questions

Introduction

The Internet continues to grow as small businesses and home users realize the opportunities available to them with a wider audience for goods. Using personalized Web sites and e-mail addresses, as well as having a permanent Internet connection, creates a closer customer experience with remote users. This closeness comes at a price as systems are made accessible 24x7. With accessibility, unwelcome guests and customers have invitations to use the network. The exploitation of vulnerabilities on a system include misusing protocols, or applications, by connecting to an IP address on an open TCP or UDP port of a system on the network. Security for the home isn't as well developed as in a corporate environment. Users often do not have the time to become experts while maintaining their businesses or working remotely.

Using *netstat* to Determine Open Ports on a System

The *netstat* command does many useful things other than determining open ports on a system, including displaying memory and network buffer usage, system route table information, and interface statistics. To understand more about those options, read the documentation online about *netstat*. The following focuses on using *netstat* to determine the open ports and whether they should be open.

When a remote system or user wishes to access a service on your computer (e.g., Web server), the underlying OS on the remote system creates a connection to a port on your computer system on behalf of the remote user.

A process listening on a port will accept incoming connections to that port. A large part of securing your system from network attack is an audit of these services. Once you know what is running, you can turn off services that have opened ports that you don't need, and make sure to secure the services you do need. It will also establish a baseline as to what should be running. When the system starts acting sluggishly, or responding in an abnormal fashion, you can quickly check to make sure there are no rogue processes running on unrecognized ports.

The *−a* flag tells *netstat* "show the state of all sockets." One understanding of a socket is as a listening port. The *-n* flags tells *netstat* to not attempt to resolve names via DNS. This is generally a good practice because you remove a dependency on working DNS, and *netstat* will return information more quickly. If you need to look up an IP-to-name mapping, you can always do that later with the *host*, *nslookup*, or *dig* commands.

Here is an example of *netstat* output using the *−a* and *−n* flags.

Sample *netstat*—Output on a UNIX Server

```
Active Internet connections (including servers)
Proto Recv-Q Send-Q  Local Address          Foreign Address          State
tcp        0      0  6.7.8.9.60072     221.132.43.179.113     SYN_SENT
tcp        0      0  6.7.8.9.25        221.132.43.179.48301   ESTABLISHED
tcp        0    120  6.7.8.9.22        24.7.34.163.1811       ESTABLISHED
tcp        0      0  6.7.8.9.60124     67.46.65.70.113        FIN_WAIT_2
tcp        0      0  127.0.0.1.4000    127.0.0.1.60977        ESTABLISHED
tcp        0      0  127.0.0.1.60977   127.0.0.1.4000         ESTABLISHED
tcp        0      0  *.4000                 *.*               LISTEN
tcp        0      0  6.7.8.9.22        24.7.34.163.50206      ESTABLISHED
tcp        0      0  6.7.8.9.62220     216.120.255.44.22      ESTABLISHED
tcp        0      0  6.7.8.9.22        24.7.34.163.65408      ESTABLISHED
tcp        0      0  6.7.8.9.22        67.131.247.194.4026    ESTABLISHED
tcp        0      0  6.7.8.9.64015     217.206.161.163.22     ESTABLISHED
tcp        0      0  6.7.8.9.22        82.36.206.162.48247    ESTABLISHED
tcp        0      0  *.80                   *.*               LISTEN
tcp        0      0  *.993                  *.*               LISTEN
tcp        0      0  *.25                   *.*               LISTEN
tcp        0      0  *.22                   *.*               LISTEN
tcp        0      0  *.21                   *.*               LISTEN
tcp        0      0  127.0.0.1.53           *.*               LISTEN
tcp        0      0  6.7.8.9.53        *.*                LISTEN
udp        0      0  127.0.0.1.123          *.*
udp        0      0  6.7.8.9.123       *.*
udp        0      0  *.123                  *.*
udp        0      0  *.65510                *.*
udp        0      0  127.0.0.1.53           *.*
udp        0      0  6.7.8.9.53        *.*
Active Internet6 connections (including servers)
Proto Recv-Q Send-Q  Local Address          Foreign Address          (state)
tcp6       0      0  *.25                   *.*               LISTEN
tcp6       0      0  *.22                   *.*               LISTEN
udp6       0      0  fe80::1%lo0.123        *.*
udp6       0      0  :: 1.123               *.*
udp6       0      0  fe80::2e0:81ff:f.123   *.*
udp6       0      0  *.123                  *.*
udp6       0      0  *.65509                *.*
```

```
Active UNIX domain sockets
Address   Type   Recv-Q Send-Q    Inode      Conn      Refs  Nextref Addr
c204c440 dgram       0      0         0 c1fd80c0       0 c2026540 ->
/var/run/lo
g
c20fd040 stream      0      0         0 c1fcd3c0       0        0
c1fcd3c0 stream      0      0         0 c20fd040       0        0
c1fd3300 stream      0      0         0 c1fd8680       0        0
c1fd8680 stream      0      0         0 c1fd3300       0        0
c2129e40 stream      0      0         0 c20db500       0        0
c20db500 stream      0      0         0 c2129e40       0        0
c204cb40 stream      0      0         0 c20fdb00       0        0
c20fdb00 stream      0      0         0 c204cb40       0        0
c20fdc00 stream      0      0         0 c2129800       0        0
c2129800 stream      0      0         0 c20fdc00       0        0
c2026540 dgram       0      0         0 c1fd80c0       0 c1f9c740 ->
/var/run/lo
g
c1f9c740 dgram       0      0         0 c1fd80c0       0        0 ->
/var/run/lo
g
c1fd80c0 dgram       0      0 cc32615c          0 c204c440       0
/var/run/log
c1fd8300 dgram       0      0 cc3260b4          0        0       0
/var/chroot/na
med/var/run/log
```

Examine the parts that have TCP and UDP ports in the first section of the output. Unless you're actively running IPv6, you can safely ignore the tcp6, and udp6 output. Additionally, UNIX domain sockets are local within the machine and not network related.

Sample *netstat*—TCP Output on a UNIX Server

```
tcp        0        0  6.7.8.9.60072   221.132.43.179.113       SYN_SENT
tcp        0        0  6.7.8.9.25      221.132.43.179.48301     ESTABLISHED
tcp        0      120  6.7.8.9.22      24.7.34.163.1811         ESTABLISHED
tcp        0        0  6.7.8.9.60124   67.46.65.70.113          FIN_WAIT_2
tcp        0        0  127.0.0.1.4000      127.0.0.1.60977
ESTABLISHED
tcp        0        0  127.0.0.1.60977     127.0.0.1.4000
ESTABLISHED
```

```
tcp       0       0  *.4000                    *.*               LISTEN
tcp       0       0  6.7.8.9.22         24.7.34.163.50206        ESTABLISHED
tcp       0       0  6.7.8.9.62220      216.120.255.44.22        ESTABLISHED
tcp       0       0  6.7.8.9.22         24.7.34.163.65408        ESTABLISHED
tcp       0       0  6.7.8.9.22         67.131.247.194.4026      ESTABLISHED
tcp       0       0  6.7.8.9.64015      217.206.161.163.22       ESTABLISHED
tcp       0       0  6.7.8.9.22         82.36.206.162.48247      ESTABLISHED
tcp       0       0  *.80                      *.*               LISTEN
tcp       0       0  *.993                     *.*               LISTEN
tcp       0       0  *.25                      *.*               LISTEN
tcp       0       0  *.22                      *.*               LISTEN
tcp       0       0  *.21                      *.*               LISTEN
tcp       0       0  127.0.0.1.53              *.*               LISTEN
tcp       0       0  6.7.8.9.53                *.*               LISTEN
```

Notice the last field contains different words like *ESTABLISHED* and *LISTEN*. This denotes the state of the socket. The sockets that show active services waiting for connections are lines that contain LISTEN. The * fields describes a port open to any IP address, so *.80 in the local address field tells us that this machine has port listening on every IP interface in this machine. Generally, a system will only have one IP address, but occasionally can have multiple interfaces.

So, a short way of getting the listening TCP ports on a UNIX system would be netstat -an | grep LISTEN, extracting only the LISTEN lines.

```
slick: {8} netstat -an | grep LISTEN
tcp       0       0  *.4000                    *.*               LISTEN
tcp       0       0  *.80                      *.*               LISTEN
tcp       0       0  *.993                     *.*               LISTEN
tcp       0       0  *.25                      *.*               LISTEN
tcp       0       0  *.22                      *.*               LISTEN
tcp       0       0  *.21                      *.*               LISTEN
tcp       0       0  127.0.0.1.53              *.*               LISTEN
tcp       0       0  6.7.8.9.53         *.*             LISTEN
tcp6      0       0  *.25                      *.*               LISTEN
tcp6      0       0  *.22                      *.*               LISTEN
```

Okay, we have a list of TCP, so let's move on to the UDP section. UDP doesn't have any state field, because unlike TCP, UDP is a stateless protocol model. Each packet is discrete and disconnected in any way to the previous packet arriving on that port. There is no provision in the protocol for retransmission of dropped packets. Applications like NTP and DNA rely on UDP.

```
slick: {9} netstat -an | grep udp
udp       0       0    127.0.0.1.123            *.*
udp       0       0    10.1.2.3.123       *.*
udp       0       0    *.123                    *.*
udp       0       0    *.65510                  *.*
udp       0       0    127.0.0.1.53             *.*
udp       0       0    10.1.2.3.53        *.*
udp6      0       0    fe80::1%lo0.123          *.*
udp6      0       0    ::1.123                  *.*
udp6      0       0    fe80::2e0:81ff:f.123     *.*
udp6      0       0    *.123                    *.*
udp6      0       0    *.65509                  *.*
```

Ignore the udp6 (IPV6) lines. The third field is the same as the TCP output from before. This is the listening address and port. The IP address of this machine is 6.7.8.9, and there is a localhost interface, 127.0.0.1, for local TCP and UDP communication. 127.0.0.1 is the localhost and not visible to the Internet.

Anything that is not recognizable and requires further information should be audited.

Sample Ports Requiring Auditing

```
tcp       0       0    *.4000                   *.*                       LISTEN
tcp       0       0    *.80                     *.*                       LISTEN
tcp       0       0    *.993                    *.*                       LISTEN
tcp       0       0    *.25                     *.*                       LISTEN
tcp       0       0    *.22                     *.*                       LISTEN
tcp       0       0    *.21                     *.*                       LISTEN
tcp       0       0    127.0.0.1.53             *.*                       LISTEN
tcp       0       0    6.7.8.9.53         *.*                 LISTEN
udp       0       0    10.1.2.3.123       *.*
udp       0       0    *.123                    *.*
udp       0       0    *.65510                  *.*
udp       0       0    10.1.2.3.53        *.*
```

Now we need to figure out what processes on the local system correspond to those services. Looking in the/etc/services file, we can determine what UNIX services usually reside on these ports. This does not mean that a service hasn't hijacked a well-known port specifically to hide its footprint, but it gives us a better idea of what could be running.

Sample /etc/services Output

```
ftp             21/tcp          # File Transfer Protocol
ssh             22/tcp          # Secure Shell
ssh             22/udp
telnet          23/tcp
# 24 - private
smtp            25/tcp          mail
# 26 - unassigned
time            37/tcp          timserver
time            37/udp          timserver
```

Looking at the audited ports, we can determine what service is potentially being served and whether this service should be open to the outside world to function correctly. Recording the information for later use will help us determine problems in the future (see Table B.1).

Table B.1 Partially Audited Ports

Connection Type	IP + PORT	Possible Service
tcp	*.4000	
tcp	*.80	Web server
tcp	*.993	IMAPS server
tcp	*.25	SMTP server
tcp	*.22	Secure shell
tcp	*.21	FTP server
tcp	6.7.8.9.53	DNS server

There is no way to know that this service is actually what is being used on the port without querying the system. We use another useful tool, *lsof*, to inspect each open port.

Determining More Information with *lsof*

Query the kernel data structures to return what process is associated with each particular port. The command that allows us to do this deep digging is *lsof*. This is a tool for listing open files on a UNIX system. In the UNIX world, pretty much everything is a file, and so *lsof* will also list open ports, and tell you which process is holding that port open.

lsof also has many flags, but we will keep it to a few simple examples. We examine a UDP connection on port 53. From the following output, we can see that it is named, which serves DNS as expected.

```
slick: {38} lsof -n -i UDP:53
COMMAND  PID  USER    FD   TYPE     DEVICE SIZE/OFF NODE NAME
named    1177 named   20u  IPv4 0xc1f5f000      0t0  UDP 6.7.8.9:domain
named    1177 named   22u  IPv4 0xc1f5f0d8      0t0  UDP 127.0.0.1:domain
```

Checking UDP port 65510, we see that it is also named. This is most likely the rndc control channel.

```
slick: {39} lsof -n -i UDP:65510
COMMAND  PID  USER    FD   TYPE     DEVICE SIZE/OFF NODE NAME
named    1177 named   24u  IPv4 0xc1f5f1b0      0t0  UDP *:65510
```

Examining TCP port 4000 with *lsof*, we see that this is a user process. We should talk to user Paul and discover what the service running on port 4000 is.

```
slick: {40} lsof -n -i TCP:4000
COMMAND   PID USER    FD   TYPE     DEVICE SIZE/OFF NODE NAME
telnet  16192 paul     3u  IPv4 0xc2065b44      0t0  TCP 127.0.0.1:60977-
>127.0.0.1:4000 (ESTABLISHED)
razors  22997 paul     4u  IPv4 0xc1ff2ca8      0t0  TCP *:4000 (LISTEN)
razors  22997 paul    16u  IPv4 0xc206516c      0t0  TCP 127.0.0.1:4000-
>127.0.0.1:60977 (ESTABLISHED)
```

Using *netstat −an*, create a list of listening ports. With *lsof*, check each of these ports to figure out what processes are actually listening, and confirm that the services match the processes as expected. Figure out if those processes are needed, and either turn them off, or set up an ACL on your firewall to allow that service through.

Using *netstat* on Windows XP

With Windows XP, there are additional flags *−b*, *-v*, and *−o* that will show additional information. *−b* displays the executable involved in creating the connection. In the following example, you can see that Apache is running on the local system and it has port 80 open. *−v* when used with *−b* will display the sequence of components that created the connection. *−o* will display the process that has the port open (see Table B.2).

```
C:\Documents and Settings\jdavis>netstat -anvb


Active Connections
```

```
Proto   Local Address            Foreign Address        State          PID
TCP     0.0.0.0:80               0.0.0.0:0              LISTENING      1268
C:\WINDOWS\system32\imon.dll
C:\Program Files\Apache Software Foundation\Apache2.2\bin\libapr-1.dll
C:\Program Files\Apache Software Foundation\Apache2.2\bin\libhttpd.dll
C:\Program Files\Apache Software Foundation\Apache2.2\bin\httpd.exe
C:\WINDOWS\system32\kernel32.dll
[httpd.exe]


TCP     0.0.0.0:135              0.0.0.0:0              LISTENING      252
C:\WINDOWS\system32\imon.dll
C:\WINDOWS\system32\RPCRT4.dll
c:\windows\system32\rpcss.dll
C:\WINDOWS\system32\svchost.exe
C:\WINDOWS\system32\ADVAPI32.dll
[svchost.exe]
```

Table B.2 Common Ports Associated with Popular Services

20 FTP data	68 DHCP	123 NTP	161 SNMP	993 SIMAP
21 FTP	79 Finger	137 NetBIOS	194 IRC	995 SPOD
22 SSH	80 http	138 NetBIOS	220 IMAP3	1433 MS SQL Svr
23 SMTP	110 POP3	139 NetBIOS	389 LDAP	2049 NFS
43 whois	115 SFTP	143 IMAP	443 SSL	5010 Yahoo! Messenger
53 DNS	119 NNTP		445 SMB	5190 AOL Messenger

Closing all ports on a system makes the system useless on a network. Anytime a browser is used, or e-mail, is read, traffic is tunneling across open ports. Protect ports by using a firewall.

NOTE

As an individual worrying about the needs of a SOHO's firewall infrastructure, also make sure you "AUDiT" your systems by following these basic security steps to better ensure the company's security:

Apply the latest patches to any systems. This could be as simple as turning on Windows Auto Updater, or downloading the latest security patches for your favorite Linux distribution.

Update any firmware on appliances you are running. This includes the firewall, the printer, the wireless router, and any other networked appliance if applicable.

Determine which data is critical data. Set up an automated process for backing up that data. Make sure to have copies of those backups in multiple locations.

Turn off unneeded services on your servers, and appliances.

Due to the small size of a SOHO, there is often a misconception that there is no need for a firewall, that the company is insignificant to any would-be crackers or script kiddies. Everyone connected to the Internet should be aware of the potential dangers inherent in the medium. Just as you don't leave your front door open for any would-be thieves, the "front door" and any other open access points into the SOHO should be protected. Every open port on an Internet-visible host is an open access point into your system.

By visiting random Web sites or opening dangerous e-mail, a user exposes himself to potential virus infections. Every time a user interacts with other systems on the Internet, his IP address is logged. Using this IP address, malicious users can hack in to the network using known vulnerabilities with standard applications. The malicious user will be looking for credit card numbers, bank accounts, or passwords to subscription Web sites, among other activities. For future abuse of the network, the malicious user could install a Trojan horse that would allow him to revisit the system later.

NOTE

A firewall doesn't solve all the potential security risks. It is a perimeter security measure that will stop a percentage of attacks. It will help prevent systems from being zombiefied and then attack other systems and networks.

Additionally, if a malicious user manages to crack a valid user's password, he can access the internal network with that user's credentials. Then it is just a matter of taking advantage of the vulnerabilities on the systems to get elevated privileges.

There are a number of Internet-ready devices on the market to address the needs of a SOHO firewall. Depending on the number of servers, and environment of the SOHO, it is also possible to install and manage a firewall built on top of NetBSD, Linux, or other familiar OSes. Some appliances come with VPN features for remote access to network and resources. By using one of the Internet-ready devices, you lower the bar to entry in getting your firewall set up and blocking the traffic needed.

This chapter and the case study explore the SOHO firewall. They examine the advantages, problems, and possible solutions, and then extend to design and implementation of a simple firewall solution that includes a VPN.

Employing a Firewall in a SOHO Environment

Any system is vulnerable to infiltration, infection, and compromise in a network. Systems can be turned into zombie systems and then remotely controlled by the attacker, and used to attack other systems and networks. E-mail, future project plans, and competitive information could expose the company to an unknown degree of liability. This would brand a company to its customers, and potential customers as less than reliable. Do not be the low-hanging fruit that is easily snatched by an attacker. Safeguard yourself, company, brand name, and customers by seriously analyzing your security needs. As one aspect of a comprehensive security solution, the firewall protects the home and small office from external attack by only allowing authorized users and applications to gain access, while allowing network pass through for authentic data.

Host-Based Firewall Solutions

Use a host-based firewall as one element in your defense in-depth strategy, but do not rely on that application alone to protect your data and systems. Zone Fire Alarm, Windows XP Internet Connection Firewall, and other host-based firewalls protect individual systems. Having a firewall that sits outside the system that runs the applications you are using means the firewall is protecting all your assets in a unified fashion, minimizing problems of application interference. If a host-based firewall solution crashes, it can take the system down with it. If an appliance crashes, only the appliance is affected. Finally, a host-based firewall uses the resources of your system to protect you. An appliance does not take away CPU, and memory resources, to protect access to resources.

Make sure to update all systems on a regular basis for patches, or updates to applications. Install antivirus software, antispyware software, and a software firewall to the host. This will harden the host considerably. Protect the system behind a firewall appliance. This creates two layers of protection for each system.

Introducing the SOHO Firewall Case Study

The following case study illustrates the design of a simple SOHO firewall intended for the average user without much hands-on systems or security experience. The user is interested in securing his networked business assets, while allowing his family general use of the broadband network access. He wants to protect all systems from attack on the outside, and prevent dangerous outgoing traffic. He also wants to encourage external traffic to a personalized company Web site, and to interact with his customers with a personalized e-mail address. This section describes the user's current situation, the problem, the proposed solution, and the implementation of the solution.

Assessing Needs

Tom Little is a sole trader in the home office space. He has set aside a room in his home as an office for tax deductions. He has two desktops in his office that are the core of his business infrastructure. One contains billing invoices, customer account information, and account management software that his wife uses in her role as secretary for the business. The other system includes all of his e-mail correspondence with vendors and customers, and his project plans for the various accounts he is currently working. Tom has a printer connected to his main work system that is shared. Tom has a networked 160GB Ethernet hard drive on which he stores backups of his files. He also uses his laptop connected to the network.

Tom's two children have their own PCs. Tom grants them Internet time while watching over them, allowing them to explore and broaden their knowledge in a supervised environment.

Tom currently has broadband access to his home. All his systems are connected via cat 5 cable from the DSL router provided by his ISP.

Tom wants to create a more segregated network. He also wants to move the kids' systems out of his office. He plans to implement a wireless solution to allow him to access his business resources remotely with his laptop. He also wants a personalized Web site and e-mail address so he can e-mail his clients from a @company.com address rather than the @yahoo.com address he has been using. Tom does a little investigation of the products available and realizes many of the solutions are well within his budget (see Figure B.1).

Figure B.1 Tom's Current Network Topology

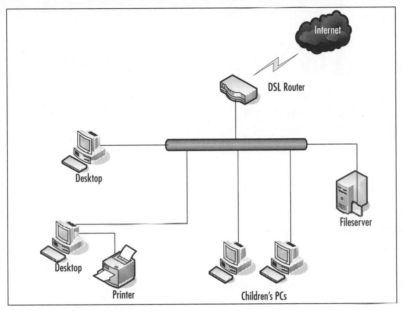

Defining the Scope of the Case Study

Tom's challenge is that he needs to protect his company's assets without interfering with the running of his business, or his family's access to the Internet. All equipment he uses must be readily available, and inexpensive.

Designing the SOHO Firewall

This section explains how Tom determines his needs, and plans, designs, and implements a firewall with VPN. Tom learns more about the available features, differences in firewall technology, and costs of different vendor solutions. Tom proceeds by:

- Determining the requirements.
- Analyzing the existing environment.
- Creating a preliminary design.
- Developing a detailed design.
- Implementing the firewall with VPN and modifying the network.

Tom begins his investigation by:

- Determining the functional requirements of his family and business.
- Talking to local user groups for recommendations.
- Drawing a physical map of his home.

Determining the Functional Requirements

The users of the network are Tom, his wife, and their children. Tom and his wife both use the Internet for recreational purposes, and for the home business. His children use the Internet for school projects, and gaming. Tom works with his family to define expectations of the home network.

Determining the Needs of the Family

Although Tom's wife sees the benefits of separating the children's PCs from the home office, she is worried that she won't be able to get the access she needs to the Internet. She also doesn't see how she will be able to supervise the kids' browsing habits.

The kids aren't sure how they will be able to print their school papers, and are concerned that a firewall will adversely affect the bandwidth that is available for their gaming. They are excited about having the computers in their own space.

Tom plans to buy his wife a laptop to facilitate her working remotely and watching over the kids, and a printer for the kids to print their schoolwork. Tom is considering either running a Web server, and e-mail server locally, or paying for hosted services. This limits his budget for modifying his network to include a firewall to $200.

Talking to Local User Groups

Tom has heard of the local user group BayLISA, a group of system and network administrators ranging in skill levels. The group meets once per month to discuss issues related to their professions. It can also be a social atmosphere. Tom decides to e-mail the group with a detailed list of his problem. He registers with the BayLISA group by sending an e-mail to the mailing list manager majordomo@baylisa.org with the body "subscribe baylisa." He follows the verification mechanism. After watching traffic for a few days, he submits his request.

Tom receives a number of responses from his query and notes all of the information. He categorizes product recommendations and experience separate from the general comments about his problems. Many users recommend he use a hosted site, as he does not have the expertise to manage a Web or e-mail server. He could accidentally expose all his private files with the Web server, and expose his business network to more vulnerabilities by having incorrectly configured servers, or nonpatched servers.

He is reassured that the process of setting up a wireless network is painless, so he can move his children's computers out of the office. Additionally, although he could set up a firewall on a Linux- or Unix-based system, he doesn't have the finances to spend on the hardware, or the expertise to support the OS, applications, and firewall tuning that would be required. He is better off purchasing a firewall appliance he just has to remember to update regularly.

Creating a Site Survey of the Home

Based on his preliminary investigations and guidance from the user group, Tom comes up with the following design considerations:

- He needs to purchase a firewall with VPN capabilities.

- He needs to purchase a wireless access point to connect the laptops and children's systems.

- He needs to purchase two wireless cards for the children's desktop computers.

- He needs to invest in a hosted service plan that will allow him to have a personalized Web site, and e-mail address.

The next step is to analyze the existing environment. This includes:

- Identifying current technology options and constraints.

- Investigating the costs.

- Weighing the costs and benefits of each solution.

Tom determines that there is an equal amount of business, school, and entertainment content being used for the broadband access. He determines the second printer for the kids is a good choice, as it will limit the access the children need to the office network. He also determines that he does not want the Web server, and e-mail server, affecting the family's bandwidth, so he has decided to remotely host these services.

Tom's existing network is very simple. The broadband service is delivered to the house from a DSL modem. From the modem, the service is wired to the PCs via a cat 5 Ethernet cable. The printer is a peripheral of his main business PC via the PC's serial port. It is shared out to the local network. The networked disk is connected via a cat 5 Ethernet cable that sits

Identifying Current Technology Options and Constraints

After talking to the local user groups, exploring the options available on the store shelves, and doing searches on the Internet using the words *SOHO firewall best practices*, Tom realizes he has several options in configuring his firewall.

Tom creates a list of the options available so he can better examine the choices he has to make. He fills out a list of important features, technical specs, and the pricing associated for each model. His list looks similar to Table B.3 with a column for each solution.

Table B.3 Vendor Feature List

Vendor		Netgear
Product	Website	Prosafe FVS 114
Features		
	Firewall Type	Stateful Packet Inspection
	VPN Type	IPSec (ESP, AH), MD5, SHA-1, DES, 3DES, IKE, PKI, AES
	Intrusion Prevention	Y
	Intrusion Detection	Y
	Antivirus Protection	N
	Content Filtering	Some
	Update Mechanism	Via Web Browser
	Licensing	NA
	Management	Via Web Browser
Technical		
	Processor	200 MHz 32-bit RISC
	OS	
	Memory	2MB Flash, 16MB SDRAM
	Ports	4
	Wireless	N
	Console/Modem	N
	Certifications	VPNC Compliant
Price		$79.99

He then populates the list with the various vendor offerings he finds at the local Fry's Electronics, Best Buy, and online listings. He would prefer to purchase the hardware locally, because if it doesn't work, he wants the ease of returning it quickly. He quickly determines that the Linksys Wireless G Broadband Router, at $59.99, and the Netgear Prosafe VPN Firewall model FVS 114, at $79.99, fit perfectly into his budget and have all the functionality he needs.

Implementing the SOHO Firewall

This section describes at a high level how Tom builds his firewall protected VPN accessible network. He approaches the implementation by:

- Assembling the network components.
- Installing the components.
- Testing the configuration from the various access points.

Assembling the Components

Tom visits his local hardware store, Fry's Electronics, and picks up a Linksys Wireless G Broadband Router, a Netgear Prosafe VPN Firewall model FVS 114, and two ASUS 802.11b/g Wireless LAN cards. He already has the cat 5 cables that will connect his business systems to the firewall.

Installing the Components

Tom is reasonably experienced with hardware installation, having previous upgraded the children's desktops. He feels comfortable having assembled the components, and tools, so he shouldn't have any problems putting the network together.

Remote Virtual DMZ

After looking at the various options available for hosting his Web and e-mail servers, Tom chooses to go with the Yahoo! Small Businesses Services site. He has been using his @yahoo.com address for years and has not had any problems with it. He knows that Yahoo! has a reliable and redundant network due to the nature of its business. He is also impressed with their use of regular snapshots, and backups of Web sites. He feels secure in the knowledge that his Web site will not just disappear at a moment's notice. Tom searches for a descriptive domain name widgets.com at http://smallbusiness.yahoo.com/webhosting. He tries tomswidgets.com, and it is available. He clicks on **compare all plans**. Looking at the disk space and other features, he realizes that for now, he just needs the starter plan. He pays a $25 setup fee and $11.95 for 5GB of space, 200 possible business e-mail addresses, and other features. He knows that it will take approximately 24 hours before his domain is live, but he is immediately able to begin editing the site. His wife logs in to the site, and replicates a brochure she made for the company using the site builder tools.

He is investing in a solution that means he doesn't have to rely on understanding all the technical decisions on how to build a reliable, fault-tolerant mail and Web server solution, and manage the spam and anti-virus protection for his inbound and outbound e-mail. For now, the space will just hold his Widget catalog, and contact information but his wife has many creative ideas on how to improve the site.

This solution has created a remote virtual DMZ that separates his Web server and mail server from his home systems. It maximizes his time in not having to manage servers that would also consume the bandwidth into his home.

Installing the Wireless Cards

Tom puts on an antistatic wristband before he opens the children's PCs. He unplugs the power, and all of the cables, and sets the systems on a flat working surface. He opens each PC in turn, attaching the wristband to the metal frame of the computer. He unscrews the screw holding the metal guard in place in front of the open PCI slot. He inserts one of the cards carefully, pushing until he feels the card firmly click into place. He repeats the procedure on the second computer. Tom closes each system, noting the MAC address for each card. He powers the systems back on after plugging them in. The Add New Hardware wizard appears, and Tom follows the instructions for installing the software for the cards. He confirms that the MAC addresses are what he expects by opening a command window with **Start | Run | command**. He types **ipconfig /all** and sees

```
Ethernet adapter Wireless Network Connection:


        Media State . . . . . . . . . . . : Media disconnected
        Description . . . . . . . . . . . : ASUS 802.11b/g Wireless LAN Card
        Physical Address. . . . . . . . . : 00-11-E6-AB-24-9C
```

He repeats this process on the second computer. While he is noting down MAC addresses, he checks the two laptops to confirm their addresses.

Configuring the Wireless Router

Tom plugs in the wireless router into the DSL modem. He follows the instructions for connecting to the wireless router that came with the packaging. He first sets the wireless network name to WiHoInc and disables the SSID broadcast. According to the user group postings, this makes it less likely that individuals trolling for wireless access will discover his wireless network.

> **NOTE**
>
> The default username and password for the wireless router is blank username, and admin for the password. Change this as soon after the basic configuration.

He enables WPA Pre-Shared key, chooses AES for encryption, and creates a reasonable length shared key "Widgets for the Win." This is a pass phrase that will be easy for him to remember, but not easy for others to take advantage of. He records it in his PDA device in an encrypted format where he keeps the rest of his passwords that access his important data.

He enables MAC filtering, which will allow him to permit only PCs listed to access the wireless network. He edits the MAC filter address and adds his children's PCs, and the two laptops.

He clicks the **Security** tab, and enables the firewall protection. Although this is not Tom's main firewall, this will protect his laptop, and kids' systems from some attacks. He makes sure Block Anonymous Internet requests is enabled. He also filters multicast and IDENT requests. He does not filter Internet NAT redirection.

He logs in to each of the children's PCs, as well as the laptops, and configures them to connect to the WiHoInc network. After confirming that the connections work, he disassembles and reassembles the children's PCs in their rooms. He could configure the wireless firewall to only allow network traffic at certain times of day to prevent his children from browsing the network while he or his wife is not around, but he feels they will follow the rules for using the Internet. Additionally, he has logging turned on so he knows exactly where the systems are browsing. He also has the capability of enabling blocking of specific sites, or keywords. The firewall on the wireless appliance is limited, so in the future he may pick up another firewall appliance to put between the network router and the wireless appliance.

Configuring the Firewall with VPN Router

Tom connects a cat 5 Ethernet cable from the wireless router to his firewall. He turns on the firewall. He then connects his computer and printer network ports to the firewall Ethernet ports. He checks that the lights for each of the ports are showing up as connected.

NOTE

The firewall separates the internal network from the other networks, keeping the interior of the network the most secure. If the wireless network is compromised, the servers on the internal network are not accessible.

He browses to 192.168.0.1 (the default IP address for this particular appliance). He accepts all the defaults allowing the wireless router to give the firewall a DHCP address, and let the firewall give his internal systems their own IP addresses.

NOTE

The default username and password for the firewall is admin, and password. Change this soon after the basic configuration.

Tom checks the Basic Settings. He can safely accept this basic configuration from the initial setup.

He then checks logging, and checks the All Websites and news groups visited, All incoming TCP/UDP/ICMP traffic, All Outgoing TCP/UDP/ICMP traffic, Other IP traffic, and Connections to the Web based interface of this Router, as he wants to get as much information as possible about what is happening in his internal network. Later, after he feels comfortable with what is normal behavior on his systems, he might turn off some of the logging so it is not as comprehensive. Tom doesn't worry about the syslog server configuration, as he does not have a logging infrastructure. For now, Tom isn't going to e-mail the logs to himself; instead, he chooses to look at them and clear them manually.

The logging is now comprehensive. The highlighted portion of the log in Figure B.2 shows Tom's access to the Administrator Interface.

On the Rules tab, Tom sees that he can configure specific rules to allow and disallow services, and actions from happening. Tom plans to watch his log for a few days and determine what if anything he needs to tune.

Tom invested in a solution that would give him VPN functionality. This allows him to connect his laptop remotely to the internal system so he can print, or access records from his porch or anywhere in his house. Now that he has the basic firewall configured, he can configure the VPN access. He clicks on the VPN wizard, and gives the connection a name. He reuses his pre-shared key, and chooses remote VPN client.

Figure B.2 Administrator Access Logged

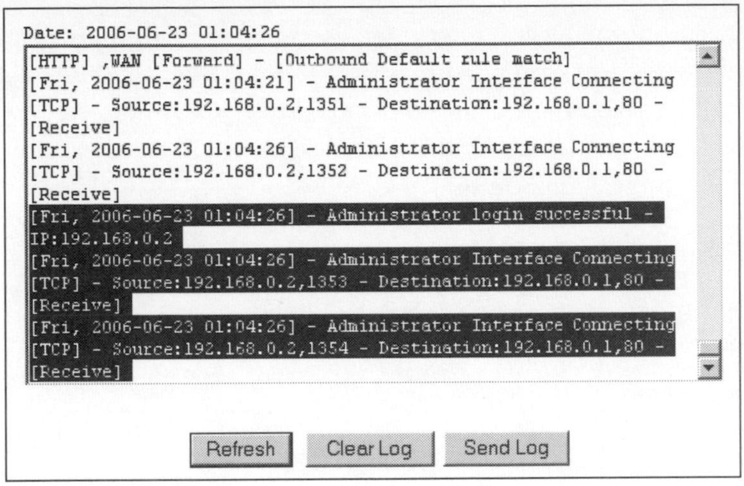

```
Date: 2006-06-23 01:04:26
[HTTP] ,WAN [Forward] - [Outbound Default rule match]
[Fri, 2006-06-23 01:04:21] - Administrator Interface Connecting
[TCP] - Source:192.168.0.2,1351 - Destination:192.168.0.1,80 -
[Receive]
[Fri, 2006-06-23 01:04:26] - Administrator Interface Connecting
[TCP] - Source:192.168.0.2,1352 - Destination:192.168.0.1,80 -
[Receive]
[Fri, 2006-06-23 01:04:26] - Administrator login successful -
IP:192.168.0.2
[Fri, 2006-06-23 01:04:26] - Administrator Interface Connecting
[TCP] - Source:192.168.0.2,1353 - Destination:192.168.0.1,80 -
[Receive]
[Fri, 2006-06-23 01:04:26] - Administrator Interface Connecting
[TCP] - Source:192.168.0.2,1354 - Destination:192.168.0.1,80 -
[Receive]
```

Refresh   Clear Log   Send Log

He downloads the Netgear VPN client software so that he can use IPSec to connect to the VPN. Optionally, he could connect direct to another VPN firewall via his firewall if he were to bring on board a remote partner using this same VPN wizard setting on the VPN firewall.

Testing the Configuration from Various Access Points

Tom first checks that his children can access the Internet. The speeds appear to be fine connecting to www.yahoo.com. He next tries to access his office printer, or his office server. Both appear to be inaccessible to his children.

Next, Tom checks that he has access to the Internet on his laptop. He knows he can browse the Web from his children's PCs, so he is not expecting any problems. He is not disappointed—the wireless works as expected. He turns on the VPN tunnel by clicking on the application software icon. He now has access to the printer, and servers, that are sitting in his office. He confirms this by accessing the printer and file shares available from his server.

Finally, Tom checks that his office servers have the access required to function within the scope of his business needs. He accesses the widget production site to download costs of materials. The connection works. He can also print from both systems, and access his backup file server. He is satisfied that his network is working the way he expects it to.

Summary

A firewall acts as a border guard, filtering packets by application proxy, packet filtering, or state inspection. Tom's final network topology is comprehensive. He has an internal DMZ that creates an untrusted network that is still protected within his network, an external virtual DMZ via the hosted service, and an internal protected network behind the firewall (Figure B.3).

Figure B.3 Tom's Network with Firewall

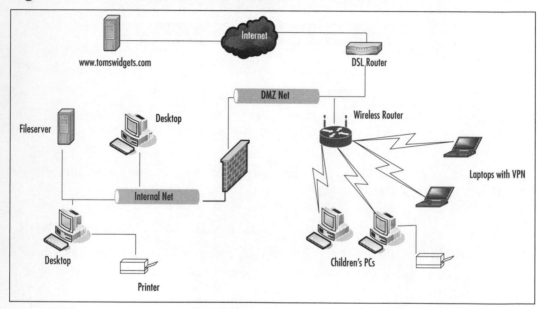

Choose the right firewall for your needs. If you don't have a GB connection, 1000Mbps is not useful. 10/100 is sufficient. DHCP, a decent management GUI for managing the firewall, wireless access points, virtual private networks, along with the type of filters, and the mechanism of firewalling are all aspects you need to analyze to determine what will be the most cost-effective with feature trade-offs. Don't implement services you won't use.

Solutions Fast Track

Introducing the SOHO Firewall Case Study

- ☑ Security is an important function that SOHO users must address as they connect to the intranet.

- ☑ Protection of networked assets can be seen as securing your house on a virtual level.

- ☑ End services you do not need so you do not have open ports on your system that could be used to infiltrate your network. Use *netstat* to determine what services are running on which ports.

Designing the SOHO Firewall

- ☑ Gaming, education, and business interactions are all components of the functional requirements.

- ☑ In the preliminary design, the user opts for a remote service hosting his Web and e-mail, a firewall, and wireless router.

Implementing the SOHO Firewall

- ☑ In the detailed design, the user assembles the components, installs the hardware, configures the software, and tests access points.

- ☑ Configuration includes examining the default settings, enabling logging, and the VPN. Further modifications to the firewall can be enabled after examining typical usage from the logs.

- ☑ Depending on the functional requirements, there are a number of solutions that range in price from $50 to $600 for small businesses, and home office users.

- ☑ Change default passwords for all appliances.

Frequently Asked Questions

The following Frequently Asked Questions, answered by the authors of this book, are designed to both measure your understanding of the concepts presented in this chapter and to assist you with real-life implementation of these concepts. To have your questions about this chapter answered by the author, browse to **www.syngress.com/solutions** and click on the **"Ask the Author"** form.

Q: How do I maintain an out-of-the-box solution firewall?

A: Check the Web site for the manufacturer of the Web site. Sign up for any mailing lists, and make sure to install any firmware patches that are recommended.

Q: One of my applications isn't working right. How do I make it work?

A: First, take the firewall out of the picture. Does it work now? If so, start working basic principles. Turn on the highest level logging on the firewall. Does it show in the logging that the connection is being refused? If so, configure a rule in the rule set to match that setting. You can figure out what settings are needed using *netstat* on the system that is running the application to see what ports it is looking for. If you aren't seeing a connection refused in the logs, check to see if you see any problems reported with this particular application and your chosen appliance. Finally, if all else fails, and you can't find the information on your own, contact the manufacturer for support. By going through these steps first, you can show that you have made a diligent effort to solve your own problem, and the support staff will be more attentive hearing the steps you have taken.

Q: If it doesn't work, whom do I talk to?

A: Contact support for the manufacturer. Check the documentation that came with the appliance, and the vendor's Web site. It is recommended to check the vendor's Web site prior to purchasing a solution to gauge the support level available. Check your favorite mailing lists, baylisa@baylisa.org, and sage-members@sage.org. Local Linux user group mailing lists like svlug@svlug.org can generally be helpful, or you can check security mailing lists.

Q: What is the cost of the out-of-the-box solution?

A: This case study showed a solution that cost $130 for the wireless and firewall appliances, and then a Web services fee of $12 per month to host the Web site. Depending on the solutions you choose, you may spend less or more based on the functionality, and vendor.

Appendix C

Glossary of Technology and Terminology

This glossary includes terms and acronyms that you may encounter during your efforts to learn more about computer security.

ActiveX: ActiveX is a Microsoft creation designed to work in a manner similar to Sun Microsystems' Java. The main goal is to create platform-independent programs that can be used continually on different operating systems. ActiveX is a loose standards definition; not a specific language. An ActiveX component or control can be run on any ActiveX-compatible platform.

ActiveX defines the methods with which these COM objects and ActiveX controls interact with the system; however, it is not tied to a specific language. ActiveX controls and components can be created in various programming languages such as Visual C++, Visual Basic, or VBScript.

Active Scripting: Active scripting is the term used to define the various script programs that can run within and work with Hypertext Markup Language (HTML) in order to interact with users and create a dynamic Web page. By itself, HTML is static and only presents text and graphics. Using active scripting languages such as JavaScript or VBScript, developers can update the date and time displayed on the page, have information pop up in a separate window, or create scrolling text to go across the screen.

Adware: While not necessarily malware, adware is considered to go beyond the reasonable advertising one might expect from freeware or shareware. Typically, a separate program that is installed at the same time as a shareware or similar program, adware will usually continue to generate advertising even when the user is not running the originally desired program.*

Antivirus Software: Antivirus software is an application that protects your system from viruses, worms, and other malicious code. Most antivirus programs monitor traffic while you surf the Web, scan incoming e-mail and file attachments, and periodically check all local files for the existence of any known malicious code.

Application Gateway: An application gateway is a type of firewall. All internal computers establish a connection with the proxy server. The proxy server performs all communications with the Internet. External computers see only the Internet Protocol (IP) address of the proxy server and never communicate directly with the internal clients. The application gateway examines the packets more thoroughly than a circuit-level gateway when making forwarding decisions. It is considered more secure; however, it uses more memory and processor resources.

Attack: The act of trying to bypass security controls on a system. An attack may be active, resulting in the alteration of data; or passive, resulting in the release of data. Note: The fact that an attack is made does not necessarily mean that it will succeed. The degree of success depends on the vulnerability of the system and the effectiveness of the existing countermeasures. Attack is often used as a synonym for a specific exploit.*

Authentication: One of the keys in determining if a message or file you are receiving is safe is to first authenticate that the person who sent it is who they say they are. Authentication is the process of determining the true identity of someone. Basic authentication is using a password to verify that you are who you say you are. There are also more complicated and precise methods such as biometrics (e.g., fingerprints, retina scans).

Backbone: The backbone of the Internet is the collection of major communications pipelines that transfer the data from one end of the world to the other. Large Internet service providers (ISPs) such as AT&T and WorldCom make up the backbone. They connect through major switching centers called Metropolitan Area Exchange (MAE) and exchange data from each others' customers through peering agreements.

Backdoor: A backdoor is a secret or undocumented means of gaining access to a computer system. Many programs have backdoors placed by the programmer to allow them to gain access in order to troubleshoot or change a program. Other backdoors are placed by hackers once they gain access to a system, to allow for easier access into the system in the future or in case their original entrance is discovered.

Biometrics: Biometrics is a form of authentication that uses unique physical traits of the user. Unlike a password, a hacker cannot "guess" your fingerprint or retinal scan pattern. Biometrics is a relatively new term used to refer to fingerprinting, retinal scans, voice wave patterns, and various other unique biological traits used to authenticate users.

Broadband: Technically, broadband is used to define any transmission that can carry more than one channel on a single medium (e.g., the coaxial cable for cable TV carries many channels and can simultaneously provide Internet access). Broadband is also often used to describe high-speed Internet connections such as cable modems and digital subscriber lines (DSLs).

Bug: In computer technology, a bug is a coding error in a computer program. After a product is released or during public beta testing, bugs are still apt to be discovered. When this occurs, users have to either find a way to avoid using the "buggy" code or get a patch from the originators of the code.

Circuit-level Gateway: A circuit-level gateway is a type of firewall. All internal computers establish a "circuit" with the proxy server. The proxy server performs all communications with the Internet. External computers see only the IP address of the proxy server and never communicate directly with the internal clients.

Compromise: When used to discuss Internet security, compromise does not mean that two parties come to a mutually beneficial agreement. Rather, it means that the security of your computer or network is weakened. A typical security compromise can be a third party learning the administrator password of your computer.

Cross Site Scripting: Cross site scripting (XSS) refers to the ability to use some of the functionality of active scripting against the user by inserting malicious code into the HTML that will run code on the users' computers, redirect them to a site other than what they intended, or steal passwords, personal information, and so on.

XSS is a programming problem, not a vulnerability of any particular Web browser software or Web hosting server. It is up to the Web site developer to ensure that user input is validated and checked for malicious code before executing it.

Cyberterrorism: This term is more a buzzword than anything and is used to describe officially sanctioned hacking as a political or military tool. Some hackers have used stolen information (or the threat of stealing information) as a tool to attempt to extort money from companies.

DHCP: Dynamic Host Configuration Protocol (DHCP) is used to automate the assignment of IP addresses to hosts on a network. Each machine on a network must have a unique address. DHCP automatically enters the IP address, tracks which ones are in use, and remembers to put addresses back into the pool when devices are removed. Each device that is configured to use DHCP contacts the DHCP server to request an IP address. The DHCP server then assigns an IP address from the range it has been configured to use. The IP address is leased for a certain amount of time. When the device is removed from the network or when the lease expires, the IP address is placed back into the pool to be used by another device.

Demilitarized Zone: The demilitarized zone (DMZ) is a neutral zone or buffer that separates the internal and external networks and usually exists between two firewalls. External users can access servers in the DMZ, but not the computers on the internal network. The servers in the DMZ act as an intermediary for both incoming and outgoing traffic.

DNS: The Domain Name System (DNS) was created to provide a way to translate domain names to their corresponding IP addresses. It is easier for users to remember a domain name (e.g., yahoo.com) than to try and remember an actual IP address (e.g., 65.37.128.56) of each site they want to visit. The DNS server maintains a list of domain names and IP addresses so that when a request comes in it can be pointed to the correct corresponding IP address.

Keeping a single database of all domain names and IP addresses in the world would be exceptionally difficult, if not impossible. For this reason, the burden has been spread around the world. Companies, Web hosts, ISPs, and other entities that choose to do so can maintain their own DNS servers. Spreading the workload like this speeds up the process and provides better security instead of relying on a single source.

Denial of Service: A Denial-of-Service (DoS) attack floods a network with an overwhelming amount of traffic, thereby slowing its response time for legitimate traffic or grinding it to a halt completely. The more common attacks use the built-in features of the Transmission Control Protocol (TCP)/IP to create exponential amounts of network traffic.

E-mail Spoofing: E-mail spoofing is the act of forging the header information on an e-mail so that it appears to have originated from somewhere other than its true source. The protocol used for e-mail, Simple Mail Transfer Protocol (SMTP), does not have any authentication to verify the source. By changing the header information, the e-mail can appear to come from someone else.

E-mail spoofing is used by virus authors. By propagating a virus with a spoofed e-mail source, it is more difficult for users who receive the virus to track its source. E-mail spoofing is also used by distributors of spam to hide their identity.

Encryption: Encryption is when text, data, or other communications are encoded so that unauthorized users cannot see or hear it. An encrypted file appears as gibberish unless you have the password or key necessary to decrypt the information.

Firewall: Basically, a firewall is a protective barrier between your computer (or internal network) and the outside world. Traffic into and out of the firewall is blocked or restricted as you choose. By blocking all unnecessary traffic and restricting other traffic to those protocols or individuals that need it, you can greatly improve the security of your internal network.

Forensic: Forensic is a legal term. At its root it means something that is discussed in a court of law or that is related to the application of knowledge to a legal problem.

In computer terms, forensic is used to describe the art of extracting and gathering data from a computer to determine how an intrusion occurred, when it occurred, and who the intruder was. Organizations that employ good security practices and maintain logs of network and file access are able to accomplish this much easier. But, with the right knowledge and the right tools, forensic evidence can be extracted even from burned, waterlogged, or physically damaged computer systems.

Hacker: Commonly used to refer to any individual who uses their knowledge of networks and computer systems to gain unauthorized access to computer systems. While often used interchangeably, the term hacker typically applies to those who break in out of curiosity or for the challenge itself, rather than those who actually intend to steal or damage data. Hacker purists claim that true hacking is benign and that the term is misused.

Heuristic: Heuristics uses past experience to make educated guesses about the present. Using rules and decisions based on analysis of past network or e-mail traffic, heuristic scanning in antivirus software can self-learn and use artificial intelligence to attempt to block viruses or worms that are not yet known and for which the antivirus software does not yet have a filter to detect or block.

Hoax: A hoax is an attempt to trick a user into believing something that is not true. It is mainly associated with e-mails that are too good to be true or that ask you to do things like "forward this to everyone you know."

Host: As far as the Internet is concerned, a host is essentially any computer connected to the Internet. Each computer or device has a unique IP address which helps other devices on the Internet find and communicate with that host.

HTML: HTML is the basic language used to create graphic Web pages. HTML defines the syntax and tags used to create documents on the World Wide Web (WWW). In its basic form, HTML documents are static, meaning they only display text and graphics. In order to have scrolling text, animations, buttons that change when the mouse pointer is over them, and so on, a developer needs to use active scripting like JavaScript or VBScript or use third-party plug-ins like Macromedia Flash.

There are variations and additions to HTML as well. Dynamic Hypertext Markup Language (DHTML) is used to refer to pages that include things like JavaScript or CGI scripts in order to dynamically present information unique to each user or each time the user visits the site. Extensible Markup Language (XML) is gaining in popularity because of its ability to interact with data and provide a means for sharing and interpreting data between different platforms and applications.

ICMP: Internet Control Message Protocol (ICMP) is part of the IP portion of TCP/IP. Common network testing commands such as PING and Trace Route (TRACERT) rely on the ICMP.

Identity Theft: Use of personal information to impersonate someone, usually for the purpose of fraud.*

IDS: An Intrusion Detection System (IDS) is a device or application that is used to inspect all network traffic and to alert the user or administrator when there has been unauthorized access or an attempt to access a network. The two primary methods of monitoring are signature based and anomaly based. Depending on the device or application used, the IDS can alert either the user or the administrator or set up to block specific traffic or automatically respond in some way.

Signature-based detection relies on the comparison of traffic to a database containing signatures of known attack methods. Anomaly-based detection compares current network traffic to a known good baseline to look for anything out of the ordinary. The IDS can be placed strategically on the network as a Network-based Intrusion Detection System (NIDS), which will inspect all network traffic, or it can be installed on each individual system as a Host-based Intrusion Detection System (HIDS), which inspects traffic to and from that specific device only.

Instant Messaging: Instant messaging (IM) offers users the ability to communicate in real time. Starting with Internet Relay Chat (IRC), users became hooked on the ability to "chat" in real time rather than sending e-mails back and forth or posting to a forum or message board.

Online service providers such as America Online (AOL) and CompuServe created proprietary messaging systems that allow users to see when their friends are online and available to chat (as long as they use the same instant messaging software). ICQ introduced an IM system that was not tied to a particular ISP and that kicked off the mainstream popularity of Instant Messaging.

Internet: The Internet was originally called Arpanet, and was created by the United States government in conjunction with various colleges and universities for the purpose of sharing research data. As it stands now, there are millions of computers connected to the Internet all over the world. There is no central server or owner of the Internet; every computer on the Internet is connected with every other computer.

Intranet: An Intranet is an Internet with restricted access. Corporate Intranets generally use the exact same communication lines as the rest of the Internet, but have security in place to restrict access to the employees, customers, or suppliers that the corporation wants to have access.

IP: The IP is used to deliver data packets to their proper destination. Each packet contains both the originating and the destination IP address. Each router or gateway that receives the packet will look at the destination address and determine how to forward it. The packet will be passed from device to device until it reaches its destination.

IP Address: An IP Address is used to uniquely identify devices on the Internet. The current standard (IPv4) is a 32-bit number made up of four 8-bit blocks. In standard decimal numbers, each block can be any number from 0 to 255. A standard IP address would look something like "192.168.45.28."

Part of the address is the network address which narrows the search to a specific block, similar to the way your postal mail is first sent to the proper zip code. The other part of the address is the local address that specifies the actual device within that network, similar to the way your specific street address identifies you within your zip code. A subnet mask is used to determine how many bits make up the network portion and how many bits make up the local portion.

The next generation of IP (IPv6 or [IP Next Generation] IPng) has been created and is currently being implemented in some areas.

IP Spoofing: IP spoofing is the act of replacing the IP address information in a packet with fake information. Each packet contains the originating and destination IP address. By replacing the true originating IP address with a fake address, a hacker can mask the true source of an attack or force the destination IP address to reply to a different machine and possibly cause a DoS.

IPv4: The current version of IP used on the Internet is version 4 (IPv4). IPv4 is used to direct packets of information to their correct address. Due to a shortage of available addresses and to address the needs of the future, an updated IP is being developed (IPv6).

IPv6: To address issues with the current IP in use (IPv4) and to add features to improve the protocol for the future, the Internet Engineering Task Force (IETF) has introduced IP version 6 (IPv6) also known as IPng.

IPv6 uses 128-bit addresses rather than the current 32-bit addresses, allowing for an exponential increase in the number of available IP addresses. IPv6 also adds new security and performance features to the protocol. IPv6 is backwards compatible with IPv4 so that different networks or hardware manufacturers can choose to upgrade at different times without disrupting the current flow of data on the Internet.

ISP: An ISP is a company that has the servers, routers, communication lines, and other equipment necessary to establish a presence on the Internet. They in turn sell access to their equipment in the form of Internet services such as dial-up, cable modem, Digital Subscriber Line (DSL), or other types of connections. The larger ISPs form the backbone of the Internet.

JavaScript: JavaScript is an active scripting language that was created by Netscape and based on Sun Microsystems' platform-independent programming language, Java. Originally named LiveScript, Netscape changed the name to JavaScript to ride on the coattails of Java's popularity. JavaScript is used within HTML to execute small programs, in order to generate a dynamic Web page. Using JavaScript, a developer can make text or graphics change when the mouse points at them, update the current date and time on the Web page, or add personal information such as how long it has been since that user last visited the site. Microsoft Internet Explorer supports a subset of JavaScript dubbed JScript.

Malware: Malicious Code (Malware) is a catch-all term used to refer to various types of software that can cause problems or damage your computer. The common types of malware are viruses, worms, Trojan horses, macro viruses, and backdoors.

NAT: Network Address Translation (NAT) is used to mask the true identity of internal computers. Typically, the NAT server or device has a public IP address that can be seen by external hosts. Computers on the local network use a completely different set of IP addresses. When traffic goes out, the internal IP address is removed and replaced with the public IP address of the NAT device. When replies come back to the NAT device, it determines which internal computer the response belongs to and routes it to its proper destination.

An added benefit is the ability to have more than one computer communicate on the Internet with only one publicly available IP address. Many home routers use NAT to allow multiple computers to share one IP address.

Network: Technically, it only takes two computers (or hosts) to form a network. A network is any two or more computers connected together to share data or resources. Common network resources include printers that are shared by many users rather than each user having their own printer. The Internet is one large network of shared data and resources.

Network Security: This term is used to describe all aspects of securing your computer or computers from unauthorized access. This includes blocking outsiders from getting into the network, as well as password protecting your computers and ensuring that only authorized users can view sensitive data.

P2P: Peer-to-peer Networking (P2P) applies to individual PCs acting as servers to other individual PCs. Made popular by the music file swapping service, Napster, P2P allows users to share files with each other through a network of computers using that same P2P client software. Each computer on the network has the ability to act as a server by hosting files for others to download, and as a client by searching other computers on the network for files they want.

Packet: A packet, otherwise known as a datagram, is a fragment of data. Data transmissions are broken up into packets. Each packet contains a portion of the data being sent as well as header information, which includes the destination address.

Packet Filter: A packet filter is a type of firewall. Packet filters can restrict network traffic and protect your network by rejecting packets from unauthorized hosts, using unauthorized ports, or trying to connect to unauthorized IP addresses.

Packet Sniffing: Packet sniffing is the act of capturing packets of data flowing across a computer network. The software or device used to do this is called a packet sniffer. Packet sniffing is to computer networks what wire tapping is to a telephone network.

Packet sniffing is used to monitor network performance or to troubleshoot problems with network communications. However, it is also widely used by hackers and crackers to illegally gather information about networks they intend to break into. Using a packet sniffer, you can capture data such as passwords, IP addresses, protocols being used on the network, and other information that will help an attacker infiltrate the network.

Patch: A patch is like a Band-Aid. When a company finds bugs and defects in their software, they fix them in the next version of the application. However, some bugs make the current product inoperable or less functional, or may even open security vulnerabilities. For these bugs, users cannot wait until the next release to get a fix; therefore, the company must create a small interim patch that users can apply to fix the problem.

Phishing: Posting of a fraudulent message to a large number of people via spam or other general posting asking them to submit personal or security information, which is then used for further fraud or identity theft. The term is possibly an extension of trolling, which is the posting of an outrageous message or point of view in a newsgroup or mailing list in the hope that someone will "bite" and respond to it.*

Port: A port has a dual definition in computers. There are various ports on the computer itself (e.g., ports to plug in your mouse, keyboards, Universal Serial Bus [USB] devices, printers, monitors, and so forth). However, the ports that are most relevant to information security are virtual ports found in TCP/IP. Ports are like channels on your computer. Normal Web or Hypertext Transfer Protocol (HTTP) traffic flows on port 80. Post Office

Protocol version 3 (POP3) e-mail flows on port 110. By blocking or opening these ports into and out of your network, you can control the kinds of data that flows through your network.

Port Scan: A port scan is a method used by hackers to determine what ports are open or in use on a system or network. By using various tools, a hacker can send data to TCP or User Datagram Protocol (UDP) ports one at a time. Based on the response received, the port scan utility can determine if that port is in use. Using this information, the hacker can then focus his or her attack on the ports that are open and try to exploit any weaknesses to gain access.

Protocol: A protocol is a set of rules or agreed-upon guidelines for communication. When communicating, it is important to agree on how to do so. If one party speaks French and one German, the communications will most likely fail. If both parties agree on a single language, communications will work.

On the Internet, the set of communications protocols used is called TCP/IP. TCP/IP is actually a collection of various protocols that have their own special functions. These protocols have been established by international standards bodies and are used in almost all platforms and around the globe to ensure that all devices on the Internet can communicate successfully.

Proxy Server: A proxy server acts as a middleman between your internal and external networks. It serves the dual roles of speeding up access to the Internet and providing a layer of protection for the internal network. Clients send Internet requests to the proxy server, which in turn initiates communications with actual destination server.

By caching pages that have been previously requested, the proxy server speeds up performance by responding to future requests for the same page, using the cached information rather than going to the Web site again.

When using a proxy server, external systems only see the IP address of the proxy server so the true identity of the internal computers is hidden. The proxy server can also be configured with basic rules of what ports or IP addresses are or are not allowed to pass through, which makes it a type of basic firewall.

Rootkit: A rootkit is a set of tools and utilities that a hacker can use to maintain access once they have hacked a system. The rootkit tools allow them to seek out usernames and passwords, launch attacks against remote systems, and conceal their actions by hiding their files and processes and erasing their activity from system logs and a plethora of other malicious stealth tools.

Script Kiddie: Script kiddie is a derogatory term used by hackers or crackers to describe novice hackers. The term is derived from the fact that these novice hackers tend to rely on existing scripts, tools, and exploits to create their attacks. They may not have any specific knowledge of computer systems or why or how their hack attempts work, and they may unleash harmful or destructive attacks without even realizing it. Script kiddies tend to scan and attack large blocks of the Internet rather than targeting a specific computer, and generally don't have any goal in mind aside from experimenting with tools to see how much chaos they can create.

SMTP: Simple Mail Transfer Protocol (SMTP) is used to send e-mail. The SMTP protocol provides a common language for different servers to send and receive e-mail messages. The default TCP/IP port for the SMTP protocol is port 25.

SNMP: Simple Network Management Protocol (SNMP) is a protocol used for monitoring network devices. Devices like printers and routers use SNMP to communicate their status. Administrators use SNMP to manage the function of various network devices.

Stateful Inspection: Stateful inspection is a more in-depth form of packet filter firewall. While a packet filter firewall only checks the packet header to determine the source and destination address and the source and destination ports to verify against its rules, stateful inspection checks the packet all the way to the Application layer. Stateful inspection monitors incoming and outgoing packets to determine source, destination, and context. By ensuring that only requested information is allowed back in, stateful inspection helps protect against hacker techniques such as IP spoofing and port scanning

TCP: The TCP is a primary part of the TCP/IP set of protocols, which forms the basis of communications on the Internet. TCP is responsible for breaking large data into smaller chunks of data called packets. TCP assigns each packet a sequence number and then passes them on to be transmitted to their destination. Because of how the Internet is set up, every packet may not take the same path to get to its destination. TCP has the responsibility at the destination end of reassembling the packets in the correct sequence and performing error-checking to ensure that the complete data message arrived intact.

TCP/IP: TCP/IP is a suite of protocols that make up the basic framework for communication on the Internet.

TCP helps control how the larger data is broken down into smaller pieces or packets for transmission. TCP handles reassembling the packets at the destination end and performing error-checking to ensure all of the packets arrived properly and were reassembled in the correct sequence.

IP is used to route the packets to the appropriate destination. The IP manages the addressing of the packets and tells each router or gateway on the path how and where to forward the packet to direct it to its proper destination.

Other protocols associated with the TCP/IP suite are UDP and ICMP.

Trojan: A Trojan horse is a malicious program disguised as a normal application. Trojan horse programs do not replicate themselves like a virus, but they can be propagated as attachments to a virus.

UDP: UDP is a part of the TCP/IP suite of protocols used for communications on the Internet. It is similar to TCP except that it offers very little error checking and does not establish a connection with a specific destination. It is most widely used to broadcast a message over a network port to all machines that are listening.

VBScript: VBScript is an active scripting language created by Microsoft to compete with Netscape's JavaScript. VBScript is based on Microsoft's popular programming language, Visual Basic. VBScript is an active scripting language used within HTML to execute small programs to generate a dynamic Web page. Using VBScript, a developer can cause text or graphics to change when the mouse points at them, update the current date and time on the Web page, or add personal information like how long it has been since that user last visited the site.

Virus: A virus is malicious code that replicates itself. New viruses are discovered daily. Some exist simply to replicate themselves. Others can do serious damage such as erasing files or rendering a computer inoperable.

Vulnerability: In network security, a vulnerability refers to any flaw or weakness in the network defense that could be exploited to gain unauthorized access to, damage, or otherwise affect the network

Worm: A worm is similar to a virus. Worms replicate themselves like viruses, but do not alter files. The main difference is that worms reside in memory and usually remain unnoticed until the rate of replication reduces system resources to the point that it becomes noticeable.

* These definitions were derived from Robert Slade's *Dictionary of Information Security* (Syngress. ISBN: 1-59749-115-2). With over 1,000 information security terms and definitions, Slade's book is a great resource to turn to when you come across technical words and acronyms you are not familiar with.

Index

802.11x wireless protocols, 126–127

A

access
    restricting to home wireless
        network, 130–131
    Windows, levels and permissions,
        18–21
accounts
    Guest, disabling in Windows XP,
        11–12
    user. *See* user accounts
Acrobat Reader, 208–209
active scripting and Web surfing,
    112–115
ActiveX controls, 106
Ad-aware, 145, 146, 147–148
addresses
    IP. *See* IP addresses
    MAC, 130–131
    spoofed e-mail, 92–93
Administrator account
    securing home system, 128–129
    Windows XP, 9–13
Adobe Acrobat Reader, 208–209
advertising
    See also spam, spyware
    adware, 140–144, 150
Aethera e-mail (Linux), 193–194
AfterSTEP window manager, 187
AirSnarf, 134
Amazon.com, 107
antivirus software
    using, 44–47
    for wireless networks, 133

application gateways, 74
applications
    in desktop environments (Linux),
        181–184
    Office application suites (Linux),
        209–214
    running Windows on Linux,
        214–217
    updating, 162
ARPNET, 86
attachments, e-mail, 87–91
attacks. *See specific attack*
authentication, CHAP protocol, 203
Automatic Update (Windows XP),
    57–60, 161
automating maintenance tasks,
    159–161

B

backing up data, 175
Backup For One, 175
BIOS (Basic Input/Output System),
    setting password in, 37–38
Blackbox window manager, 187,
    188–189
blocking
    cookies, 108–109
    e-mail file attachments, 89–90
    ports via firewall, 227
    spam, 94
Bloomberg cyber-extortion, 105
booting into Safe Mode (Windows),
    174
bots described, 43
Brain virus, 43
browsers (Linux), 202–209

Brute Force Attacks, 36
Bugtraq vulnerability information, 57

C

cable/DSL routers
  firewalls, 74–80
  and NAT, 70, 112
CAN-SPAM Act, 95, 97
CDE (Common Desktop
    Environment), 185
certificates, digital, 116–117
CHAP (Challenge Handshake
    Authentication Protocol), 203
childproofing the Web, 119–120
Code Red worm, 48
Cohen, Fred, 43
Comcast's spam blocking, 96
Common Desktop Environment
    (CDE), 185
communication ports, 223
Computer Management Console
    (Windows XP), 9–11
computer networks. See networks
computers. See PCs
configuring
  home wireless networks, 130–131
  Internet Explorer security zones,
    113–115
  log file size, 168
  screen savers, 26–27
  Windows Firewall, 76–80, 170–171
  Windows services, 22–24
  Windows user accounts, Security
    Groups, 8–16
  ZoneAlarm firewall, 79
connections

  configuring for home wireless
    networks, 130–131
  verifying hotspot, 135
content filtering, Web, 119–120
cookies, and security, 106–109
cracking passwords, 35–36
crime on the Web, 105–106
CrossOver Office suite, 216–217
cryptography. See encryption
cumulative patches, 55
cyber-extortion, 105

D

data, restoring, 175
defragmenting
  hard disks, 158–159
  and performance, 155
denial-of-service (DoS) attacks, 76
desktop environments (Linux),
    180–185, 189
devices
  Plug and Play, 23
  running NAT, 70
DHCP (Dynamic Host
    Configuration Protocol), 226
Dictionary Attacks, 35–36
digital certificates, 116–117
dir command, 25
disabling
  file sharing, 17–18, 134
  firewall logging, 78
  Guest accounts (Windows XP),
    11–12
  Simple File Sharing (Windows XP),
    17–18
  Windows services, 22–24

disaster response, event log-checking, 166–167
Disk Cleanup, 155–157
disk cleanup for PCs, 155–157
Disk Defragmenter, 158–159
displaying
 See also viewing
 Windows Display properties, 26–27
DNS servers, and IP address handling, 225
DoS (denial-of-service) attacks, 76
DSL cable
 and firewalls, 74–80
 and NAT, 70, 112
 and wireless networks, 126

E

e-mail
 attachments, 87–91
 evolution of, 86
 hoaxes, phishing, 97–101
 migrating from Windows to Linux desktops, 196–201
 and PIM clients (Linux), 190–196
 and PIM software (Linux), 96–201
 resources on safe, 102
 spam, 93–97
 spoofed addresses, 92–93
 Web-based and POP3, 91, 136
education and the Web, 104–105
Employee-Monitoring.com, 145
emulator software, 214–216
enabling
 firewall logging, 78
 Security event logging, 167–169
encryption

password, 135–136
 using with home wireless networks, 131–132
Enlightenment window manager, 187
erasing pagefiles, 157–158
event logs, 80, 166–169
Event Viewer, using, 166–167
Evolution e-mail (Linux), 190–192
exporting e-mail from Outlook, 199–201

F

FAT32 vs. NTFS, 16
file and folder security, disabling sharing, 134
file attachments, opening e-mail, 86–91
files
 See also specific file type
 and disk cleanup for PCs, 155–157
 hidden extensions, 24–25
 Windows, security, 16–21
filtering
 packet, and firewalls, 72–73
 ZIP files, 90
financial transactions over the Web, 118–119
Firefox browser, 203–204
firewalls
 application gateways, proxy firewalls, 74
 generally, 69–71
 packet routing and filtering, 72–73
 personal, 74–80, 133–134
 resources about, 84
 routers and ports, 71–72
 security considerations, 227–228

stateful inspection, 73
in wireless networks, 124
folders, Windows Security, 16–21
FVWM window manager, 187

G

Galeon browser, 204
gateways, application, 74
Gnome desktop environment
(Linux), 181–185
GNU Project, 181
Groups, Windows Security, 13–15
Guest accounts, disabling in Windows
XP, 11–12

H

Hancom Office suite, 214
hard disks
defragmenting, 158–159
disk cleanup, 155–157
heuristic scanning, 47
hidden file extensions, 24–25
HIDS (host-based intrusion detection
system), 80–81
HijackThis tool, 148, 149
hoaxes, 97–101
home wireless networks, securing,
128–133
host-based intrusion detection system
(HIDS), 80–81
hosts, and IP addressing, DNS,
224–226
Hotmail Web-based e-mail, 91
hotspot security (wireless), 133–134
HTML (Hypertext Markup
Language) and Web pages, 106
HTTP port 80, 223

Hybrid Attacks, 36

I

iCalendar, 201
ICS (Windows Internet Connection
Sharing), 70
identity theft. *See* phishing
IDSs (intrusion detection systems), 69
IIS (Internet Information Services),
disabling, 23
importing
bookmarks into Linux, 206
importing Outlook mail into
Mozilla, 198–199
Internet Calendaring and Scheduling
Core Object Specification
(iCalendar) standard, 201
Internet Explorer
setting security levels in, 113–115
vulnerabilities of, 57
Internet Information Services (IIS),
23
intrusion detection systems (IDSs),
69, 80–83
IP (Internet Protocol), 222
IP addresses
described, 225
managing, 226–227
and network traffic flow, 70–72
spoofed e-mail, 92
IPSs (intrusion prevention systems),
69, 80–83

J

JavaScript, 106
JDBGMGR hoax, 99

K

KDE desktop environment (Linux), 181, 183–185
KDE suite/KMail, 192–193
keylogging, 144
KOffice suite, 213–214
Kolla, Patrick, 145
Konqueror browser, 205
KWin window manager, 187

L

L33t-5p34K G3n3r@t0r, 35
Lavasoft, 145
legislation, CAN-SPAM Act, 95
LibPST conversion application (Linux), 199
licensing, GNU Public License, 181
links, and phishing, 100–101
Linksys wireless routers, 128
Linux
    common desktop environments, 180–185
    e-mail and PIM clients, 190–196
    e-mail and PIM software, 196–201
    Office application suites, 209–214
    summary, 218
    Web browsers, 202–209
    X Window system, window managers, 185–189
logging
    enabling and disabling, 78
    enabling Security event, 167–169
    security event logs, 166–167
logins, Windows XP, 7
logs, event, 80

M

MAC Media Access Code) addresses, 130–131
Macromedia Flash (Linux), 206–207
Macromedia Shockwave/Director, 207
maintenance, general PC, 154–161
Malicious Software Removal Tool, 50
malware
    See also spam, spyware
    described, 5–6
    e-mail security concerns, 86–91
    history of, 43–44
    removing, 49–51
    resources on, 52
McFee malware removal tools, 50
McFee VirusScan, 45–46
Melissa virus, 43
memory, erasing pagefiles, 157–158
Messenger, Windows, disabling, 23
Metacity window manager, 186
Microsoft Exchange, and Evolution, 192
Microsoft Internet Explorer, vulnerabilities of, 57
Microsoft Outlook Express
    migrating e-mail to Linux desktop, 197–199
    vulnerabilities, 92, 94
Microsoft PowerPoint, 211
Microsoft Security Bulletins, 55, 162
Microsoft Windows. See Windows
migrating
    bookmarks to Linux, 206
    e-mail from Windows to Linux desktops, 197–199
    from Windows to Linux desktops, 189

money transactions over the Web, 116–119

monitoring
  Internet traffic, 28
  Web activity, 145

Mozilla Mail/Thunderbird browser/e-mail, 194–195, 198–199, 202–203

N

NAT (Network Address Translation), 70, 75, 112, 226–227

Net Nanny, 120

NetVizor, 145

Network Address Translation (NAT), 70, 75, 112, 226–227

network-based intrusion detection system (NIDS), 80–82

network traffic, firewalls' handling of, 69–73

networks
  computer protocols and ports, 222–224
  IP addresses and DNS, 224–226
  peer-to-peer (P2P), 72
  virtual private (VPNs), 136
  and Windows security, 6
  wireless. See wireless networks

NIDS (network-based intrusion detection system), 80–82

NTFS vs. FAT32, 16

O

Office application suites (Linux), 209–214

opening e-mail attachments, 87–91

OpenOffice.org, 209–213

Opera browser, 205

Outlook Express
  migrating to Linux desktops, 197–199
  spam blocking, 94
  spoofed addresses, vulnerability, 92

P

packet filtering, 72–73

packet routing, firewalls and, 72–73

pagefiles, erasing, 157–158

Password Safe, 37

passwords
  See also permissions
  cracking, 35–36
  keeping secure, 32–35
  protecting in wireless networks, 135–136
  setting in BIOS, 37–38
  storing, 36–37
  strong, 12
  use and security of, 30–31
  weak, 6
  and Windows access levels, 18–21
  Windows XP Administrator account, 12–13

patches
  for PCs, 161–162
  precautions, 60–63
  purpose and procedures, 55–60
  resources on, 64
  terminology, 54–55

PCs (personal computers)
  booting into Safe Mode, 174
  general maintenance, 154–161
  Linux. See Linux
  patches and updates, 161–162

resources on securing, 164

restoring system, 173–174, 176–177

scanning events, log data, 171–172

scheduling maintenance tasks, 159–161

Windows XP Security Center, 162–163

PDF files, 208, 212

peer-to-peer (P2P) networking, 72

perimeter security

firewalls, 69–80

introduction to, 68–69

intrusion detection and prevention, 80–83

permissions

See also passwords

and Windows access levels, 18–21

personal firewalls, 133–134

PGP encryption program, 135

phishing, 100–101, 119

physical security, 6

points, setting system restore, 62

pop-up spam and Windows Messenger Service, 4

POP3 (Post Office Protocol) e-mail

servers, 72

vs. Web-based e-mail, 91, 136

ports

communication, 223

firewalls and, 71–72

PowerPoint, 211

preventing

spyware, 145–150

virus and worm infections, 49–51

privacy

adware and, 149

and anonymous Web surfing, 109–112

profiles, user account, 8

protocols

See also specific protocol

802.11x wireless, 126–127

computer, TCP, UDP, 222–224

proxy firewalls, 74

PSW.Win.32.WOW.x Trojan horse, 30–31

public wireless networks, using safely, 133–134

R

RAM (random access memory), erasing pagefiles, 157

RealPlayer plug-in, 207–208

rebooting in Safe Mode, 172

Registry, Windows, disabling Remote Registry, 23

removing

malware, 49–51

spyware, 145–150

renaming

admin accounts, home wireless systems, 128–129

Windows XP Administrator account, 12–13

resources

e-mail safety, 102

on firewalls, 84

hoax databases, 100

keeping PCs secure, 164

on malware, 52

on passwords, 39

on patching, 64

PC recovery, 177

spyware and adware, 150

Web surfing privacy, safety, 121

Windows security, 28

wireless network security, 136
restore points, setting, 62
restoring Windows XP, 173–175
Roboform (password program), 37
rollups described, 55
rootkits described, 43
routers and firewalls, 71–72
RSA Security's survey on password
    security, 31
running Windows applications on
    Linux, 214–217

S

Safe Mode, booting into, 172, 174
Sawfish window manager, 186
scanning, antivirus, 45–47
scheduling
    antivirus scans, 46–47
    Internet Calendaring and
        Scheduling Core Object
        Specification (iCalendar)
        standard, 201
    maintenance tasks, general PC,
        159–161
screen savers, Windows, 25–27
scripting, active, and Web surfing,
    112–115
Secunia's vulnerability information,
    57
Secure Password Generator, 35
securing
    home wireless networks, 128–133
    passwords, 32–35
security
    See also specific product or platform
    e-mail. *See* e-mail
    firewalls. *See* firewalls
    hotspot, 133–134

of passwords, 30–31
perimeter, 68–69
physical, 6
SSL connections, 116–117
Web surfing safely, 104–112
Windows XP Security Center,
    using, 162–164
Security Bulletins (Microsoft), 55
security event logging, enabling,
    167–169
Security Focus's Bugtraq, 57
Security Groups, Windows, 13–21
Service Pack 2 (Windows XP), 5
service packs described, 55
Service Set Identifier (SSID), 129,
    135
services, Windows, 21–24
session cookies, 107
sharing files, folders (Windows),
    16–21
Shockwave/Director, 207
Simple File Sharing (Windows XP),
    17–18
Simple Mail Transfer Protocol
    (SMTP), 71
small office/home office (SOHO)
    perimeter security, 68–69
    personal, cable/DSL router firewalls,
        74–75
SMTP port, 223
SMTP (Simple Mail Transfer
    Protocol), 71
Snort IDS program, 82
software
    See also specific product or application
    antivirus, 44–49
    compatibility layer, 215–216
    malware, 5–6, 42–43

SOHO (small office/home office), 68–69, 74–75

spam
  e-mail, 93–97
  and Windows Messenger Service, 4

Spector Pro monitoring program, 120, 145, 148

spoofed e-mail addresses, 92–93

Spybot Search & Destroy, 145, 148

SpyCop, 148

spyware
  adware, 140–144
  generally, 144–145
  introduction to, 140
  preventing and removing, 145–150
  resources on, 150

SQL Slammer virus, 43–44, 56

SSDP Discovery Service, 22–23

SSID (Service Set Identifier)
  changing, 129
  and wireless encryption, 135

SSL (Secure Socket Layer) and shopping safety, 116–117

Star Writer, Star Impress, Star Calc, Star Web (Linux), 209–212

StarOffice suite, 213

stateful inspection, 73

storing passwords, 36–37

streaming video, 207

strong passwords, 12, 33–35

surfing the Web, privacy of, 109–112

Sylpheed e-mail application, 195–196

Symantec, 146

system restore, Windows XP, 173–174

T

Tab Window Manager (TWB), 187

TCP/IP (Transmission Control Protocol/Internet Protocol), 223–224

Thunderbird (Mozilla), 195

traffic
  firewalls' handling of, 69–74
  monitoring incoming and outgoing, 228

transactions, financial, over the Web, 116–119

Trend Micro's HouseCall, 51

Trend Micro's PC-cillin software, 45, 46–47, 79, 171

Trojan horses
  described, 43
  PSW.Win.32.WOW.x, 30–31

TWB (Tab Window Manager), 187

TXT files, 88–89

U

UDP protocol, 224

Universal Plug and Play (UPnP), 22–23

updating
  antivirus software, 47–49
  patches, 55, 58–60
  security on PCs, 161–162

UPnP (Universal Plug and Play), 22–23

URLs (universal resource locators) and spoofed addresses, 92–93

user accounts
  Windows configuration, 7–13

Windows XP home account types, 15–16

V

VBScript, 106
Vcalendar standard, 201
Vcard (Virtual Card standard), 201
viewing
  Event Viewer Security logs, 169
  installed services, 21–24
Virtual Card standard (Vcard), 201
virtual memory, erasing pagefiles, 157–158
virtual private networks (VPNs), 136
viruses, 42–43, 52
VPNs (virtual private networks), 136
vulnerabilities
  patches and, 54–56
  Windows file and folder sharing, 16–21

W

wardriving, 125
weak passwords, vulnerability of, 6
Web, the
  and active scripting, 112–115
  content filtering, 119–120
  cookies, 106–109
  resources for using safely, 121
  shopping and financial safety, 116–119
  threats and vulnerabilities, 104–106
Web-based e-mail, 136
Web browsers (Linux), 202–209
WEP (Wired Equivalence Privacy), 131–132

WinBackup, 175
window managers (Linux), 185–189
WindowMaker window manager, 187
Windows
  access levels and permissions, 18–21
  Automatic Update (Windows XP), 58–60
  FAT32 vs. NTFS, 16
  file and folder security, 16–21
  hidden file extensions, 24–25
  migrating to Linux desktops, 189
  screen savers, 25–27
  security groups, 13–15
  Security Groups, 13–15
  services, 21–24
  threats and vulnerabilities, 5–13
  update site, 161–162
  vulnerabilities generally, 4–5
  XP. See Windows XP
Windows Disk Defragmenter, 158–159
Windows Event Logs, 80, 166–167
Windows Firewall, 76–80, 170–171
Windows Internet Connection Sharing (ICS) and NAT, 70
Windows Messenger Service
  disabling, 23
  spam and, 4
Windows Services Console, 21–24
Windows System Restore feature, 61–62
Windows XP
  Administrator Tools, 9–11
  Automatic Update, 57–60
  Backup Utility, 175–176
  disabling Guest accounts, 11–12

home account types, 15–16
logging in, 7
password security, 33–35
System Restore feature, 173–174
user account configuration, 7–13
Windows Firewall, 76–80
Windows System Restore feature,
    61–62
Windows XP Home, auditing
    security, 167, 166–167
Windows XP Security Center, using,
    162–163
Windows XP Service Pack 2, 5
Wine emulator, 216
WinZip, 89, 135
Wired Equivalence Privacy (WEP),
    131–132
wireless networks
  basics and protocols, 124–127
  hotspot security, 134–137
  public, using safely, 133–134
  securing home system, 128–133
  security resources, 136
World of Warcraft (WoW) Trojan,
    30–31
World Wide Web. *See* Web, the
WorldWide WarDrive (WWWD),
    125
worms, 42–43, 52
WPA (Wi-Fi Protected Access),
    131–132

X

X Window servers, 187–188
X Window system, window managers
    (Linux), 185–189

Xfce desktop environment (Linux),
    185

Y

Yahoo's Web-based e-mail, 91

Z

ZIP files, 89–90
zombies described, 43
ZoneAlarm firewall, 79–80, 108–109,
    112

Syngress: *The Definition of a Serious Security Library*

Syn·gress (sin-gres): *noun, sing.* Freedom from risk or danger; safety. See *security.*

Syngress IT Security Project Management Handbook

Susan Snedaker

The definitive work for IT professionals responsible for the management of the design, configuration, deployment and maintenance of enterprise-wide security projects. Provides specialized coverage of key project areas including Penetration Testing, Intrusion Detection and Prevention Systems, and Access Control Systems.

ISBN: 1-59749-076-8

Price: $59.95 US $77.95 CAN

Combating Spyware in the Enterprise

Paul Piccard

Combating Spyware in the Enterprise is the first book published on defending enterprise networks from increasingly sophisticated and malicious spyware. System administrators and security professionals responsible for administering and securing networks ranging in size from SOHO networks up to the largest enterprise networks will learn to use a combination of free and commercial anti-spyware software, firewalls, intrusion detection systems, intrusion prevention systems, and host integrity monitoring applications to prevent the installation of spyware, and to limit the damage caused by spyware that does in fact infiltrate their networks.

ISBN: 1-59749-064-4

Price: $49.95 US $64.95 CAN

Practical VoIP Security

Thomas Porter

After struggling for years, you finally think you've got your network secured from malicious hackers and obnoxious spammers. Just when you think it's safe to go back into the water, VoIP finally catches on. Now your newly converged network is vulnerable to DoS attacks, hacked gateways leading to unauthorized free calls, call eavesdropping, malicious call redirection, and spam over Internet Telephony (SPIT). This book details both VoIP attacks and defense techniques and tools.

ISBN: 1-59749-060-1

Price: $49.95 U.S. $69.95 CAN

SYNGRESS®

Syngress: *The Definition of a Serious Security Library*

Syn·gress (sin–gres): *noun, sing.* Freedom from risk or danger; safety. See *security*.

Syngress: *The Definition of a Serious Security Library*

Syn·gress (sin-gres): *noun, sing.* Freedom from risk or danger; safety. See *security.*

Phishing Exposed

Lance James, Secure Science Corporation,
Joe Stewart (Foreword)

If you have ever received a phish, become a victim of a phish, or manage the security of a major e-commerce or financial site, then you need to read this book. The author of this book delivers the unconcealed techniques of phishers including their evolving patterns, and how to gain the upper hand against the ever-accelerating attacks they deploy. Filled with elaborate and unprecedented forensics, Phishing Exposed details techniques that system administrators, law enforcement, and fraud investigators can exercise and learn more about their attacker and their specific attack methods, enabling risk mitigation in many cases before the attack occurs.

ISBN: 1-59749-030-X

Price: $49.95 US $69.95 CAN

Penetration Tester's Open Source Toolkit

Johnny Long, Chris Hurley, SensePost,
Mark Wolfgang, Mike Petruzzi

This is the first fully integrated Penetration Testing book and bootable Linux CD containing the "Auditor Security Collection," which includes over 300 of the most effective and commonly used open source attack and penetration testing tools. This powerful tool kit and authoritative reference is written by the security industry's foremost penetration testers including HD Moore, Jay Beale, and SensePost. This unique package provides you with a completely portable and bootable Linux attack distribution and authoritative reference to the toolset included and the required methodology.

ISBN: 1-59749-021-0

Price: $59.95 US $83.95 CAN

Google Hacking for Penetration Testers

Johnny Long, Foreword by Ed Skoudis

Google has been a strong force in Internet culture since its 1998 upstart. Since then, the engine has evolved from a simple search instrument to an innovative authority of information. As the sophistication of Google grows, so do the hacking hazards that the engine entertains. Approaches to hacking are forever changing, and this book covers the risks and precautions that administrators need to be aware of during this explosive phase of Google Hacking.

ISBN: 1-93183-636-1

Price: $44.95 U.S. $65.95 CAN

SYNGRESS®

Syngress: *The Definition of a Serious Security Library*

Syn·gress (sin-gres): *noun, sing.* Freedom from risk or danger; safety. See *security*.

Syngress: *The Definition of a Serious Security Library*

Syn·gress (sin–gres): *noun, sing.* Freedom from risk or danger; safety. See *security.*

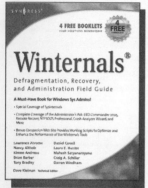

Winternals Defragmentation, Recovery, and Administration Field Guide

Dave Kleiman, Laura E. Hunter, Tony Bradley, Brian Barber, Nancy Altholz, Lawrence Abrams, Mahesh Satyanarayana, Darren Windham, Craig Schiller

As a system administrator for a Microsoft network, you know doubt spend too much of your life backing up data and restoring data, hunting down and removing malware and spyware, defragmenting disks, and improving the overall performance and reliability of your network. The Winternals® Defragmentation, Recovery, and Administration Field Guide and companion Web site provide you with all the information necessary to take full advantage of Winternals comprehensive and reliable tools suite for system administrators.

ISBN: 1-59749-079-2

Price: $49.95 US $64.95 CAN

Video Conferencing over IP: Configure, Secure, and Troubleshoot

Michael Gough

Until recently, the reality of videoconferencing didn't live up to the marketing hype. That's all changed. The network infrastructure and broadband capacity are now in place to deliver clear, real-time video and voice feeds between multiple points of contacts, with market leaders such as Cisco and Microsoft continuing to invest heavily in development. In addition, newcomers Skype and Google are poised to launch services and products targeting this market. *Video Conferencing over IP* is the perfect guide to getting up and running with video teleconferencing for small to medium-sized enterprises.

ISBN: 1-59749-063-6

Price: $49.95 U.S. $64.95 CAN

SYNGRESS®

Syngress: *The Definition of a Serious Security Library*

Syn·gress (sin‑gres): *noun, sing.* Freedom from risk or danger; safety. See *security.*

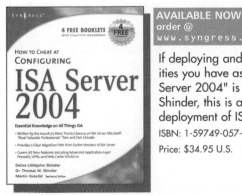

Syngress: *The Definition of a Serious Security Library*

Syn·gress (sin–gres): *noun, sing.* Freedom from risk or danger; safety. See *security.*

Syngress: *The Definition of a Serious Security Library*

Syn·gress (sin–gres): *noun, sing.* Freedom from risk or danger; safety. See *security*.

Syngress: *The Definition of a Serious Security Library*

Syn·gress (sin–gres): *noun, sing.* Freedom from risk or danger; safety. See *security.*

How to Cheat at Managing Windows Server Update Services

Brian Barber

If you manage a Microsoft Windows network, you probably find yourself overwhelmed at times by the sheer volume of updates and patches released by Microsoft for its products. You know these updates are critical to keep your network running efficiently and securely, but staying current amidst all of your other responsibilities can be almost impossible. Microsoft's recently released Windows Server Update Services (WSUS) is designed to streamline this process. Learn how to take full advantage of WSUS using Syngress' proven "How to Cheat" methodology, which gives you everything you need and nothing you don't.

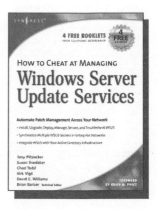

ISBN: 1-59749-027-X

Price: $39.95 US $55.95 CAN

How to Cheat at IT Project Management

Susan Snedaker

Most IT projects fail to deliver – on average, all IT projects run over schedule by 82%, run over cost by 43% and deliver only 52% of the desired functionality. Pretty dismal statistics. Using the proven methods in this book, you'll find that IT project you work on from here on out will have a much higher likelihood of being on time, on budget and higher quality. This book provides clear, concise, information and hands-on training to give you immediate results. And, the companion Web site provides dozens of templates for managing IT projects.

ISBN: 1-59749-037-7

Price: $44.95 U.S. $64.95 CAN

SYNGRESS®

Syngress: *The Definition of a Serious Security Library*

Syn·gress (sin‑gres): *noun, sing.* Freedom from risk or danger; safety. See *security*.

How to Cheat at Designing a Windows Server 2003 Active Directory Infrastructure

This book will start off by teaching readers to create the conceptual design of their Active Directory infrastructure by gathering and analyzing business and technical requirements. Next, readers will create the logical design for an Active Directory infrastructure. Here the book starts to drill deeper and focus on aspects such as group policy design. Finally, readers will learn to create the physical design for an active directory and network Infrastructure including DNS server placement; DC and GC placements and Flexible Single Master Operations (FSMO) role placement.

ISBN: 1-59749-058-X

Price: $39.95 US $55.95 CAN

Exam 70-291: Implementing, Managing, and Maintaining a Microsoft Windows Server 2003

ISBN: 1-931836-92-2

Price: $59.95 US

Exam 70-293: Planning and Maintaining a Microsoft Windows Server 2003 Network Infrastructure

ISBN: 1-931836-93-0

Price: $59.95 US

Exam 70-294: Planning, Implementing, and Maintaining a Microsoft Windows Server 2003 Active Directory Infrastructure

ISBN: 1-931836-94-9

Price: $59.95 US

SYNGRESS®

Syngress: *The Definition of a Serious Security Library*

Syn·gress (sin-gres): *noun, sing.* Freedom from risk or danger; safety. See *security*.

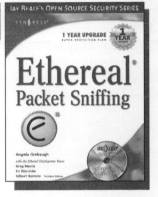
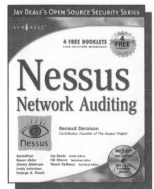

Syngress: *The Definition of a Serious Security Library*

Syn·gress (sin-gres): *noun, sing.* Freedom from risk or danger; safety. See *security*.

Buffer OverFlow Attacks: Detect, Exploit, Prevent

James C. Foster, Foreword by Dave Aitel

The SANS Institute maintains a list of the "Top 10 Software Vulnerabilities." At the current time, over half of these vulnerabilities are exploitable by Buffer Overflow attacks, making this class of attack one of the most common and most dangerous weapons used by malicious attackers. This is the first book specifically aimed at detecting, exploiting, and preventing the most common and dangerous attacks.

ISBN: 1-932266-67-4

Price: $34.95 US $50.95 CAN

Programmer's Ultimate Security DeskRef

James C. Foster

The Programmer's Ultimate Security DeskRef is the only complete desk reference covering multiple languages and their inherent security issues. It will serve as the programming encyclopedia for almost every major language in use.

While there are many books starting to address the broad subject of security best practices within the software development lifecycle, none has yet to address the overarching technical problems of incorrect function usage. Most books fail to draw the line from covering best practices security principles to actual code implementation. This book bridges that gap and covers the most popular programming languages such as Java, Perl, C++, C#, and Visual Basic.

ISBN: 1-932266-72-0

Price: $49.95 US $72.95 CAN

Hacking the Code: ASP.NET Web Application Security

Mark Burnett

This unique book walks you through the many threats to your Web application code, from managing and authorizing users and encrypting private data to filtering user input and securing XML. For every defined threat, it provides a menu of solutions and coding considerations. And, it offers coding examples and a set of security policies for each of the corresponding threats.

ISBN: 1-932266-65-8

Price: $49.95 U.S. $79.95 CAN

SYNGRESS®